Hollywood Secrets of Project Management Success

James Persse

PUBLISHED BY
Microsoft Press
A Division of Microsoft Corporation
One Microsoft Way
Redmond, Washington 98052-6399

Library of Congress Control Number: 2008927282

Printed and bound in the United States of America.

1 2 3 4 5 6 7 8 9   QWT   3 2 1 0 9 8

Distributed in Canada by H.B. Fenn and Company Ltd.

A CIP catalogue record for this book is available from the British Library.

Microsoft Press books are available through booksellers and distributors worldwide. For further information about international editions, contact your local Microsoft Corporation office or contact Microsoft Press International directly at fax (425) 936-7329. Visit our Web site at www.microsoft.com/mspress. Send comments to mspinput@microsoft.com.

Acquisitions Editor: Ben Ryan
Developmental Editor: Devon Musgrave
Project Editor: Victoria Thulman
Editorial Production: P.M. Gordon Associates
Cover Illustration: John Hersey

Body Part No. X14-71548

To

Julie, Gaye, Marie, Sue

and

Angela

Contents at a Glance

Table of Contents

What do you think of this book? We want to hear from you!

Microsoft is interested in hearing your feedback so we can continually improve our books and learning resources for you. To participate in a brief online survey, please visit:

www.microsoft.com/learning/booksurvey/

Part III **Production**

What do you think of this book? We want to hear from you!

Microsoft is interested in hearing your feedback so we can continually improve our books and learning resources for you. To participate in a brief online survey, please visit:

www.microsoft.com/learning/booksurvey/

Introduction

Thomas Edison patented the world's first motion picture camera, the Kinetograph, in 1897. His associate W. K. L. Dickson set up the camera in a tarpaper-clad shed dubbed the Black Maria and began to roll film. His first subject was Fred Ott, a local man with the ability to sneeze on cue. Then came jugglers and circus animals and the world's first on-screen kiss. In 1903 Dickson shot and edited The Great Train Robbery, *an exciting story—a full 15 minutes long—of a Wild West holdup. The public watching in Nickelodeons everywhere ate it up, and presto! the movies were born. Soon enough, early entertainment pioneers like Samuel Goldfish, Carl Laemmle, and Jesse Lasky were buying tracts of California farmland and setting up their own studios. They had movies to make, yes, but they also had something bigger to do: They had an industry to invent.*

Some 70 years later, in 1982, The Maynard Corporation appointed its first chief information officer (CIO), Robert Trowlers. Trowlers' initial assignment was to integrate an emerging blend of computing resources—mainframes, midrange systems, and personal computers (PCs)—into a unified landscape, one that would support a vast new potential for the collection, analysis, and dissemination of information. Soon other CIOs would emerge, many others. Today there are thousands of CIOs spread across the American business landscape. But back then, it was the dawn of a new world—the Information Age. And the early CIOs had little history to guide them. They too had business to conduct, and plenty of it. But surely many of them felt—as many may yet feel today—that there was also a business to invent.

Gates of Heaven, Worlds of Water

In the spring of 1980, United Artists (UA)—the famous movie studio founded in 1919 by Charlie Chaplin, Mary Pickford, and Douglas Fairbanks—was about to go under.

Some $40 million of its money—much of it leveraged against assets—had disappeared in a single place, Kalispell, Montana. That's where one of its filmmakers, Michael Cimino, was working on his magnum opus, *Heaven's Gate*, a fictional retelling of the 1890s Johnson County cattle wars. The film's original budget had been set at $11.6 million, about average for the time. But Cimino, whose previous film, *The Deer Hunter*, was being hailed as a contemporary masterpiece, had other ideas. He wanted larger crowds, he wanted more smoke, he wanted more horses, he wanted more film, he wanted more time. He wanted more Art. UA was under fairly new management then, and that management team wanted to prove to the industry that it could produce big, prestige pictures like the rest of Hollywood. So they sent more money for extras (and costumes and makeup and food). And then more money for smoke and horses (and smoke machines and wranglers and oats). And then money for more film, and then money for that most expensive of all movie-making elements, time. The budget doubled, then tripled, then grew again. UA management was no doubt sweating but must have been too busy watching the checks going out to check the rough cuts coming in. Because what Michael Cimino ultimately delivered was a movie that made very little dramatic or visual sense to anyone. It was a mess—a four-hour-long mess. Its premiere in New York was so disastrous that the studio yanked it from national distribution after a week, not wanting to throw good money after bad with additional print and shipping expenses.

As a consequence, the general public at the time had no chance to see *Heaven's Gate*. But UA's parent company, the conservative insurance giant Transamerica, had its sights locked on UA. Such laissez faire business practices were not to its liking, so executive management stepped in. Heads rolled, and many people were never to work in Hollywood again. More than that, the ordeal left such a bad taste that Transamerica wanted UA off its books, more out of disgust than because of real financial harm. So it quietly agreed to an offer from MGM to buy UA. After 60 illustrious years, Chaplin's, Pickford's, and Fairbanks' studio was no more.

How did things get so far out of whack that such a prestigious studio with such a prime lineage could fall in the wake of one of its own projects? Many people would blame the director as an obsessed artist with no appreciation for the contribution of his backers. Some would say that the new management at UA was just too inexperienced with entertainment deal making and risks. Still others would say that's just Hollywood for you—egos out of control, inevitable decadence sprung from uncontrolled plenty.

Today, *Heaven's Gate* sits with *Cleopatra*, *Camelot*, and *Paint Your Wagon* as a legend of rampant misspending, mismanagement, and missed signals.

Here's another story, more recent but just as famous. The sci-fi adventure *Waterworld* was a Universal/Kevin Costner project that came about because of his runaway success at the box office beginning in 1990 with the western *Dances with Wolves*. *Dances with Wolves* cost $19 million to make and grossed $424 million for its backers. The very next year, his adventure film *Robin Hood: Prince of Thieves* was another huge hit. It cost an impressive $50 million (success always ups production budgets) but returned $440 million to the studio. Could this guy do no wrong? Studio executives were very solicitous: "Mr. Costner, your sensitive treatment of the Indians was most inspiring. And your reimagining of the Robin Hood tale would have thrilled even Errol Flynn. What, sir, are you thinking of next?"

Kevin Costner and his director friend Kevin Reynolds wanted to make a movie about a world of melted ice caps, one almost completely submerged in water. Bands of renegades and heroes would compete for what little land existed. "Very interesting." Universal Studios thought it might want to jump on board with this project too. "Would there be any Indians in it? No? Okay, no problem. Could it maybe be a Robin Hood at sea sort of thing? No? Hey—just asking. How much money might you need?"

The initial budget for *Waterworld* was set at $60 million. A big budget, yes, but the high concept of the adventure piece could be seen to justify that level of risk. Universal could handle that. And so production began, and it began with such enthusiasm from the creative leads that they insisted the picture be shot on location—not in a studio tank or in an enclosed seaside lagoon even, but on the ocean. *Out* on the ocean. Way away from shore. That's when the problems began.

First off, the design and engineering issues were formidable. Transporting a movie crew— upwards of 200 people—to a location in, say, Kalispell, Montana, is complicated enough in and of itself. But to locate the company out on water required camera platforms that floated, and special crew riggings, special power requirements, special safety precautions, a fleet of boats at the ready for back-and-forth transportation. The list goes on and on. Then there were the sets themselves—they had to float, too. The engineering bills were huge, and they were huge early on. But the project went forward.

Next there arose continuity issues. The surface of the ocean is amazingly dynamic. It can change by the hour, and by the hour on this shoot it did. What the creative team saw was that from shot to shot, the scenes weren't matching. Four hours of work from one angle didn't cut with the four hours of work from the other angle. Accordingly, scenes had to be reshot and reshot.

Then the weather did not cooperate, which is problem enough on dry land but something quite different on the water. One storm destroyed a good portion of the sets. And they didn't just topple over—they sank. So the engineers had to be called back in.

And these were just the big issues. The constant delays began to cause conflict on the set, high up in the creative chain, unfortunately. The star, who was also the producer, eventually fired his friend the director over creative differences and took charge of the shoot. That, of course, required another extension of production time.

By the time all was said and done (most of the saying being done in the press), the original $60 million had turned into $175 million, making *Waterworld* the most expensive movie ever made. At the date of its release, what with all the negative publicity, the odds were stacked against it. Businesswise, the film would need to outsell the megahit *Jurassic Park* simply to break even. And even if *Waterworld* could manage to become one of the Top Ten box office successes of all time, it was still likely to end up a massive financial loss. Sure enough, all of the dire predictions appeared to come true. The film grossed only $88 million at the U.S. box office and initially was considered to be one of the biggest flops ever made. Again, heads rolled, and many people involved in the production departed Hollywood for good.

So here at the beginning of this book are two crazy stories from Hollywood. As a point of interest, both had something of a Hollywood-style happy ending. Through rentals, ancillary markets, and the gift of time, *Heaven's Gate* has finally been able to break even, making back its money on the spreadsheets at least. And many critics reassess it now as a film with its own certain awe and pageantry. *Waterworld* did even better. U.S. audiences may have stayed away in droves, but the rest of world bought tickets, and the film eventually turned a profit of $100 million for Universal. So the picture that merely broke even still managed to achieve a degree of artistic success. And the one that had been judged to be a silly cartoon still managed to bring in strong financial returns. Regardless of either outcome, however, Hollywood still considers both to be catastrophes.

And that brings us to the theme of this book: *Heaven's Gate* and *Waterworld* may be wonderful stories of Hollywood excess, the kind the public has craved since the days of silent-screen comedian Fatty Arbuckle, but they are *atypical* stories. They stand out and garner attention in exact proportion to the degree to which they are atypical.

In actuality, however, the vast majority of Hollywood productions are amazingly well run. They come in on time, on budget, and with the full breadth of the script on display on screen. Issues of originality or story intelligence aside, that's a pretty impressive performance. In 2006 the mainstream studio system put out just over 300 theatrical releases. That's over 300 brand-new products, all financed, designed, planned, staffed, and manufactured from scratch. The size of that production package in total is right around $600 billion. That's an annual number. And the dozen or so studio executives I spoke to estimate that less than 10 percent of that figure is for overages.

The perception may well be that Hollywood is footloose and fancy free when it comes to project management. The truth, however, is that Hollywood may be about the best project management machine on the planet.

Project Management in the World of Information Technology

Here's another interesting misperception: Hollywood thinks the information technology (IT) world is much, **much better** at project management than it is.

In preparing this book, I visited with 22 motion picture executives and producers from studios such as Warner Bros., Paramount, Legendary Pictures, Parallel Entertainment, Universal, Intermedia Films, and others. When I told these industry professionals about the theme and purpose of this book, they all gave me funny looks at first. I explained that I wanted to better understand their methods for staying on schedule, staying on budget, and delivering a product that firmly represented initial specs, and that I was after this because my industry—the IT industry—had problems doing that. When they asked how bad the problem was, I low-balled the answer each time: "We'd like to operate consistently at no more than, say, 10 to 15 percent over any of those thresholds." Frequently, jaws dropped; sometimes only the eyeballs bulged a little. But the response was always the same. Bill Fay, president of Legendary

Pictures, summed it up succinctly: "We'd *never* get by on numbers like that." In Hollywood, running even 2 or 3 percent over is going to require a lot of explaining on someone's part. I didn't mention that more than a few industry studies put overall IT performance regularly at 30, 50, even 100 percent off the mark.

When we IT professionals hear stories about *Heaven's Gate* and *Waterworld*, we probably laugh like everyone else, but inside we probably wince a little too. Those of us who work as project managers or program managers in one capacity or another can easily relate to stories of runaway or misguided projects, either from secondhand knowledge or from firsthand experience. Because project management sits at the heart of project activities, it is the project managers who must deal with the initial fallout that comes when project controls dissipate, and who must then continually work under those conditions to mitigate subsequent effects. My own experience in the industry bears this out. In working with companies like Pitney Bowes, BellSouth Science & Technologies, MCI, AT&T, GTE, CIBER Defense Systems, Macy's, Kohl's, American Healthcare, British Petroleum, Johnson Controls, and others, I have seen a distinct pattern: Project performance is highly variable. The ability of a technology organization to develop a product in sync with budget, schedule, and functional expectations is soft at best.

But *why* is it soft? And *how* soft is it? To answer these two starting-line questions, let's begin by putting them in the proper context: the unprecedented success of the technology industry.

An American Success Story

Today's IT professionals—project managers, executives, technical experts—are part of the most successful social and technological revolution since the Industrial Revolution of the 1770s. In the span of a few decades, a single generation has transformed the world. Information flows, communication channels, integration points, exchange avenues, commonality of form—these are the hallmarks that solidify a working civilization. And because of the recent and rapid advances in technology, these markers have never been more plentiful or more efficient than they are today. What's involved here is not just inventive or innovative technologies but integrative technologies, the work that corporate American IT shops engage in on a daily basis to shape the needs of business, commerce, and culture.

That's a big job, and to be honest, the industry hasn't had a lot of time to learn it. Computers as a business tool have been with us in earnest only since the late 1950s. Back then, only the biggest or the most transaction-intensive–type companies used them. They were complex, mainframe systems, very expensive and very unwieldy. In the 1960s, computers got a little smaller and a littler smarter; less expensive, mini- and midrange systems became available. During this period, a wealth of prepackaged, generic-type software solutions had been developed, so automation spread throughout most of the Fortune 500 landscape, from accounting departments to shipping and receiving to sales and marketing. At the time, these data processing operations typically fell under the management venue of administration and ended (most usually) at the office of the organization's chief financial officer (CFO). In the mid-1970s, the microcomputer was developed, and another real change began to evolve: Little businesses began to automate, and big businesses began to distribute their computing resources even more widely, setting micros on the desks of more and more workers. By the mid-1980s, the IBM Personal Computer had washed over corporate America, and a new third party software applications industry had been born. Users who once sat quietly at keyboards in front of "green screens" now swished mice around pads, keyed in Lotus macros, printed fancy documents, and asked for more. The "personal" side of computing usurped a great deal of computing's "business" side. The Data Processing Age now gave over to the Information Age.

This really was a business revolution, a true paradigm shift. It's conceivable to draw a line down the middle of the year 1982 to mark the divisions BPC and ADP—"before personal computing" and "after data processing." This year could also be seen as the birth of modern IT project management: The vast success and popularity of the new computing brought with it a vast array of new needs, and those needs quickly turned into new projects—*lots* of new projects. The Nickelodeon revolution that ushered in the new movie industry was indeed impressive for its day, but even that was nothing like this scope of change.

Managing the Projects

All of this was rapidly changing the shape of corporate America. New IT shops were now being blocked onto organizational charts, new CIOs were being appointed, and new computing capabilities were spreading throughout the organization. The growth of the IT industry over the last 25 years or so has been phenomenal. In 1982, it was sized at about $400 million; today, it is sized at just over $1.3 *trillion*.[1] Perhaps more significant is the size of the IT customer base. Data processing concerns were once centered on a few select groups within an enterprise. Today IT touches, almost without exception, everybody in the enterprise. (The same thing happened in the movie business. In 1905 there were zero theaters showing movies in the United States. By 1930, there were 97,000. In the same time span, movie attendance went from zero to 300 million annually.[2]) The single thing that came out of this was work, a new kind of work: the development of business automation solutions now and for the first time *within* an organization. Perhaps the least-anticipated element of this new paradigm was the volume of work. IT shops were born from the get-go as project shops—not out of vision, but out of necessity.

As quickly as it became evident that the size and throughput of IT would trend for the foreseeable future as a northbound line, continuing to grow, so did the need for more active

---

[1] Matt Asay, "IT Spending Set to Fall," *C/Net Magazine*, February 11, 2008.

[2] David A. Cook, *History of Narrative Film*, W. W. Norton & Co., 1996.

project management become apparent. Previously, project management on technology projects had been more of an administrative and internal coordination function: A look at project management in a discipline like construction will show pretty much the same thing. That's not to say that those job roles are free of complexity or the need for analyses and proactive positioning. But they do operate in environments that can be considered (at least to some extent) predictive. What project management faced in the new paradigm of technology development was that traditional needs for cost, schedule, and quality control were dumped with little preparation into an arena of change in which speed-to-market, feature flux, business missions, competitive positioning, and multiple agendas all required the same high level of attention.

The result was three-faceted:

1. A lot of work got done; the industry's success is testament to that.

2. In doing that work and in meeting that business mission, a method of production (in some places overt, in others covert) evolved.

3. Embedded within that method was a high degree of chronic waste.

The third point is the kicker. That's the catalyst for this book, as it's been the catalyst for many, many books about technology strategy, management, development, and deployment. IT people readily acknowledge the problem of a high level of waste. A common misperception, however, is that the source of this waste is project management—but that's confusing the point of measurement with the point of generation. The real issue is not that project management needs to get a handle on things so that things will run smoother. The issue—explored in this book—is that the source of the problems is an inherent organizational design that, in the domain of IT, is immature with respect to product development. (After all, at 25 you might be super smart and irrepressibly energetic, but how mature can you really be?) Good project management is a maturing discipline in any organization; it helps make an organization more mature. In IT shops, it can help make the shops more responsive, more effective, and more accountable. The key, then, is not to fix project management. It's to introduce *more* project management.

The Cost of Success

This is not a book designed to bash project management, or to paint upper-level technology management as being soft or short-sighted. Nevertheless, although the success of IT across the business landscape—its ubiquitous proliferation and its undeniable effectiveness—is readily visible, it's important to acknowledge that this success has been accompanied by a kind of production-predictive deficiency. (IT people have a hard time saying up front how their projects are likely to turn out.) This awareness is essential because of the fundamental importance of IT within today's business enterprise: Because IT has become such an integrated part of business strategies, business tactics, and business operations, its effectiveness can no longer be separated from the business. Today, a reasonable claim might be that as goes IT, so goes the business. That level of integration, considered along with the required investment of capital and resources and competitive positioning, leads to an inescapable conclusion: If IT shops are not operating within practical ranges of efficiencies, the bottom line for the business will suffer.

Here's a quick survey across 25 years of performance.

- In 1982, the insurance company Allstate set out to automate all of its office operations using the new technology of micro computing. Management set a 5-year transformation timetable and gave it an $8 million budget. But six years and $15 million later, the offices were a long way from being automated to any appreciable degree. Management reassessed and reestablished a new budget. What had begun as $8 million was now set at $100 million.[3]

- In 1988, the financial institution Westpac Banking Corp. decided on a strategic initiative to redesign its information system's data and work flows. This major effort was engineered against a 5-year timetable, an $85 million budget, and an expanded workforce augmented by hundreds of technology specialists. Three years later—mid-1991—project expenditures had topped $150 million, with little to show for it. With no assurance of future success and with nothing to salvage from the effort, Westpac management decided to cut its losses: It canceled the project cold and eliminated 500 development jobs.

- In 1994, the Standish Group released its infamous Chaos Study. Through surveys of Fortune 500 IT shops, the study concluded that the average IT project ran 189 percent over schedule and 222 percent over budget, with 30 percent of planned functionality missing in delivered products. Nearly 30 percent of all projects begun were canceled before completion.

- In 1997, KPMG conducted a survey of Canadian IT performance. In working with 1,450 companies, it found that 61 percent of all projects failed in some degree to meet performance expectations. Greater than 74 percent overran their schedules by 30 percent or more. The report concluded that annual unbudgeted project expenditures probably approached the $25 million (Canadian) mark.

- In 1998, a study by Peat Marwick found that about 35 percent of 600 firms surveyed had at least one runaway software project for that year.[4]

- In 2001, a Robbins-Gioia survey looked at big project performance in the realm of enterprise resource planning (ERP) implementations. Here is how 232 respondents described their projects: 51 percent said they were unsuccessful. Of those shops, 56 percent had a project management office in place, but only 36 percent of them reported

---

[3] Steve McConnell, *Rapid Development: Taming Wild Software Schedules*, Microsoft Press, 1996.

[4] Robert Charette, "Why Software Fails," *IEEE Magazine*, September 2005.

success. A 2001 Conference Board survey that looked at the same area worked with 117 companies and found that 40 percent reported ERP implementations that failed to achieve business goals within the first year. On average, implementation costs were 25 percent over budget. Only 34 percent of shops were "very satisfied" with how the implementations turned out.

- In 2004, the Standish Group released its new Chaos Study. What it found was an improvement over the 1994 results, but the numbers still showed real performance issues: Only 29 percent of projects could be described as unqualified successes; 53 percent of projects could be described as challenged or seriously compromised; 18 percent failed completely—canceled or not used. The average schedule overrun was now 84 percent (better than 1994, when it was 164 percent). The average cost overrun was 56 percent (better than 1994 at 180 percent). That same year, *Computerworld Today* reported that one third of all IT spending went to repair botched projects. Supporting the Chaos results, Deborah Weiss of the Meta Group found that 72 percent of all IT projects were either late, came in over budget, lacked functionality, or were never delivered.[5]

- In 2005, the giant English food retailer J Sainsbury had to write off an investment of U.S. $526 million in an automated supply-chain management system because the massive project stalled midway through. Integration issues caused Sainsbury merchandise to get stuck in the company's warehouses. As a result, the inventory was not getting through to many of its stores. Sainsbury, now without a system of any kind, was forced to hire about 3,000 additional clerks to stock its shelves manually.[6]

Three things to note about these stories: First, the stories recount big failures and big findings. That's intentional. It's simply more interesting to read about big failures than about smaller ones. Second, the numbers don't really add up: The study data and numbers don't consistently agree. Are projects on average 25 percent over budget, or is it 110 percent? Is schedule slippage endemic at 12 weeks or 54 weeks? There's probably no way to really know.

Third, and perhaps the real point, all of the data point in the same direction. The numbers may not agree, but they do seem to beg the same question: How far off the mark do most projects fall? (Versus over or under the mark.) Specific, pinpoint conclusions may be risky with these data, but the general conclusion is pretty obvious. Most managers may never have been involved in a $500 million chargeoff, but they probably have seen the smaller kind in action. Perhaps of deeper concern is the degree of acquiescence that may have grown around those trends. The industry has a tendency now to accept slippage as part and parcel of the package. A summary look at the bottom line might encourage reexamination of this tendency. This year, IT expenditures will exceed $1.4 trillion worldwide. Of all projects initiated, 5 to 15 percent are likely to be abandoned; 20 to 40 percent are likely to run well over

---

[5] Siohban McBride, "Poor Project Management Leads to Higher Failure Rate," *Computerworld Today*, October 15, 2004.

[6] Jeff Attwood, "The Long Dismal History of Software Project Failure," *Coding Horror Ezine*, May 15, 2006.

budget and schedule. On this basis, compromised technology projects have the potential to cost the economy $60 billion to $70 billion.[7]

The Project Management Landscape

So why does the IT industry report project performance rates that would make other industries blush? A likely answer, mentioned earlier in this chapter, is that performance problems in the domains of technology development typically do not stem from any failings of project management. In fact, such "problems" may be better thought of as organizational traits, particular to certain kinds of product development, that put pressure on classical approaches to project management. These traits are not anomalies so much as they are nuances of landscape. They frame IT projects as in-sourced efforts within a larger business environment. As such, they are not things executive managers, program managers, or project managers should seek to avoid. (By their nature, they are unavoidable.) Rather, they are traits that organizations and IT shops should work to identify, engage, and then manage.

As borne out by my own experience, certain of these traits seem to be dominant. They tend to appear in most IT shops to one degree or another, and they tend to have a direct impact on project management's ability to shepherd a production effort through its life cycle phases. Here's a quick look at these nine traits.

1. **Technology is integrated.**   It's connected to all other facets of the business enterprise. And its main job is to further the business missions of the organization—so it does not have sole input into what business projects might be initiated (and thus turned into technology projects). From time to time, therefore, it may be obligated to engage in projects that are not always based on optimal technology drivers. Furthermore, many IT shops lack assessment methods or evaluation criteria for determining, in a common and objective way, project challenges, risks, and likely investment requirements, as a tool to help the organization prioritize project selection. Consequently, project managers often get handed projects that have been compromised right from the start, and these professionals are charged with shaping as much of a success out of them as they can.

2. **Portfolios are complex.**   The data centers and operating environments that run corporate business systems are complex entities, and they grow more complex every year. A large part of this complexity, perhaps the largest part, comes from integration. Systems support one another; they exchange data; they share data; one reports from another; this one supplies that one. Unfortunately, corporate IT is not very good at portfolio management. Most IT departments have a very limited understanding of the data architectures that drive their business flows. The potential for fallout is very real. Changing one system can easily alter how another works. A successful new transaction

---

[7] Robert Charette, "Why Software Fails," *IEEE Magazine*, September 2005.

in one place can instigate a faulty move in another place. By default, IT projects are becoming more complex, so project management is becoming more complex. This complexity brings with it a need for additional assessment, analysis, and planning activities, but this need often is overlooked or underemphasized at the corporate level.

3. **Scopes are aggressive.**   This is a common project management complaint. Upper management sets unrealistic deadlines for complex work and then cheerleads for the impossible (while the players get beaten up on the field). This is probably true of any business, business being the competitive entity that it is. Speed-to-market can heavily influence a company's ability to attract and retain market share. So that push to move faster while carrying more will probably always be there—yet another burden that project management is asked to shoulder. Project management strategies that address this requirement, however, are available: Iterative and Agile methods can be used to deliver incrementally more complete products across a life cycle while still achieving a market presence, but upper management must support this with an operational shift from traditional development practices that it is often uncomfortable with.

4. **Resources are stretched.**   There never seem to be enough people—enough of the good people anyway—to attack project work with the appropriate strength of force. Departments are encouraged to work as "lean" as possible. People are pulled from one project to the next. They are asked to do double duty. Turnover may be high. These resource problems combined with the three foregoing traits engender the classic IT crunch: too much work and not enough people. Talented project managers may be forced to spend most of their time shuffling resources, interviewing, talking to staffing agencies. They become mini–human resources departments within a project effort. Out of this comes a very natural temptation: to fill seats with bodies—talented or not—so that the work won't stop. Unfortunately, with a team that's inexperienced or unskilled, the work may never stop.

5. **Business needs shift.**   Another major complaint out of project management is that it's not possible to pin down the focus or the scope of the project. That's because business needs shift. The market place is dynamic. And the larger or more complex the project, the greater the propensity for shift. Project managers have been known to walk out the door over this issue. What, if anything, can be done to address this instability? Not much, because business needs will always be shifting. This shifting becomes particularly problematic when conditions continue to be regarded as static and performance is expected to reflect that stasis. A more valid complaint, then, is that upper management, which is almost always a contributor to that ebb and flow (it okays the changes), still evaluates performance and progress based on fixed costs and fixed schedules. This project management complaint may greatly diminish if upper management would acknowledge the dynamism and provide support to promote replanning and adjustments.

6. **An IT-business gap persists.**   This may be the single biggest impactor of project management success in the technology realm. From it, all these other conditions can spring. It's the gap of understanding and appreciation that exists between the domains of IT and business. Business people think technology is mysterious magic, and technology people think business is simple: an input here, an output there. This separation has some basis in fact: IT units specialize in technology issues, whereas business units specialize in business flows. But rational though it may be, such separation provides a disconnect in that business people often do not garner an understanding of how technology projects are managed or engineered, so they tend to ask for things that may seem logical but are really impractical. At the same time, technology people may not appreciate the complexities of business flows and the challenges that come with automating them in full detail. Accordingly, they may become frustrated when clarifications and changes (perhaps seen as new requests) begin to flow. This condition requires a cultural awareness that promotes and actively fosters close partnerships between IT and business units. And in most places, that awareness has not yet developed.

7. **Change control is dicey.**   Change control is one of the most important of project management tools. The methods used to request changes, to evaluate their impact, and to decide on their suitability will often determine whether a project stays in control or drifts out of control. The problem is that it is often seen solely as a project management tool, when it should be seen as an organizational tool—better yet, even a business tool. As has been shown in the foregoing items, change is inevitable. All projects will experience it. The key is to order it. But when change control sits as an internal project attribute, it can be seen from the outside as an impediment to change, as a tool of procrastination, or as a wall set up to shield the technology teams from the business teams. So people look for ways to get around change control. Favors are called in. Back doors are opened. And this happens even within well-modulated change environments. The challenge presented here to project management is to present change control as a facilitator of change, an expediter of change, and then to operate it so that those benefits become visible.

8. **Stakeholders are diverse.**   You can't make all the people happy all the time. That's mainly because so many different people want so many different things. This holds true in any business enterprise, but it's especially true with technology projects. Because technology touches so many people, technology projects have to deal with a host of stakeholders: project sponsors, system users, operations folks, maintenance folks, upstream systems folks, downstream systems folks, and so on. A project may touch each in a different way. What's more, it may require a different contribution from each. Part of the task of project management is to help ensure that stakeholders coordinate and collaborate across the project lifecycle. But with competing agendas, even the best of project managers working within the best of systems can find this responsibility to be demanding, with the need to apply different measures of success across stakeholder groups.

9. **Communication attenuates.**   Effective communications is a challenge in any business environment. Put together a collection of people with different sets of specialties and organize them into teams, and the communication problems will start. That's a trait of any organization. Smart organizations focus on how to make communications effective. Most organizations focus on how to make communications efficient. Efficiency, however, is a source of many communication problems. The ease of communications— e-mails, PowerPoint slides, memos, and so on—can encourage poor communication, and a lot of it. Communicating is a major task of project management. Some see it as *the* major task. But very often project management must operate in an environment of attenuating communications. The further away the message gets, the more diluted it becomes. As a result, an environment in which communication channels are filtered, thinned, or blocked will by default have a difficult time managing project activities and achieving project targets.

All of these traits are in place in every IT shop. Each of these traits has the potential to affect the control and success of a technology project. So taken together, their effects can be substantial and even overwhelming in terms of outcome. But again, these are not elements of project management; rather, they are reflections of organizational design and culture. The point is that they simply tend to evidence themselves most readily in project management results.

So what's the answer, then? Is it to resign ourselves to suboptimal performance levels and perhaps simply amortize overage as a cost of doing business? This is actually a route many companies take. It's easy, it's fast, and it's also somewhat invisible, thanks to certain mechanisms in accounting practices,. But it's not much of a business response. By contrast, a valid, valuable, and proven business response exists. Most of us in project management and many of us in the IT industry at large know just what to do to address and manage these traits.

Solutions Are Available

It's surprising to some, but for about 25 years the world of IT has had available to it a suite of management tools and frameworks developed specifically to address issues of project management and product development in the domains of technology. Each of these takes a somewhat specialized and unique view of the subject, but they are all shaped to achieve the same things: (1) They provide mechanisms for identifying and managing the scope of the work. (2) They provide guidelines for managing the work within schedule and budget expectations. (3) And they provide avenues for ensuring the achievement of established quality and performance goals.

Perhaps most important, each of these solutions has been proved to work in technology shops; they enhance a shop's ability to control project activities in line with preset expectations. As mentioned earlier, Hollywood's studio production system is an effective, systematic approach to creating a motion picture. The following standards and frameworks are very much like that system. They can each serve as the foundation for developing a technology production system tailored to a specific IT shop. Let's take a quick look at each.

The Project Management Institute's *Project Management Body of Knowledge*

In the mid-1980s, the Project Management Institute (PMI) codified its *Project Management Body of Knowledge* (PMBOK). The PMBOK contains a set of nine Knowledge Areas that professional project managers should know. Initiation covers project identification and kickoff. Scope Management covers requirements development. Cost Management covers the creation and control of the project budget. Time Management focuses on the definition of project activities and, from this, a project schedule. Quality Management stresses two facets of quality: quality control and quality assurance. Communications Management covers status, progress, and performance reporting. Risk Management covers risk identification, tracking, and mitigation. Vendor Management covers supplier sourcing and acquisition. The PMI is widely recognized as an authoritative voice in the domain of technology project management. Its practices conform to four common phases of product development: initiation, planning, execution, and closure. And many organizations today look for project managers who have been certified in the PMBOK through the PMI's Project Management Professional (PMP) designation.

Iterative/Agile

The iterative approach to product development, most often encompassed in the Agile method, is a way to manage a project so that a product, especially a complex one, can be built in ordered increments, with proper attention being paid to each increment so that quality, reliability, and dependability are ensured. The central idea behind Agile is agility—the ability to stay flexible in order to meet a customer's need. The prime motivation of the incremental or Agile approach is customer satisfaction; this is realized through the continuous delivery of workable solutions. A key approach to Agile is incremental development, which means taking a big idea, working out functional components, and then building on these sequential functional foundations. Agile places special emphasis on active communications over passive documentation. It relies heavily on continuous customer collaboration and feedback. It promotes quality and simplicity in design and uses teams that self-organize to maximize the talent pool contained therein. Above all, Agile promotes responsiveness to change. It welcomes change across the project life cycle, with the belief that so long as the customer and the technical team can agree regarding the change, then project harmony and business consistency will be maintained.

Capability Maturity Model Integration

Capability Maturity Model Integration (CMMI) is a product development and process improvement framework sponsored and developed by the Software Engineering Institute. Like the PMBOK, it was first introduced in the mid-1980s. The framework describes a set of Process Areas that contain a series of practices proved to support product quality goals. Five of these Process Areas directly address project management concerns: Project Planning focuses on estimation and plan development. Project Monitoring & Control emphasizes tracking progress to the plan. Risk Management contains practices for identifying, tracking, and mitigating risks. Integrated Project Management focuses on collaboration and coordination among stakeholders. And Quantitative Project Management is a high-maturity process area that establishes quantitative performance goals for project management activities. Other Process Areas like Requirements Management, Configuration Management, and Supplier Agreement Management also support tangential project management concerns. Many organizations that have adopted CMMI have reported significant improvements in schedule allegiance, cost control, productivity rates, and product quality.

International Standards Organization's ISO 9001:2000

ISO 9001 is an international quality standard that was also established in the mid-1980s by the International Standards Organization. It is a "generic" quality standard in that it can be applied in any environment that's engaged in product development, whether that product is coat hangers or software systems. The focus of the standard is on fulfilling customer requirements through a documented quality management system. The core of the standard consists of five sections. The first section covers the establishment of a quality management system (QMS) through documented policies and procedures. The next section addresses management's responsibility as the owner and sponsor of the QMS. The third section provides requirements for providing the proper resources to support the QMS. The fourth section addresses the need to provision the product in a way that supports visibility, inspection, and traceability. The fifth and final section provides requirements for product measurement and continuous improvement. ISO 9001 can be used as an umbrella program under which effective project management business processes can be defined and described. ISO has proved beneficial to many technology shops. Its generic nature provides a very flexible and tailorable approach to any organization that wishes to better formalize its project management approach.

Microsoft Solutions Framework/Six Sigma/The Custom Approach

Still other methods and frameworks are available. The Microsoft Solutions Framework (MSF) wraps additional management and production practices around existing methods like Agile and CMMI. Six Sigma is a system to improve existing management and development processes. It has been widely popularized by such companies as Motorola, GTE, and Ford Motors. And then there's the custom approach, which may be the best approach of all. The bounds and tenor of project management can be highly reflective of the organizational culture, so many companies—while perhaps using elements of some of the standards mentioned previously—develop their own project management programs.

The message is clear. The industry is aware that project management requires special attention, so various bodies within it have developed tools that can provide this needed attention.

A caveat: Once in place, such systems must be used.

Available Does Not Mean *Used*

Although all of the foregoing methods and approaches have value, that value cannot be realized if they are not used. As noted previously, most corporate IT shops do not use them at all. (Some studies place the percentage of IT shops with no formal methodology at 73 percent.) Perhaps the most curious example is the lack of PMBOK use. I have seen shop after shop set up project management offices and hire in teams of project managers. Their recruitment ads set up the requirements that applicants must be PMP-certified, so they bring in a team of PMPs. But the shops stop there. They fail to use the PMBOK from an organizational standpoint. Management seems to assume that practicing the PMBOK falls into the personal purview of each project manager. That, of course, is a backward assumption. A PMP operating in the absence of PMBOK practices (or other methods) is managing in an ad hoc, reactive manner.

Similarities with adoption of ISO 9001, CMMI, Agile, and the others also are common. Management may *want* to operate in those realms but lacks the commitment necessary to develop those realms. For example, becoming a CMMI Maturity Level 2 shop requires a degree of organizational change. But first it requires management to understand what CMMI asks of a shop, confirmation that it fits in with current business strategies, and then the dedication of resources to make the transformation. All of this is going to take a certain amount of time, and upper-level managers may feel that the organization does not have the luxury of that time. Furthermore, they may feel that although the PMBOK, Agile, ISO 9001, CMMI, and other systems have gotten some good press, the hard evidence for a promising return on investment (ROI) is essentially lacking.

The central message of this book is that the practices embodied in these models and standards really do work to enhance project management activities and outcomes. Numerous examples demonstrating how and why many of them work so well are presented throughout. These examples of good business practice come from what at first may seem like an unlikely source.

Why the Association with Hollywood?

As noted earlier, Hollywood may be the finest-tuned project management machine on the planet. Large-scale motion picture productions routinely come in on time, on budget, and to spec. By contrast, project management in the IT world has not been able to match that level of consistency or predictability. The cause here is not really one that stems from project management. The typical landscape of technology development places a series of hurdles and obstacles in the path of development activities. These hurdles and obstacles may often cause a project to veer off course. But the fact is that IT product development and motion picture development are conducted in strikingly similar environments. Moreover, a closer look will show that the hurdles and obstacles that pop up in the technology landscape are also present in the entertainment landscape. Of the numerous similarities, eight in particular stand out:

1. Both deal in intangible product development.

2. Both are shaped to directly address a deadline-oriented business need.

3. Both require significant investments.

4. Both are built against a specification open to change.

5. Both rely on specialized production protocols and technologies.

6. Both require the integration and collaboration of specialized teams.

7. Both require careful analysis, design, execution, and integration.

8. Both must be thoughtfully delivered to their target audiences.

Let's consider each of these in turn.

Developing the Intangible

Most industries that deal in project management are in the business of creating something tangible, like a bridge or a house. But in the worlds of Hollywood and IT, things are different: They both work to create amorphous products. There is little to no intrinsic value in a motion picture, and the same is true for a piece of software. In physical terms, a motion picture is about 10,000 feet of celluloid, worth (with the reel and can) perhaps $7. A software system can easily fit onto a CD. The value there: maybe 2¢. Hollywood and the IT industry use significant investments and resources to develop intangible products. If the project entails building a car and the car turns out to be a failure, it's at least possible to salvage some parts and sell the scrap metal. But if a movie is a dud, all the studio will have to show for it is the film, no matter how many millions it spent to get that film. And if an IT shop's software or system architecture is a dud, the same thing applies: All the shop is left with are bits, bytes, and maybe a little paper.

Shaped to a Business Need

A motion picture is not produced simply because some producers somewhere think they've got hold of a great story. Potential projects are analyzed in minute detail. The style of the story is assessed; the performances of similar stories are evaluated; audience trends and preferences are mapped. The studio is after one thing: a popular success. So projects are undertaken to meet a demand in the market place, a demand that will evidence itself in ticket sales. The same holds true for IT projects. Rarely are projects initiated simply for the sake of technological advances. Rather, business drivers form the catalysts that kick IT projects into gear. Behind most IT projects—and the technology teams that work them—is a business unit with teams of business specialists who are seeking some form of enhanced business operations. Add to this the driver of a deadline. In the same way that a movie must be ready for, say, the Summer Season or the Christmas Season, so too are IT projects driven by business deadlines.

Significant Investments

Both Hollywood and corporate IT departments operate through significant investments in time, resources, and money. A typical motion picture costs $65 million, takes a year to produce, and employs at different times about 200 people. A typical corporate IT department looks pretty much the same—an annual budget in the tens of millions and dozens of teams focused on the work at hand. Both are big business. And what's more, motion picture production and technology production are enterprises with relatively thin margins of success. For both, then, there is a real need to operate effectively and efficiently, with reliable controls over budgets, schedules, and resource utilization. Accordingly, predictable project management is crucial to both fields.

Specifications Open to Change

Another peculiarity shared by Hollywood and corporate IT is that they both work to specifications that are open to change. In Hollywood, the script is the starting point, but as production unfolds, it will often undergo rewrites, adjustments, and other kinds of changes. Change is famous in the IT world. Requirements can remain in a state of flux across the development life cycle. That's why change control is so important, on a movie set and within a tech team. Because the investments are so large and the success of the end product directly affects the ongoing success of the business, change needs to be managed in a coordinated and orderly fashion. The single trait that often separates well-run projects from well-worn ones is the attention paid to change control.

Specialized Production Protocols and Technologies

The terms and methods encountered in a technology department can appear alien to the business stakeholders the technology teams may interface with from time to time. For many outside parties, what goes on within the walls of IT is something akin to magic. It's technological mystery. Accordingly, it is often incumbent on IT to "translate" for its stakeholders, to foster a stream of communications that relieves its partners of technical details and focuses instead on business issues. The same thing occurs in Hollywood. The production system there relies on increasingly sophisticated techniques for how images, sound, music, editing, special effects, and other components are integrated into a seamless whole. The terms and methods that drive communications on a movie set can easily confuse the casual observer. Over the years, Hollywood has developed communication channels and reporting mechanisms that shield key stakeholders (executives and investors) from the details of the method while emphasizing production objectives, goals, and performance levels.

Specialized Teams

Movie making requires the use of many specialized teams: a producer's unit, a director's unit, a camera crew, a sound crew, the makeup department, the props department, the art department, costume, hair, electrical crew, catering, and so on. Each team has a specific job to perform and a specific contribution to make to the production. One key of project success here is the smooth coordination and collaboration among teams. The same need exists in the IT world. IT projects require the use of many specialized teams also: architects, designers, programmers, technical writers, testers, deployment specialists, and so on. These teams likewise provide specific services to the project as a whole. And just as in Hollywood, it is critical that these teams move in a synchronized manner.

Common Life Cycle

A distinct feature that Hollywood shares with corporate IT is a similar production life cycle. Both industries move a project through series of production phases. In Hollywood, the phases are development, preproduction, production, post-production, and distribution. The (typical) corresponding IT phases are initiation, planning, execution and control, closure, and deployment. The same kinds of activities occur in each phase. In phase 1, projects are assessed, selected, and initiated. In phase 2, projects are planned and—to a degree—designed. In phase 3, the project is executed according to plan. Phase 4 sees the final integration of product components. And phase 5 deals with the coordinated release of the product out to its users.

Strategic Delivery

Finally, in both industries, the final end products must be thoughtfully and carefully delivered to their target audiences. In the film industry, this involves marketing and promoting the movie through campaigns aimed at certain audiences. It also includes making release prints, which are then distributed to theaters. In short, the movie is packaged so its audience can easily find it. The same approach holds true for the IT industry. System deployment is a crucial but often overlooked capstone on a project. Proper documentation needs to be developed, training needs to be conducted, implementation schedules need to be worked out, and installations need to be undertaken. With both movies and software, this is where the true value of the product begins to become evident. A high-quality product given proper distribution will be met with the endorsement of its audience. That ensuing degree of customer satisfaction typically ensures the opportunity to engage in a new project.

These eight traits paint a synchronous clockwork shared by the motion picture industry and the world of IT. There is a difference, though: Hollywood has figured out how to make these traits work to its favor. And that brings us to the purpose of this book.

The Purpose of This Book

The main purpose of this book, then, is a simple one: to provide a set of practical guidelines and techniques that can be applied to the management of technology projects so that anticipated outcomes can be more fully realized. Throughout, this set of practices and techniques is borrowed from an industry known for its ability to achieve predefined outcomes: the motion picture industry. We'll work toward this using a three-faceted approach.

First, a range of problems commonly encountered within the domains of technology project management will be identified. These are the kinds of problems known to be the *dominant* causes of cost, schedule, and quality drifts. (It's impossible to look at all sources of project problems; there are just too many of them, and each with many incarnations.) Certain problems arise out of specific organizational cultures, industry focuses, competitive positions, market demands, and so on. Such problems can be called the "special" problems of project management; they are born out of particular environments. The focus, however, will be on the "general" problems of project management: those common ones that most shops, in one way or another, continually wrestle with. Being general, they are the ones that can most readily get a shop into trouble. But at the same time, their generality makes them amenable to modulation and control through management action.

Next, with these source problems identified and described, we'll leave the corridors of corporate American IT shops for the avenues of Hollywood. Keeping these problems in mind, we'll look at some of the practices and pathways that motion picture studios follow when they congregate a team to produce a movie. The idea here is not to find philosophical similarities that may exist between IT and Hollywood, or to look for a kindred spirit or shared management ethic. It's to point out concrete actions that deliver tangible measurable results when put into practice, actions that can tie directly to identified needs within technology projects. For example, how does Hollywood control its requirements? How does it use configuration management, performance reporting, or change control? How does it coordinate stakeholder involvement? How does it assess the business value of projects before committing to them? Once we identify these actions, we'll move back to our domain.

Finally, these Hollywood lessons will be transcribed for successful application across technology projects. Naturally, as with any management technique, some adaptation will be required. But the focus here is on minimal adaptation; the practices identified—the lessons presented—do not require a stretch in order to be useful. That's the major premise of this book: that the way Hollywood manages its projects is almost exactly the same as what's been recommended to American IT for the management of its own projects. Recommended by whom, or what? By the PMI (PMBOK), by the Agile Consortium (Agile and SCRUM), by the Software Engineering Institute (CMMI), by the International Standards Organization (ISO 9001), and so on.

The purpose of the book, then, may be to remind ourselves (through proof from others) that what we've been telling ourselves for a while now about effective project management has been right all along.

The Audience for This Book

This book is really intended for anyone who deals with technology product development and would like to explore ways in which the production process can be shaped to be better managed with more predictable end results. Specifically, however, it is aimed at three traditional roles within an organization: program and project managers, upper-level managers, and CIOs. Let's take a very quick look at each category.

Program and Project Managers

Project managers run individual projects. Program managers run, or oversee, collections of projects. These are the job roles that more often than not deal with the virtues and vices of product development. They are expected to deliver on the virtues and therefore are rarely given credit for them as they occur. But they get the full brunt of the vices—the problems, shortfalls, diversions, and disconnects—even when they are not provided the means for dealing with them. So they are the chief audience group for this book. Of note, as the prime audience, this group of readers won't be provided with a magical list of new lessons or techniques; rather, the book will show that those lessons and techniques they may already be familiar with really do work and in fact have been proved to work very well, with some variance, in the motion picture industry. My hope, then, is to provide program and project managers with the support they may need to reshape these practices for integration into their own shops.

Upper-Level Technology Managers

Program and project managers often have very solid ideas about how their projects ought to be managed; they typically have the background, experience, and training (usually through the PMI) for the mature development of such opinions. But upper-level managers—who may have to deal with a whole slew of other responsibilities and business demands—may not have the benefit of similar experience or exposures. As a consequence, they sometimes can't relate to the ideas presented to them, especially if they perceive that such concepts have potential to affect their domain cultures. For this reason (even though backed by sincere intentions), they have problems taking such suggestions at face value. They can't envision the benefits. The ideas presented in this book can provide a bit of the background and proof-of-concept data they may be looking for or curious about. Armed with these basics, they may begin to realize how they can apply some of these lessons, and then work with their program and project managers to effect coordinated, beneficial change.

CIOs

Throughout this book, it's emphasized that technology shops can improve fiscal and technical performance by adopting a project management methodology that follows the spirit of Hollywood's studio production system. No specific methodology, like the PMBOK or ISO or Agile or CMMI, is promoted here. The point is to establish *some* kind of system—big or small, heavy or light, custom or standardized. As noted earlier, most IT shops lack any system at all. As leaders in their organizations, CIOs are agents of change. As leaders, they should also be ultimately accountable for the effectiveness of their project management practices and product development performances. This book is intended to serve as a catalyst for change: CIOs who read it and acquire a new understanding of various elements of project management may then see the need for change and take advantage of some of the lessons in this book to start the change process.

How This Book Is Organized

This book is organized into five general parts. The order of those parts conforms to the sequence in which they occur within the Hollywood system. Of note, they also occur in this same general order in the traditional life cycle of a technology development project. (That, of course, is one of the themes of this book.) A brief overview follows.

Part I is titled **Development.** Here we look at a series of topics that deal with how projects are identified, initiated, and—from a corporate perspective—controlled. These topics include:

- The value of working to a project management methodology

- The importance of portfolio management

- The use of project concept assessment

- The advantage of working with strong business requirements

- The application of Agile methods to fix appropriate scopes

Most of the topics and the lessons we can derive from these subjects probably apply at the upper management level of an organization. They deal in executive decision-making domains that provide a strategic focus to technology management. From these domains, program and project management activities stem.

Part II is **Preproduction.** Here we look at issues and topics that focus on how projects are planned and staffed, and how sponsorship and commitments are obtained. These topics include:

- The creation of requirements analyses and work breakdown structures (WBSs)

- Establishing realistic budgets and schedules

- Identifying and providing qualified resources

- The value of enlisting the help of periodic performance audits

- Obtaining business sponsorship and commitments

These subjects apply at the program and project levels of an organization, and they also reach across into the business units of an organization. They focus specifically on the ways projects are analyzed and planned, how appropriate resources are identified, and how business and technology teams form common commitments to project goals.

Part III is **Production.** In this section we look at the kinds of topics that influence how projects are monitored, tracked, and controlled; and how progress is reported on. The focus here is on the somewhat specific details of pro forma project management. The following topics are discussed:

- The importance of focusing on requirements delivery

- Techniques to determine and assign work tasks

- Approaches to schedule, budget, and performance reporting

- The need to plan and begin verification activities early

From these topics are derived lessons that center on the day-to-day tasks of project management, with an emphasis on some controls that can be set into place to ensure that cost, schedule, functional, and quality objectives are continually being met.

Part IV is titled **Post-Production.** In the movie world, post-production deals with finishing a film through editing and mixing. Here we look at topics that center on the end of a project's life cycle, specifically on how product components are tested, packaged, and delivered. These topics include:

- The value of verifying requirements delivery

- The importance of user acceptance testing

- The incorporation of business feedback before delivery

The lessons that emerge in this part highlight the importance of a working partnership of business and technology teams to ensure that as a project nears its end targets, the developed product does indeed meet its business and operational objectives.

Part V, **Wrap-Up**, summarizes the themes of the book by revisiting the general needs of project management within corporate America. The topics touched on here at the end include:

- A reminder to follow the project management system (large or small) that the shop develops

- A quick relisting of the individual lessons

From Principles to Practice

The shape of the book as just outlined can serve to remind us of activities we probably know we should already be doing on projects. The stories presented in the following chapters provide proof that these activities really can work for us—that they do work for the movies and work really well. Let's begin with a look at Hollywood's studio production system and explore the lessons it has to share with us.

Find Additional Content Online

As new or updated material becomes available that complements developer books, it will be posted online on the Microsoft Press Online Developer Tools Web site. The type of material you might find includes updates to book content, articles, links to companion content, errata, and sample chapters. This Web site will be available soon at www.microsoft.com/learning/books/online/developer, and will be updated periodically.

Part I
Development

Here we look at a series of topics that deal with how projects are identified, initiated, and—from a corporate perspective—controlled.

Chapter 1
Know the System

This is not a book about process improvement or about the adoption of any particular process model to power information technology (IT) businesses. But a look at the techniques used by Hollywood production companies to manage their projects will clearly show the value that process brings to the table. Motion picture production is a process-driven system, and it's been that way since about 1920. In the 90 years since, the entertainment industry has refined and matured this process so that today, not only is it common *for an $80 million, two-year project to come in on budget, on schedule, and according to script, but it's* expected *as well.*

Things are different in the much younger technology industries. Software, systems, and hardware shops have yet to embrace process with the same enthusiasm or faith. Yet this is beginning to change. More and more chief information officers (CIOs) and senior managers are moving toward process-supported production methods. Industry support groups and organizations have responded in kind.

A look at the project management guidelines developed by the Project Management Institute and expressed in the Project Management Institute's (PMI) Project Management Body of Knowledge *(the PMBOK) will show a very methodological approach to this aspect of production. Likewise, the requirements of the International Standards Organization's (ISO) 9001:2000 generic quality standard incorporate practices that can support quality management in IT shops, as well as on the factory floor. And a review of the Software Engineering Institute's (SEI) Capability Maturity Model Integration (CMMI) process framework will reveal a model for technology development that emphasizes consistency, repeatability, and continuous refinement. Technology management and improvement guides such as Six Sigma, Agile, and Information Technology Infrastructure Library (ITIL) are based on the same kinds of concepts.*

The benefits of looking at Hollywood's studio production system in this context are readily identifiable. Both industries—the IT industry and the movie industry—share striking similarities in the life cycle of production. Because of these similarities, it's easy to observe firsthand the successful application of management concepts that have a direct impact on motion picture project success. With slight modification and adaptation, many of these practices can be integrated into IT shops, with expectations for similar success.

This opening chapter begins with an overview of the Hollywood system and shows how it ties in numerous ways to the life cycle of technology product development.

Two Percent Over, with a Lot of Explaining to Do

When you sit in Bill Fay's office, you know you're smack in the metaphorical middle of Hollywood, even though the office is in Burbank.

Bill is the president of Legendary Pictures, a production company in partnership with Warner Bros. Legendary's offices are in Building 26 on the Warner lot, a building that sits right in the shadow of the iconic Warner Bros. water tower. No steel and glass towers here—the compound is composed of cream stucco two- and three-story office buildings with Art Deco flourishes that radiate the heyday of 1940s studio production. When I arrive for my 10 o'clock meeting, the guard at Gate 4 checks me in, gives me a badge, and points to a parking space. Bill's office is on the second floor of Number 26. His assistant takes me up and shows me in. The exterior wall of the office is a long row of glass windows that look out on the water tower; the opposite wall is decorated with a series of movie posters that I take to be recent Legendary productions. The most prominent is a very large one for the picture *300*, a story about the battle of Thermopylae in 480 B.C. The movie, which mixes live action with extensive computer-generated imagery, was a huge hit for Legendary and Warner's. Bill tells me that this is one project he was especially pleased with—exactly on time, exactly on budget. At this interview, one of my first of many for this book, Bill begins to articulate how he and his people managed to achieve this outcome. The basic message echoes across all of those other interviews in almost the exact same way: The key, says Bill, is "the system."

People in Hollywood aren't bragging when they talk about "the system" like that, the way some IT people seem to be doing when they claim, for example, "We're CMMI Level 5 . . . " (which brings into question whether they really use the standard on a regular basis). In Hollywood, using the system is not a special achievement. It's a de facto management approach, one that all studios, all production companies, all independents adhere to—because it works. The Hollywood system is not 100 percent effective all of the time, and famous stories of the system gone haywire continue to be told. For the most part, however, it is a highly reliable way of conducting the business of movie making.

Hollywood, as we'll see throughout the chapters of this book, operates very much like the world of systems and software development. Both deal with amorphous products, both involve the use of specialized but integrated teams, both function under very real business deadlines and constraints, and both involve, to one degree or another, the use of "magic"— technical magic or creative magic. The U.S. IT industry is sized in the billions. The U.S. motion picture industry also is sized in the billions. The advantage Hollywood has—and one reason why it's been able to work out a manageable system—is simply one of age. The birth of the film industry can be dated to 1905 (the year the Lumière brothers presented the first public showing of short films in Paris), giving it about a century of learning that IT hasn't yet had. As Bill emphasizes, however, the system is not so much about controlling the magical, creative elements of film making as it is about managing the business aspects.

Here's how he paints the average motion picture project: To get a typical movie "in the can" takes about a year and a half of planning and work; it requires a talent pool (off and on) of about 200 to 300 people, spread across maybe 20 specialized teams; and it will need a capital investment (again the average) of about $65 million. That doesn't include the costs of promotion and distribution later on. That's just to get the movie *made*. Another cycle of work and perhaps an additional $35 million will get it on the screen.

When that much time, that many people, and that kind of money are involved, somebody somewhere better have some kind of system to manage it all. If you think about it, Bill says, you can see that the system is in place to ensure sound business practice across the life cycle of a picture project. He names five business attributes on which good practice is based: consistency, predictability, accountability, communications, and trackability.

Consistency   By this Bill means consistency of vision, a common agreement, reached through communications and reviews, regarding the purpose, scope, and tone of the project. The system helps ensure that all key players and department heads (the production chief, the director, the star, the production designer, the prop master, and on and on) share this vision and have agreed to shape their efforts in pursuing and achieving this vision. (That's one reason why contracts flourish so in Hollywood; they capture that consistency of vision in writing.)

Predictability   The system defines a preset work flow that can be mapped out, planned, and followed, thereby ensuring that essential work phases are not skipped and critical milestones are not missed or ignored. The schedules that drive productions are built around these phases and milestones. The budgets take into account the required system activities. The advantage of following a system like this is twofold. First, it should be possible to know on any day how well the project is proceeding according to plan. This knowledge is essential, given that a single day in production can cost $200,000. It should then be possible to judge what needs to be done today and where the process needs to be tomorrow. Second, this predictability adds visibility into the project: Not only should the production head know this information, but everyone else can leverage it, too, from the studio production chief on down the line. The system is a map, and others can intelligently follow your progress across that map.

Accountability   With a project with 20 teams and 200 people and $65 million on the hook, a lot of people must be accountable for a lot of different things. Slipping 10 percent over budget is a $6 million slip, so it's helpful to know who did the slipping and why. The system builds accountability into every phase of production. The production system pays very close attention to job descriptions. Part of this comes from the union- and guild-based talent pools that provide the workers in the movie industry. But the point is that job definitions (which in the IT world can often be murky) are firmly in place across a production team. Each person undertakes a specific role, makes specific contributions, is allocated a specific portion of the budget, and regularly reports on his or her performance. This level of accountability allows the producer's team to keep production targets always in focus, and to make appropriate adjustments and plan deviations when needed.

Communications   Another big benefit of the system, as emphasized by Bill as well as many other producers I interviewed, is the way it promotes communication—both informal, casual communications and formal, binding communications. Producing, at its heart, is a communications job. In the same way, IT project management also should be largely a communications job. You can't manage well by working solely from paper reports at a desk remote from the action. You need to be engaged with the people who are performing the work, the large jobs and the small jobs. The Hollywood system promotes this engagement through well-established communication channels that facilitate reviews, approvals, discussions, and myriad forms of on-the-go decision making.

Trackability   Finally, and perhaps of most importance (at least to the producers and studio chiefs), the system promotes regular and deep-reaching measures of progress. This progress tracking begins on day 1 and does not end until the lid on the can of the final cut is taped shut. The system brings with it daily "hot cost" reports (day-by-day expenditures), weekly cost reports, labor reports, schedule reports, scene completion reports, and call sheets for upcoming work: measurement, measurement, measurement, both up and down the chain. Rigorous adherence to this aspect of the system is essential; otherwise, people tend to run out and do their own things, unguided and unchecked. The end result can be a *Heaven's Gate* or a *Waterworld*, with people scratching their heads and asking, "Wasn't this Paul's office yesterday?"

Two features of these five attributes are noteworthy. First, they essentially translate to basic management techniques. As well-worn adages of Business 101, they're likely to be encountered, in some form or other, in just about any business enterprise. Second, the use of a system—any kind of a method or approach—to embed these traits into routine activities seems essential to the success of a business culture. And yet in my years in technology development, working in shops of all shapes and sizes, I have only rarely encountered development methodologies or process approaches of this kind.

Like many IT professionals, I've worked on technology projects run by capable managers and staffed with solid technical talent, and I've watched my fair share of these slip into an escalating spiral of cost and schedule overruns, some by well over 100 percent. Plenty of these stories abound—and they almost always come from system-less shops. When I tell a couple of these stories to Bill Fay, he shakes his head in disbelief. "That wouldn't fly in this business," he says. He explains that no able producer or competent production team would ever allow a project to drift so far off base. He mentions that all productions begin with a 10 percent contingency. Any time a project looks like it might have to tap into the contingency, bells go off, notifications go out, and analyses are made. And should a project come in at the end with a 2 or 3 percent overage of budget or schedule, someone will have a lot of explaining to do.

I do not mention to Bill that in the IT world, a 2 or 3 percent drift would be considered a wild success. Instead, I focus back on the system, because I've been caught with a different kind of surprise: The system he's been describing sounds like an apt framework for managing a technology project.

The Hollywood System of Production Management

The Hollywood production system really is a formal system. It's not a buzzword or a cliché or a pseudonym for big studio clout. It's the established way of engaging in motion picture production.

The system consists of five separate and distinct phases, each one leading from and building on the previous. Whether you're Paramount, Warner Bros., Metro-Goldwyn-Mayer (MGM), Miramax, Parallel Entertainment, or Legendary Pictures, you use the system. Ask Bill Fay or fellow studio executives Pat Crowley, Marty Ewing, Michael Beugg, Amy Kaufman, and Clayton Townsend to describe the system, and you'll get the same answer each time.

Figure 1-1 depicts how the Hollywood system, with its five phases, is structured. These phases are discussed next.

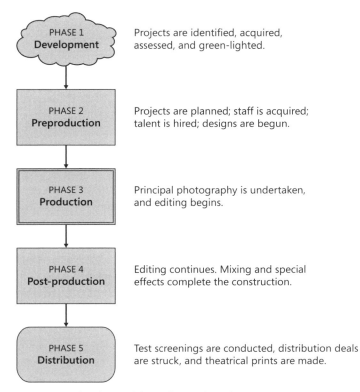

PHASE 1 Development — Projects are identified, acquired, assessed, and green-lighted.

PHASE 2 Preproduction — Projects are planned; staff is acquired; talent is hired; designs are begun.

PHASE 3 Production — Principal photography is undertaken, and editing begins.

PHASE 4 Post-production — Editing continues. Mixing and special effects complete the construction.

PHASE 5 Distribution — Test screenings are conducted, distribution deals are struck, and theatrical prints are made.

FIGURE 1-1 The shape of the Hollywood production system

Phase 1: Development

The first phase in motion picture production is *development*, the activities a studio performs to develop a concept or idea into a producible product: the movie. Many people in the industry would argue that development is the most important stage in successful production. It is here that the product first begins to take shape, where its form and function are initially determined. If the initial assumptions and decisions are valid, the picture stands a better chance of meeting its market and audience potentials. But if the assumptions and decisions are off the mark, the picture may founder.

The most popular example of a project plagued by incorrect assumptions, cited by a few of the studio executives I spoke to, is the 1995 adventure movie *Waterworld*. In development, the producers decided that for the sake of verisimilitude the movie—about a world submerged by a single vast ocean—would be shot out on the ocean, not in a studio tank or a harbor. What they failed to take into account was picture continuity; from shot to shot the sea surface is never the same, so scene cuts often would not match. This led to delay after delay caused by waiting for appropriate conditions and reshooting. The producers also did not fully account for the engineering solutions required for a movie set to float. Sets sank. The wild budget and schedule overruns on *Waterworld* have since become the stuff of legend, and the movie's cool public reception served to reinforce the value of realistic decision making in the development phase.

All studios, production houses, and independent producers move through a development phase for their projects. Development of a project may take three or four months, or it may take a year or two. But to one degree or another, the development phase encompasses six common activities: market analysis, property analysis, concept development, script development, packaging, and financing. These activities are discussed next.

Market Analysis

Studios don't develop movie projects because they have a romantic attachment to a particular theme or story hook. They move on a particular project because they understand the marketplace, they know what's been performing well, and they know how audience preferences are morphing; from this knowledge, they derive what might sell. The longevity of the genre film is evidence of the benefit of this kind of analysis: the western, the courtroom drama, the coming-of-age story, the romantic comedy, the fantasy. These are product formulas whose popularity rises and falls in the marketplace. Studios are in business in large part to understand how the market is changing. Their production decisions are based largely on how well a current idea fits perceived market demands.

Property Analysis

For any given IT project, according to an adage in the technology world, the following decision will be necessary at some point: do we make, buy, or reuse? The preference, of course, is to reuse something the shop already has—it's cheaper. And if it worked well the first time, it'll probably perform well again. It's the same with the studio. Columbia Pictures, together with Marvel Enterprises, owns the Spiderman franchise. MGM owns the James Bond franchise. These are two very popular series, so if the studio already has an investment in that property, why not continue leveraging it? It's probably a safer bet than putting those dollars into a totally new superhero or international secret agent. Studios are highly aware of their existing properties, and they are always looking for the right market opportunity to recycle that successful character, story line, or landscape.

Concept Development

Many studios and production companies employ "creative producers." These professionals are not really producers in the business sense of production management. Rather, they work to develop unformed concepts and storylines into feasible production proposals. Often this concept may arise from a promising or popular book—would this translate into a good movie? Or it may take the form of an existing script that a writer's agent submits to a studio. Alternatively, it may be the potential of a popular performer to cross over from the stage into motion pictures. Whatever the catalyst may be, the job of the creative producer is to see whether the concept can grow from an attractive idea into a bankable project. Creative producers may work on any number of projects at once, often with a team of analysts working under them. If their results reveal a concept with solid entertainment value, the studio may move forward. If not, the project goes into a cardboard box to be set on a shelf somewhere, perhaps never to see the light of day again.

Script Development

Two additional practices common to development (before financing) are script development and packaging. These activities can be carried out at any time during development, but they typically come about because a certain project carries with it solid market potential. The script may be the single most essential product that comes out of development. It is the foundation on which all subsequent decisions and activities are based. The script (for more on this topic, see Chapter 4, "Invest in a Solid Script") not only will contain the developed story and concept lines but will also reflect the market and property characteristics that marked it as bankable.

Packaging

With a draft script ready to go, the next step is to package it with known creative talent. Successful packaging is a near-guarantee that a project will move into production.

Packaging is the activity whereby the studio takes a script and attaches a "Name" to it, perhaps a well-known actor, or maybe a noted director. This packaging together of talent with script establishes the magnetism of a project—its ability to attract financing, press attention, and audience curiosity. Once a project has been packaged, the studio can derive an initial estimate of production costs and comfortably begin to explore investment channels.

Financing

At the end of the development phase, here's what has happened so far: A solid idea—derived either from an existing entertainment property or from a perceived market need—has been generated; that idea has been developed to see if it can sustain the weight of production; if so, a first-round script has been developed and circulated among potential creative partners. The bankability of the project has now been established. The studio can decide to finance it itself or to seek outside capital support, or both. Either way, a cost-benefit analysis (CBA) is then typically run to objectify the likely investment that will be required. Deals are struck, contracts are signed, and bank accounts are filled.

In the foregoing overview of development, the activities described seem to rely in large part on creative imagination and innovation. But the central focus, and the reason for the conduct of these activities, is a business consideration: market viability combined with production validity. Once financing is secured, the project can move forward.

Phase 2: Preproduction

Studio executives and production chiefs like to emphasize the importance of the development phase. This emphasis is understandable, because it's in development that most of the major studio-level decisions are made. But ask executive producers or line producers which state is most important, and you'll probably get a different answer. They're likely to say preproduction.

Preproduction is the planning stage of movie making. It's where the details of shooting are carefully worked out. More than that, it's the phase in which the production team is first brought together; where the tone, look, and feel of the movie are established; where performances are rehearsed; where milestones and deadlines are established. Preproduction anticipates and shapes the flow of production. And, as noted, because a typical shooting day on a mainstream movie set can cost upwards of $200,000, the need to go in prepared is paramount. More often than not, bad planning leads to bad movie making.

Preproduction lasts from three months to a year (depending on the project), and it is awash in activity: staffing, planning, script refinement, casting, location, scouting, and design. These six major tasks of preproduction are described next.

Staffing

In the software/systems world, each project is staffed with a set of key players: a lead architect or designer, a project manager, business analyst, database designer, lead programmer, test manager, technical writer, and user interface (UI) specialist. Hollywood has its own roster of key players, and these people are brought into the project during the early stages of preproduction. They are known as department heads—they lead the camera department, the sound department, the art department, make-up, costumes, and so on. The roles are well known: director, director of photography, production designer, location manager, editor, sound designer, costume designer. A key word here is "design," because that's really what these people do. They design very specific elements of the picture, in very much the same way that a technical team designs various aspects of, say, a software system. These people are brought on board under contract and given a span of time (for a major production, usually no less than three months) to shape their respective parts of the project.

Planning

Planning is the major activity of preproduction. In the development phase, a general budget is established by one of the producers to kick the project into gear. Now that the project has been green-lighted, a detailed budget and schedule need to be put together. To do this, the producer, the unit production manager, and the first assistant director analyze the script, organize the scenes into a logical shooting order, and—through consultation with the available department heads—flesh out a shooting schedule and a production budget. Both of these documents are highly detailed. It's not unusual for a production budget to run to 60 very full pages. Shooting schedules account for script progress by every one-eighth of a page.

A serious commitment is made by the studio and the producers to ensure the quality of these two planning activities. After all, the budget and the schedule that emerge will serve as a contract between all stakeholders in the project. These documents set risk limits for the studio. They designate performance expectations for the creative and management teams. They establish obligations for the performing talent. And because the parties involved all have the opportunity to give feedback during plan development and because they will eventually sign a work-for-hire contract tied directly to the budget and schedule, they all are expected to fulfill their commitments.

Script Refinement

Like business and functional requirements in the technical domains of the business enterprise, the script is likely to go through a series of revisions and refinements during preproduction. This refinement process may be to align its scope more closely to the budget or schedule, or to adjust parts of its storyline or character arcs to mesh better with the attributes of certain cast members, or simply to punch up parts that need to be stronger. The basic shape and essence of the script, however, will remain intact—that was the basis for moving forward in the first place. It is rare that a script will need—or be allowed—major rework once preproduction is under way. A script in that state runs counter to the needs for detailed planning and design work. If such rework is needed, preproduction is usually shut down, and the project may stall. In Hollywood, the explanation "the script is back in development" is a sign that the script and the project are in serious trouble. But that's actually a sign of maturity in the enterprise: Management will not move ahead if the basic requirements of the project—as embodied in the script—are not ready to be realized.

Casting

Primary casting of the movie's stars usually takes place in the development phase, as part of packaging. But a movie also features other actors, in a variety of supporting roles. During preproduction, the production team, working with a casting director or a casting agency, will talk to interested parties, review resumes, hold auditions, and perhaps shoot some screen tests, all to fill the other roles for the picture. An adage in Hollywood states that casting is 80 percent of the battle. Get the right faces up on the screen, and the magic that the studio is looking for will come more naturally. A parallel in the world of technology development is building technical teams with the necessary skill sets. Armed with the right skills, they'll be able to produce good work more quickly and with more predictable outcomes.

Location Scouting

I was surprised to learn that one of the biggest expenses associated with any movie project is transportation. Every time a production unit has to hit the road, it's like moving a small army to a new base camp, or moving a circus to a new town. That's why location scouting is so important. Working with the other department heads, the location manager analyzes the script to get a feel for what locations will be needed. The idea is to compress the story's needs into as few moves as possible, to condense the geographic spread into as small a landscape as possible while retaining the required look, feel, and verisimilitude of the story. Location scouting is similar to equipment acquisition and allocation in the technology industries. When IT projects begin, it's helpful to procure the computing resources, development environments, and tools that will be needed to accommodate specific types and levels of technical work. If these resources are not ready when the team arrives, little productive work can be accomplished.

Design

After planning, design may be the next most important job in preproduction. In IT vocabulary, the design of the project represents the technical solution for the requirements and the architecture that will express that solution. In the movie world, design includes the construction of sets, the creation of costumes, styles for hair and makeup, types of props, the tenor of the sound, the rhythm in the editing, the lighting and look of the visual images, and many other elements.

These decisions spring from the script and are guided by the chief creative manager, the director. His job is to synthesize all of these approaches into a single vision. It is critical that these decisions occur in preproduction; by the time production rolls around, a vast machine has been set into motion, and little time will be available for entertaining significant redesign considerations. Even more so, these design choices have been fed as raw material into the budget and schedule. Any big design changes, once agreement has been reached, could risk exceeding the established schedule and budget constraints.

Phase 3: Production

Production—with its sound stages, exotic locales, lights, cameras, and hubbub of activity—comes across to most people as the truly exciting part of movie making. That may be true for the chief artists and performers, but for most of the other folks on the lot, it's the most prosaic. And in fact, that's the way it should be; that's the way the producers prefer it. The magic movie-making machine has now been turned on, and the producers want it to smoothly turn out a movie, just as planned. For research for this book, I was allowed on the sound stage of the upcoming romantic comedy, *He's Just Not That into You.* For about half an hour, watching a certain scene being shot, I did feel a bit of excitement. But after that it started to get very repetitive. Everything was so orderly; everyone had a job to do, and they didn't fuss about it—they just did it. It was clear that they were all parts of that well-tuned movie-making machine.

Four major activities—shooting, rough cut editing, production reporting, and adjustments—occur during the production phase. Let's take a quick look at each.

Shooting

Shooting is the phase of principal photography, when the story is actually filmed. In Hollywood, a typical shooting schedule is 55 to 65 workdays. After many, many months of development and many, many months of preproduction, the team now has about three months to get the thing in the can. Using the schedules, teams, and designs established earlier, the production unit executes according to plan.

Rough Cut Editing

While the shoot is still running, the editing team begins "testing" the quality of the output. Rushes (film sequences shot that day) are examined and assessed every evening (with the film director and the director of photography [DP]), and the team begins to cut the scenes together to ensure that the story itself is becoming a coherent whole and that all the necessary imagery is being accounted for. Later on, after production wraps, the director will join the editing team to prepare a final, nuanced cut of the picture.

Production Reporting

Progress and expense reporting is a big job in movie making. It's a big reason for why producers even exist. Although this reporting begins as early as development and preproduction, it really ramps up during the production phase. The reason is obvious: Production is the most expensive part of the whole endeavor. Investments are required in development, in preproduction, and in post-production—often significant investments. But the real money—up to $500,000 a day—leaves the bank during production. Accordingly, production reports are constantly being generated and circulated: daily production reports (scenes shot, film stock exposed, and so on), script progress and continuity reports, daily hot cost expense reports, and weekly consolidated expense reports. And all are meticulously studied up and down the management and creative chains.

Adjustments

Finally, an Agile-like quality is inherent in the production phase. This quality comes from the series of regular (and to-be-expected) adjustments that naturally affect any plan or project, no matter what the industry or what that industry produces. Change is a constant during the production phase: Scripts may be adjusted, locations may need to be shifted, cast members may need special accommodations, rising costs in one place may necessitate a reduction of costs elsewhere. That's one of the reasons the producer's unit (i.e., the members of the management team) always travels with the production team—because production requires ongoing project management. And it's essential that this management be conducted in a very interactive, collaborative, and coordinated manner.

Phase 4: Post-Production

Once production wraps, the project now moves into *post-production*. This is a period of usually between 16 and 24 weeks, during which all of the separate elements of the movie come together. The picture, dialog, sound effects, music, special effects, transitions, and titles are integrated into a seamless whole. And from this integrative process, the movie is born.

The three chief activities of post-production are final editing, mixing, and audience testing, as discussed next.

Final Editing

During the actual shoot, the editing team examined shot footage and began assembling the shots into a rough cut. In the IT field, we'd probably call this kind of work integration testing. The intent up to this point has been to make sure that the right parts are being produced and that they will fit together in a logical order. When production wraps, the director will join the editing team to produce a final edit.

At this stage, the picture is cut into final form to establish rhythm, pace, texture, emotional drive, and story momentum. The final edit is one with all of the director's desired nuances accounted for.

Mixing

Mixing is really an extension of final editing. It is at this stage that all of the multiple presentation layers of a film are blended together. The images are cleaned up, dialog levels are honed and balanced, music is scored and laid in, sound effects are added, and special effects are cut in. In systems and software projects, this activity is akin to system testing after integration testing (i.e., the final edit) has been completed. The result is a final, compiled and integrated product, ready for test marketing.

Audience Testing

A critical aspect of post-production is audience testing. It is also one of the most nerve-racking for the production team to endure. Audience testing is just what it sounds like: The studio's marketing folks rent out a theater and invite a crowd with what they consider to be the right demographic mix. Then they show the movie.

Afterwards the screeners hand out opinion cards with a series of questions that delve into what the viewers did or did not like about the picture. IT people can recognize this kind of polling as user acceptance testing in its most venerable form. Positive responses tell the studio it has a winner. Conversely, a high proportion of negative responses indicates the need for another round of editing, or the addition of some new elements, or maybe even the shooting of some new scenes.

The purpose of testing is not to praise or point out the failures of the production team. It is to establish a business basis for marketing the picture. The studio wants to put out a product that appeals to the audience as much as possible, so it will make any adjustments it can practically make at this point, given the potential return on investment (ROI), in order to capture, leverage, or maximize that audience appeal.

When the movie is as finished as it's going to get, it's ready for distribution.

Phase 5: Distribution

A movie, which can take two years from conception to release, has only about two or three weeks in the theaters to prove its market strength. That period will reveal if the picture has "legs"—that is, if it will play successfully for weeks or months. Also established during this period is the likelihood that the picture will have a strong ancillary life in international markets, DVD sales, cable TV, and other outlets. This *distribution* phase includes three main activities: marketing and advertising, printing, and release.

Marketing and Advertising

Software and systems development professionals appreciate the need to prepare the user community to work with the solutions they deploy into operating environments and data centers. This preparation process typically entails the development of orientation materials, user guides, maintenance guides, training materials, and so on, all designed to meet the needs of the various user communities. Hollywood does the same thing in preparation of its releases. Its marketing and advertising specialists design ad campaigns, theatrical trailers, posters, and other promotional materials that will communicate to the marketplace what the picture is about and what makes it worth seeing. This step is always a major consideration for any motion picture project. A studio can easily spend on promotion half what a picture costs to make, sometimes much more.

Printing

Almost as expensive as advertising is the process of striking release prints. These are the copies of the movie that are shipped out to the theaters. A release print can cost about $2,000. So if the plan is to open in wide release, say, in 2000 theaters, investment of another $4 million or so in the project will be required. This high cost of printing is another reason why the system is so methodical in its focus on quality and detail. If the movie is a hit, those prints will have a productive circulation life. If it is not, the studio will have a lot of cans of film that no one really wants to see. And there's no real residual value in those cans: Each is worth perhaps $3 in aluminum and cellulose. It's the same with software. Your IT shop can invest $10 million in a project just to end up with some software stored on a $30 jump drive. If no one likes the software, all you'll have to show for it is a jump drive.

Release

After the movie goes out to the theaters., it's up to the audience to establish the real level of success. Now that the film has been released, the studio needs to wait for the box office results to start coming in. In this context, a difference between the film and software worlds is worth noting: professional success versus commercial success. If IT projects are professionally successful—that is, if they meet the customers' needs within their constraints—then by default they will be considered a business success, because they have addressed the business needs of scope, budget, and schedule. And although a movie (for any number of mysterious reasons) may not be a commercial success, under certain circumstances it may still be considered a professional success. If it met its own scope, budget, and schedule constraints, then it can at least be respected as a professional product. This possibility may not be a comfort to the investors, but it should be seen as a tribute to the system. Hollywood may produce many pictures that people consider "bad," but it rarely puts out a picture that comes across, from a presentation viewpoint, as inept. Even the silliest movies tend to look pretty good. Rarely does a movie audience see sloppy craftsmanship. In large part, viewers have the system to thank for that.

It took Bill Fay of Legendary Pictures a little under an hour of his time to describe the Hollywood system to me. I could tell two things by his casual yet orderly explanation. First, he knows this process backwards and forwards, and the other producers who succeed in this business know it equally well. Second, it's a real system, a living system, a practical, hands-on approach that's put to the test every day.

That's Bill's high-level picture of motion picture production. When people refer to Hollywood as the "Dream Factory," *factory* is just as relevant as *dream*. A factory in this sense may not be quite the same as a Campbell's Soup facility housing a can-stamping machine. But the same kind of preset pathway is in place to foster repeatability, predictability, and consistency.

The first major theme of this book is that this methodology can be used to show technology shops that a process similar to the Hollywood system can indeed work to enhance efficiency and quality in industries that create products that are intangible in many ways. Such products include both movies, which are little more than light bounced off a reflective screen, and software or system schematics. By looking at the performance of production companies as reflected in their ability to work on budget, on time, and to spec, we might be better able to visualize a similar kind of performance for our IT shops.

The second major theme of this book is that we can actually take some of these production practices and, with slight modification or adjustment, directly apply them as management aids in our shops. To expound a little on this, let's now move back to the world of corporate IT.

A Similar Model for the Technology Industries

Most IT professionals who have developed systems and software, managed technology projects, or helped guide technology organizations understand the intricacies inherent in complex projects. Taxed resources, changing technologies, competing stakeholder agendas, evolving requirements—these are just a few of the elements that need to be successfully juggled across even a simple project's life.

Many people cite this reality as a reason to avoid process. What they do in their shop, they maintain, is too unique for process to apply. Or process by definition is heavy and will weigh down performance and creativity. Or they just don't have the time to develop a process. Or systems development is more art than science (or engineering) anyway. And on and on.

The feelings that drive people to take those positions are understandable; healthy organisms, humans included, tend to resist change and to avoid the unknown. But the evidence shows that their reasoning is not valid. In fact, shops that operate without any formal system or development approach tend to exhibit three common traits:

- They rely on the efforts of highly talented persons—so-called heroes—to push work through.

- They push an overtime work ethic, a get-it-done-at-all-costs management style (that seems to be levied only on the line workers).

- They are due date–oriented—that is, they prefer cycles of rework, revision, and re-release over upfront planning and design activities.

If you managed a bakery shop that way, you probably wouldn't be in business long. Same for a tailor shop, or a doctor's office, or a coat hanger factory. Likewise for a motion picture project. Yet many, maybe even most, technology shops in corporate America run without any kind of system. In my years of consulting with small, large, and in-between technology organizations, I have found this condition to be curiously prevalent. It's especially strange because what would never fly in, say, the shipping and receiving unit of a business enterprise, too often makes it through that company's IT unit without notice. Even if we set aside the amount of money invested in IT budgets, the pressures of taxed resources, changing technologies, competing stakeholder agendas, and evolving business requirements are specific enough reasons for adopting process.

The answer to this challenge of fostering process and control in a business environment of change and uncertainty in part already exists for corporate American IT.

Readers who are educated in general business management disciplines or perhaps have earned the Project Management Professional (PMP) certification from the PMI, or who are familiar with quality standards such as CMMI, ITIL, Agile, and ISO 9001, or those who work in true engineering shops, will readily recognize the principles of the five-phase motion picture production system just described. That's because it has a lot in common with the classic system development life cycle (SDLC) the software world knows well. Even more so, it practically mirrors the management phase approach supported by the PMI for structuring projects. These PMI phases (the technical term is "process areas") are initiating, planning, executing, control, and closure. Projects are planned, managed, and monitored around these phases.

For the remainder of this chapter, I'll use this approach, with my own "deployment phase" added in, to begin tying motion picture production practices to practices recommended for adoption in technology shops to manage IT projects more effectively.

Figure 1-2 shows the relationship between the phases of the Hollywood system and the phases that the PMI's PMBOK describes for organizing the processes that control project management.

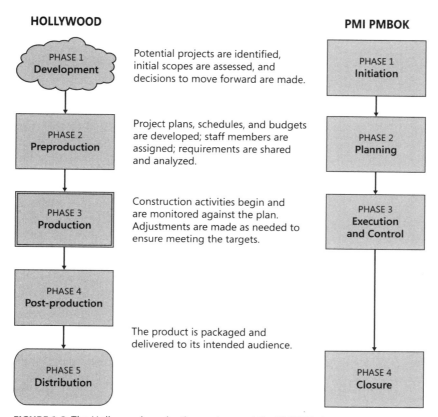

FIGURE 1-2 The Hollywood production system and the PMBOK phases

Phase 1: Initiation

The *initiation* phase in the IT world can work very much like the development phase in the entertainment world. The chief goal here is to identify projects that will contribute to the business mission of the enterprise and then provide resources for those projects to take shape. In the Hollywood system, studios look at market trends, assess their current portfolios, appraise available concepts, develop scripts, package the script with stars, and then set financing in place. The IT world could benefit by adopting similar practices. Three such development-like practices are business analysis, project development, and project scoping, all of which probably should be implemented at the upper management level. These practices, summarized next, can be used to shape the strategic direction and tactical focus of a development organization.

Business Analysis

In corporate America, sometimes it seems that IT projects get pushed into production on the basis of either the "decibel principle" (whoever yells loudest) or the "density principle" (whoever can throw the most weight around). CIOs and their executive staffs often find that they are viewed by external business units as *producers* of products (i.e., solutions), rather than *shapers* of products. Accordingly, they are expected to deliver whenever called on, often caught downstream of the initial decision to act. That line of separation, however, is not a productive one to follow. The business side of business and the technology side of business have become so integrated that there are no "sides" anymore, and well-thought-out technology solutions are essential to continued business success.

Business units, therefore, should work up front in partnership with their IT shops to explore potential opportunities, assess their costs and benefits, weigh impacts on the existing portfolio, and then establish a protocol for project selection. (For some practical guidelines in this area, see Chapter 2, "Know Your Properties," and Chapter 3, "Establish Green-Light Rules.")

Project Development

Once a movie gets the green light, it goes on the studio's production sheet as an official in-the-works project. An executive producer is then assigned to get the thing in shape. This same sequence is required when the enterprise selects an IT project to undertake: The organization at large needs to demonstrate its commitment to the project; this usually takes the form of capital investment. Then the sponsor needs to be identified, who typically is a business manager that will facilitate the exchange of work between the business specialists and the technology specialists. Two documents should emerge from the initial interactions between those parties. The first is a project charter, a formal description of the purpose and reach of the project. The second is the beginning of what might be called a script: a first draft of the business requirements, which will be used to guide the project. (For some practical guidelines in this area, see Chapter 4.)

Project Scoping

By the end of Initiation, the organization may have appointed a specific project manager (or perhaps a program manager) to begin scoping the project. Based on the business analyses conducted as described, together with the charter and the business requirements, the major boundaries of the effort can now be established. Here the size, general cost, relative schedule, and release dates are documented; from these boundaries, detailed project planning can begin. (For some practical guidelines in this area, see Chapter 5, "Time Box the Projects.")

Phase 2: Planning

The *planning* phase described in the PMBOK is just like Hollywood's preproduction phase. The goal here is to work out the details of project activities so that the effort can be tracked and controlled in an efficient manner, to meet the project's initial boundaries of scope, cost, and schedule. Three events should occur in some form at this stage of an IT project: business and functional requirements development, plan development, and staff acquisition.

Requirements Refinement

Hollywood's projects always begin with a script, even though it may undergo a series of revisions over its life. But a script is always the starting point. Technology projects need the same kind of starting point. Without some baseline set of requirements, it's difficult to plan, manage, or monitor a project. For this reason, the job of eliciting and documenting business and functional requirements tends to be an upfront consideration. The process of requirements development, however, does pose something of a conundrum: How can the requirements be defined until the project is under way? But how can requirements development be managed unless it's part of the project?

Two good solutions are possible here. One is to treat the requirements definition activities as a project unto itself, with a fixed amount of time and resources in order to establish a baseline. The other is to use the available business requirements as a benchmark for initial scope, plan from there, and then provide for appropriate change control. Either way, the process starts off with a picture of what the end product probably should look like. The alternative strategy—and it's the one many shops are drawn to, probably because it gives the impression of rapid progress—is to simply jump ahead into the unknown, trying to formulate a plan in the absence of solid expectations or common understandings. (For some practical guidelines on scope management, see Chapter 6, "Strip Board the Script.") The importance of developing a realistic, formal plan becomes obvious.

Staff Acquisition

Hollywood production teams hire on department heads during preproduction. Technology projects should likewise appoint key team members during the planning phase. The reason for early staff acquisition is twofold. First, it can take time to identify and connect with the right resources. Talented, competent people are essential to the success of any project. A process will never replace that need; it complements it. Second, adequate staff preparation is essential. In all probability, the project manager has reached this stage with an objective, a charter, some set of requirements, and some initial planning data. It now becomes important to identify these "department heads"—the lead designers, lead business analysts, database administrators (DBAs), whatever expertise and talent the team may be composed of—and involve them a couple of ways. They can use this time for orientation, for familiarizing themselves with the demands of the project, for thinking about possible approaches and technical options. The project manager also can solicit planning data from them, such as time and resource estimates, the kind of expert insight that will make the plan realistically achievable. (For some practical guidelines in this area, see Chapter 7, "Staff to the Genre.")

Plan Development

Planning is just as important for technology projects as it is for movie projects. The big costs of an IT project come during execution, when the designers are designing, the coders are coding, and the testers are testing. A thorough and realistic plan will help the project manager control this capital- and resource-intensive phase of project work. Budgets, schedules, and logistics need to be worked out in detail, preferably with input from the project's key stakeholders. As the saying goes, if you fail to plan, you plan to fail. Together with the project charter and the requirements, the project plan should be seen as the project's chief management tool, the yardstick that will be used to measure and gauge performance across the entire life cycle. (For some practical guidelines in this area, see Chapter 8, "Budget to the Board.")

Phase 3: Execution and Control

The "real" work of the project is now ready to be implemented. The team assembles and begins working out a technical solution to the business need. This is the focal point of resource and capital expenditures, and it's where most of the visible work gets done. This phase of *execution and control* can be considered the equivalent of the shooting stage of film making in the Hollywood system. Three major management activities occur here: design, development, and testing; change control; and progress and performance reporting.

Change Control

As with a movie production team, change will be inevitable for a technology production team. Change may come from any number of sources: requirements, human resources, facility use, and so on. The key is to not see change as disruptive but as a necessary component of solution realization. Change becomes problematic only when it's out of control, when it is effected without coordinated purpose. Rampant and disjointed change can sink any project into a morass of budget, schedule, scope, and quality slippages. To help prevent such problems, project management should ensure that a proper form of executive-endorsed change control is in place for the project. The protocols set aside for this process should allow for the orderly submission of change requests, the evaluation of change impacts, and a manner of scoring or weighting the approval of change requests. (For some practical guidelines in this area, see Chapter 9, "Sign on the Dotted Line.")

Design, Development, Testing

Design, development, and testing constitute the main work of execution, the production phase counterpart for technology shops. Alternatives are evaluated, solutions are designed, designs are implemented, documentation is prepared, testing cycles are run, and so on. This three-pronged activity represents the heart of any project, and it's typically where the most focused work takes place. If the project has been well planned and is being intelligently monitored and controlled, it should be a somewhat predictable phase, too. Most of the major business and management decisions should have been made by now. The major stakeholders should be in close agreement regarding what the project is all about and how to reach its goals. What's left is for the building blocks to be set in place. Because most technology shops are really good at technology, the kinds of problems that impede project success are usually not technology problems. Rather, they are scope, commitment, and communication problems. Prepare well, monitor well, control well—if the project manager focuses on these tasks, then the technical folks should find themselves free to productively focus on their tasks and not have to deal with the ad hoc push and pull found in ill-managed environments. (For some practical guidelines in this area, see Chapter 10, "Stick to the Script," and Chapter 11, "Work to the Call Sheets.")

Progress and Performance Reporting

As noted by Bill Fay, producing is a "walking-around" type job. In other words, you can't do it well solely from behind an office desk. You've got to actively communicate.

IT project managers have that same responsibility. Communication should be a proactive, ongoing ingredient to all project activities. From communications comes information, and from information comes an understanding of where the project teams stand in relation to progress and performance. That's the kind of reporting all project participants need—upstream and downstream—to appropriately focus their activities. Progress reports are akin to general status reports. They typically summarize schedule, budget, and resource utilizations against predefined benchmarks. Performance reports complement these by summarizing performance data as related to predefined performance and quality targets. Both are extremely useful when it comes to charting the ongoing course of the project. (For some practical guidelines in this area, see Chapter 12, "Ante Up the Completion Bond," and Chapter 13, "Manage the Hot Costs.")

Phase 4: Closure

Closure is considered to represent the contractual end of the project, the point at which all work has been completed and all commitments have been met. Paperwork is now complete, and resources can be released to move on to new project work. Three activities typically take place around the time of closure: user acceptance testing, resource release, and a review of lessons learned.

User Acceptance Testing

Hollywood tests its movies with test audiences before releasing the final version into theaters. The technology world does this kind of testing too. IT people call it *user acceptance testing*. After unit testing, integration testing, system testing, and regression testing (if required), the users are asked to take a look at what the IT shop has created. The idea is for them to work with the system and confirm that it really does meet their business needs and that it is solid enough to go into production. If the users agree that those conditions are met, the development team can move forward and package the product for release. If some important bugs or other problems are discovered, some rework may be needed.

Alignment and involvement of the project team with the users at this point are crucial. To forgo this step and move directly into production risks implementing a solution that may not address the right problem. Worse still, it may inadvertently introduce new problems. But worst of all, skipping user acceptance testing sends a silent message to the business community—that the technology folks place little value on their relationship with technology products. This message will serve only to push the two parties apart when the goal is to work closer and closer together. When addressed as a key item right from the start of a project, user acceptance testing can serve as a tool to foster close relationships between business and technology teams. (For some practical guidelines in this area, see Chapter 14, "Cut as You Go," Chapter 15, "Edit to the Investment," and Chapter 16, "Study the Test Cards.")

Resource Release

At this point, the project manager probably is ready to formally release the project's team members. This may sound like a trivial clean-up step, but it's actually quite important, especially in larger organizations. A formal, prescribed release activity will help notify business units and teams across the organization that particular people are now free for assignment elsewhere. This coordinated control of resource availability lends itself to more effective planning and coordination on upcoming projects.

Lessons Learned

The last step in closure is usually to conduct some form of a "lessons learned" session. Sometimes this is called a *postmortem*, a term appropriate, perhaps, for failed projects. The idea is to congregate the project's major stakeholders and take an objective and critical look at performance. What went well on this project and how can that be carried over to other projects? Were there any trouble spots? And how can similar problems be avoided in the future? This activity is one geared to continuous improvement, and it's valuable for any organization that wants to consider itself conscious, that wants to succeed by shaping its destiny, not merely reacting to it. These lessons are taken from the key stakeholders and then shared with other members of the organization. If there is a management system in place that guides how projects are run, then these lessons can be used to make the process better.

By this continuous cycle of work and examination, the organization can be expected to grow stronger over time. (See Chapter 17, "Count the Box Office.")

The hypothetical technology system just described, based mainly on the PMBOK with some other sources added in, is designed as a project management process that incorporates those five business attributes—consistency, predictability, accountability, communications, and trackability—of the Hollywood system used by motion picture production companies. The essence of this process can be summarized as the first lesson of this book.

> **Lesson 1:** **Establish a project management system** that the enterprise can use to identify, estimate, plan, manage, monitor, and measure technology projects in ways that further the business missions of the company.

Management Objective: The Project from the System

At the time of this writing, Legendary Pictures has five new movies slated for release: *Where the Wild Things Are*, an adaptation of Maurice Sendak's classic children's story; *Dark Knight*, a new Batman adventure; *10,000 BC* (probably without the furry mini-skirt); *Kung Fu*, a big-screen remake of the 1970s hit TV show; and the Halloween omnibus, *Trick R Treat*. That's a full docket for any production company, as Bill Fay readily acknowledges. A quick take on the numbers (using my estimates), based on what's been presented in this chapter, suggests a necessary commitment of approximately 1500 workers with an operating budget of maybe $600 million.

That's about the size of the entire IT operation at many well-known companies, including Home Depot, Kohl's Department Stores, Macy's South, Coca-Cola Enterprises, Jonson Controls, Kraft Foods, and the Ralph's Grocery Store chain.

In other words, Bill is running his own technology shop, the only difference being that his "technologies" are centered on entertainment tools. The company's previous releases—*300*, *We Are Marshall*, *Superman Returns*, *Batman Begins*—delivered on their investments. Bill gives a due amount of credit for that success to the studio production system. This approach, from carefully assessing the marketplace, to selecting viable properties, to developing them with talent, to producing them under careful controls, is a proven method to maximize the enterprise's ROI. Nothing is guaranteed, of course, but applying this business approach is certainly safer than simply putting Christian Bale in front of the camera and then looking for the "on" button.

No one in Hollywood—no professional, at least—would think about running a production company or a production unit in the absence of the established system. Likewise, it's hard to imagine a CIO running an American IT operation in the absence of some type of similar management system or process approach, be it light or heavy, externally developed or homegrown. The size, complexity, and reach of IT are just too vast these days to operate with an on-the-fly or do-it-down-line attitude. Yet that's often what happens. And I suspect that working without such a system in place is more the rule than the exception.

I have been consulting with technology shops for 15 years. I have worked with all types of organizations across an array of disciplines, but most of my clients have been large shops attached to Fortune 500 companies. Unfortunately, such shops are the very ones in which the tactics of program and project management tend to be delegated well below the levels of executive and upper-level management, with little visible support from either level. Failure to adequately address this need for a management process is a risky way to do business, and it's often a recipe for trouble. A brief but telling example follows.

Case in Point: Modernization Project at the Internal Revenue Service

Around 1998, the Internal Revenue Service (IRS) engaged in a project to update its aging file-keeping computer system with modern technology. It brought in a prime contractor and got to work. The contractor's approach was to throw bodies and enthusiasm at this huge initiative but failed to include an overall project management strategy. This omission was unfortunate because, looked at up close, the project was a complex integration of related subprojects. The IRS, for its part, was not adept at pushing a different, perhaps preferred approach, or at anticipating the management demands inherent in such complex IT projects. This initiative, then, was christened not so much with a strategy as with faith—faith that both parties would see the work through. In hindsight it's easy to see the risk both parties had opened themselves up to. And it's easy to trace that risk to the inevitable fallout. The project went forward, but after years of work, progress was practically nil. The original budget had been set at $8 billion, but by the time $1 billion had been spent, the production teams were already at a 40 percent overage. All five of the subprojects that made up this huge uber-project were over budget and behind schedule. In fact, the project was so far behind schedule that the contractor was notified that unless its performance improved, the government would have no choice but to fire it.[1]

At that point, the IRS and the contractor both had to scramble, and in such situations, the smart tack is to scramble together (to avoid embarrassment as much as anything). Project scope was drastically scaled back; the once-big vision was narrowed to include far more modest aspirations. A series of tight controls and audit points was then introduced as oversight to this diminished domain. The work went on. I don't have any data tracking the project after that. Trails from these kinds of big government contracts have a way of going cold when things go wrong. A safe assumption, however, in the absence of a Freedom of

---

1   David Johnson, "At I.R.S., a Systems Update Gone Awry," *New York Times*, December 11, 2003.

Information Act request, is that the level of waste involved would cause the board of directors of even the largest business enterprise to blanch in horror. Further dissection of this project probably would identify many causes for its problems of efficiency and progress failure, but a good bet is that each of them stemmed from a central lack of a cohesive approach to the work—from the lack of a system to guide activity. The bulk of this book works from this perception, that IT shops can derive tangible benefits from the use of a project management system. Upcoming chapters will look at some practices, proven to be effective, that can be considered for inclusion in such a system.

Chapter 2
Know Your Properties

Project management is an integral part of business operations for any IT shop: To the CIO, the shop itself is a strategic project. The domains of vice-presidents can be viewed in much the same light. The collected systems under program managers are essentially development efforts in motion. Project managers, of course, are responsible for development operations at the most fundamental level. With such different responsibilities and different viewpoints, is it not surprising that unexpected mission conflicts may arise?

Perhaps what's needed is a way for the organization to maintain current mappings and models of its operational systems so that activities at all of these levels— refinements, extensions, and modifications—can be made in an efficient and effective manner. One approach used to provide this control is the practice of portfolio management. Its emerging importance stems from the complexity of most technology environments. Few business systems operate in isolation. Touching one system typically means touching many others, often without effort or even intent. Without some form of portfolio management, then, executive, program, and project management can move only with a greatly diminished view of the enterprise's sphere of operations. That narrowed view can curtail organizational and project performance in very real ways. This chapter looks at the fundamental importance of portfolio management, to underscore why an IT shop needs to understand what properties it has, how those properties contribute to operational success, and how those properties may be affected by the initiation of new projects and implementations of new functionality.

Rocky XXIII, *Friday the 13th Part 14*, and *Titanic 2— Makin' It to the Top*

A look at international box office results for the last five years will show that the top-grossing movie for each year was a sequel, a revisit to familiar territory. Table 2-1 gives the breakdown, with worldwide grosses in U.S. dollars.

It's fashionable to bash the studios for such repetitiveness. Hollywood is famous for touting originality while falling back time after time on formula. That may not be the most admirable artistic path, but it's a pretty good business practice. Take a look at three of the major studios: Paramount, Warner Bros., and Buena Vista. Each grossed about $1.4 billion in 2007. That's big business. And they did it with the significant help of existing properties. In a classic

TABLE 2-1 Top-Grossing Movies, 2002–2006

Year	Movie	Earnings
2006	*Ice Age: The Meltdown*	$169,461,800
2005	*Harry Potter and the Goblet of Fire*	$602,100,000
2004	*Harry Potter and the Prisoner of Azkaban*	$540,263,485
2003	*The Lord of the Rings: The Return of the King*	$741,451,682
2002	*Harry Potter and the Chamber of Secrets*	$614,700,000

Source: Box Office Mojo. Available at boxofficemojo.com (accessed January 4, 2008).

embrace of portfolio management, the studios leveraged what they already owned—what had already proved valuable—and generated new value from it.

Value management is a prime consideration in Hollywood. But other business advantages come through the use of portfolio management as well. For starters, it helps the studio prioritize which projects it should concentrate on. There is no shortage of ideas in Hollywood when it comes to movie concepts. A studio's existing portfolio—combined with an understanding of how it did last year, how it's doing this year, and what the outlook is for next year—points the organization toward projects that will best fit into that portfolio. Portfolio management also helps the studio avoid project overlaps, redundancies, and potential conflicts. There are even well-known stories about studios cooperating with one another to avoid releasing similar movies in the same time frame.

Perhaps of most importance, portfolio management helps the studio with the practical, business side of picture production. A franchise is by definition a known entity. Its look, feel, scope, and drive all have been established. Many of its components can be reused. As a result, that kind of project can be much more effectively planned, its ultimate quality better predicted, and its potential ROI more reliably calculated. That's why studios love sequels. That's why they are forever on the lookout to develop new franchises. An original picture may be a hit for one season, but a solid and extensible franchise can be a hit for twenty seasons.

Portfolios exist in the world of corporate IT as well. They are portfolios of the systems that run business operations. Like Hollywood, corporate IT has made significant investments in the development and deployment of these properties. American IT, however, does not generally manage its portfolios with the same degree of strategic attention or data-driven decision making that Hollywood uses. It's a good possibility that this lack of attention contributes significantly to IT's troubles with project management.

IT Portfolio Management as Strategic Positioning

In the American business enterprise, a company's applications portfolio is hard at work every day, throughout the organization. In its most obvious form, it's the raison d'être for data and operations center facilities. The job of IT divisions is to make sure that all of this work proceeds at a smooth, sustainable, uninterrupted pace—and that's a really big job. Forrester Research reports that the typical IT organization expends almost 78 percent of its human and capital resources maintaining an ever-growing inventory of applications and supporting infrastructure. According to a recent report by AMR Research, however, a sizable majority of these organizations have little insight into the overall makeup of their portfolios; moreover, they use nonrepeatable, ad hoc planning processes in spending that 78 percent to maintain them.[1]

Applications portfolio management (APM) is an emerging discipline that attempts to provide a strategic framework around IT's investment decision process. It seeks at the start to identify the full and current family of solutions at work within the enterprise so that their integration points, dependencies, and duplications can be modeled. From this approach come three distinct management benefits:

1. The organization can ascertain the business value of each of its properties;

2. The organization can identify and prioritize current IT activities; and

3. The organization can manage the strategic shape of the portfolio into the future.

These three capabilities may be the ultimate mark of an effective IT shop. They may also encapsulate the chief responsibilities of a CIO or chief technology officer (CTO). Without those capabilities, an IT shop is like a person who accumulates stock certificates in a safety deposit box—let's call it a black box. Solutions may be acquired but they are not managed; their values are not tracked; and new acquisitions may have little to do with promoting the overall worth of the portfolio. This black box model of portfolio management leads directly to the issue explored next: the need for APM. Figure 2-1 depicts these benefits.

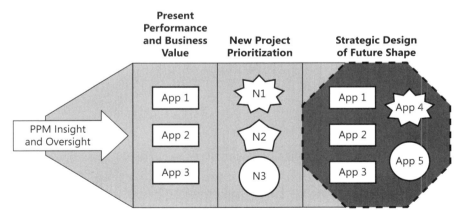

FIGURE 2-1 Applications portfolio management can deliver distinct benefits for an IT shop, benefits that emphasize control over value and priorities. PPM, project portfolio management.

---

1 Todd Datz, "Portfolio Management Done Right," *CIO Magazine*, May 1, 2003.

Another discipline closely related to APM is *project portfolio management*, which deals with how the enterprise identifies and selects the projects it wants to initiate. Project portfolio management often works hand in hand with APM (or systems portfolio management, as it is sometimes called). We'll look at project portfolio management in more depth in the next chapter, "Establish Green-Light Rules." But for now, Hollywood's approach to portfolio management can be summarized as the second lesson of this book.

> **Lesson 2:** **Implement applications portfolio management** as a way to assess and better ensure new project appropriateness, fit, and viability.

The Need for Applications Portfolio Management

Most people to whom I describe this discipline readily acknowledge APM as a good idea. They can relate it to their personal world, to their 401(k) plans or their own investment portfolios. It sounds fine because it seems like the responsible thing to do. But they often don't recognize the very real drivers that push this discipline to the forefront of effective IT management. As discussed next, four major drivers need to be appreciated and acknowledged in just about any IT shop: the complexity of environments, the need for a known starting point, the expense of software development, and the need to establish scope for effective planning.

Environments Are Complex

Environment complexity is the big one. It's the reason portfolio management exists at all. Without this complexity, it might be possible to manage properties without having to be so organized about it. But the complexity is there, and IT environments are growing ever more complex. To manage the business driven by the enterprise, the makeup of that enterprise must be known.

Directed Growth Requires a Known Starting Point

An ancient Chinese proverb states: "If you don't know where you're going, any road will do." A related dictum is attributed to the software process guru Watts Humphrey: "If you don't know where you are, a map won't help." Both sayings allude to the value of knowing where you are and knowing what you've got before seeking out new ground. The complex intertwining that makes up the enterprise needs to be developed in a way that promotes value not only through new capabilities but through embedded efficiencies as well. Portfolio management gives executives and managers the clear starting point they need to effectively direct their IT activities.

Software Development Is Expensive

After salaries and benefits of the workforce, IT expenditures represent one of a company's most significant capital obligations. IT is an expensive business. Whether engaged in planning, developing, deploying, operating, or maintaining information systems, the organization is spending a lot of money and committing the efforts of a lot of people. If any portion of that is going for projects that are redundant, half-baked, or in conflict with business missions, then management is making poor use of its resources. A big contribution that portfolio management can make to an IT shop is to give management the bird's-eye view it needs to intelligently assess proposed work in light of the influence and impact of the project across the landscape at large.

Effective Planning Begins with Scope

The fourth reason why portfolio management is so desirable is probably the most practical one; it's surely the most immediately applicable: APM aids in effective project planning. Planning sets expectations for the schedule, budget, and resource requirements for a project. But the scope of the project must be known for the estimates in each of those realms to be reliable. If project scope is open-ended, the estimates cannot be expected to reflect the realities of implementation. Naturally, a degree of uncertainty will always be present when it comes to planning and estimation, but a sound, well-documented portfolio provides the picture of dependencies and interactions needed to better pinpoint scope. And with a firmer handle on scope, plans can begin to truly reflect the demands of a project.

The Adverse Consequences of Black Box Management

The preceding four realities exist in just about every IT shop. They beg for some degree of portfolio management. When a shop opts out on this discipline, it's effectively putting on management blinders. These blinders may allow a view of the path ahead, but they obscure any obstacles to the right or the left.

Project management does not ride a one-way stream of production, in which a product is launched to sail gloriously into the sunset. Efforts put into production will shape what comes back in the form of new projects. With portfolio management, it's possible to proactively shape that cycle of production and thereby better manage value, efficiencies, and opportunities for improvement. The alternative to portfolio management is black box management (putting on the blinders)—which, as noted earlier, affords very little insight into the actual nature and status of the organization's assets.

Without the necessary planning and oversight, the enterprise faces a wide variety of risks that carry the ability to derail almost any type of project. Discussed next are the top seven project management fallouts faced by black box–managed IT shops: scope fluctuations, lost stakeholders, amorphous boundaries, redesigns, added work, problematic implementations, and ambiguous test results.

Scope Fluctuations

Without a picture of the current portfolio, project scope becomes hard to pin down, especially early on in the project life cycle. Because the true reach of the project can't be established with certainty, it's hard to estimate things like schedule, costs, and resource needs. This uncertainty weakens planning up front. At the same time, the project is subject to unexpected shifts in scope as the true reach of the solution is potentially discovered through progressively deeper engineering activities.

Lost Stakeholders

In the absence of up-to-date portfolios, projects run the risk of inadvertently omitting the involvement of key stakeholders at certain project phases. As a result, considerations, opinions, and approvals that are essential to the solution's integrity may be circumvented. Participations important to the design, testing, or implementation of the solution may be missing. Perhaps worst of all, negative performance or operational impacts may be visited on unsuspecting systems because the appropriate stakeholders were left out of the production mix.

Amorphous Boundaries

The boundaries here that are changing are of two types. The first are those boundaries set up to contain the project: the schedule, the budget, the resources. With scope in flux and key stakeholders hard to pin down, these management boundaries exhibit unpredictable volatility. The second type deals with scope (as described previously). The issue is not only that scope will fluctuate, but that little insight into *how* it will fluctuate can be achieved. The amorphous nature of these boundaries opens up the possibility of some very big surprises— of the discovery of a true scope that can easily and quickly outweigh the shop's ability to adequately address it.

Redesigns

Without sound portfolio management, designs that looked fine on paper may fail to account for all of the interactions the business requires. The only solution may be to revisit the design—adding to it, enhancing it, and modifying it so that it plugs smoothly into the reality of the environment. This process can be especially painful because the need for such changes usually is discovered only after a solution has been developed to the point that it is ready for preproduction testing. Much of that thinking and working may have to be redone.

Added Work

Taken together, the adverse consequences of black box management presented thus far add up to one thing: rework. The bottom-line outcome with most project management problems is the same: having to do the same work over again in order to make it right. That's the IT industry's number one schedule killer, budget killer, and resource killer. Sound portfolio management may not clear away all rework issues, but it will help constrain the problem by establishing up front just what the true reach of the project is.

Problematic Implementations

In the absence of APM, the act of installing a new system into production can introduce unanticipated problems. This risk is related to the redesign issue described previously. The particular issue here, however, is that the origin of the problem becomes much less clear. Its source can be easily clouded by nebulous environmental factors. When a new product is plugged into an existing portfolio but the shape of that portfolio is not well understood, what once worked well may not work at all. Or something may not be working quite right, but it's hard to say why. ("Is it something we did? Have we uncovered a hidden flaw elsewhere?") This may indeed result in redesign work, but it also may result in operations investigations, or even in operational downtime. All of this negative activity will affect not only the tenor of the specific project from which the problems sprang but also the larger performance of the operating environment, perhaps even the business itself.

Ambiguous Test Results

When IT portfolios go unmanaged, test results become suspect. By the time a project team has committed to testing activities, the product has begun to take on something of a solid shape. With any suspicion that production-like conditions may not be represented in test plans and test cases, the test team will probably feel an obligation to hedge on its quality reports, providing less than full assurance of solidity.

Before we continue, let's look back at Hollywood and review how the studio system uses portfolio management to deliver the same kinds of insights and controls that could benefit IT shops.

Hollywood and Portfolio Management

As noted previously, Hollywood is a business heavily focused on investment value. And so a major studio goal is to assemble a portfolio of proven properties that perform well over time. The fact that the studio has to actually *make* movies in order to do that is simply one of the costs of doing business. When Turner Broadcasting acquired MGM in late 1986, it did so not for that company's production capabilities but instead for its library of TV shows and films (like *Gone with the Wind*).

This focus on revenue generation and market expansion helps explain why the studios practice portfolio management so religiously. It is the framework on which all other activities hang. Portfolio management serves three purposes:

- To help the studios identify new, potential investments
- To help the studios analyze and assess the value of their present portfolios
- To help the studios leverage their portfolios to maximize future value

Identifying Investment Value

All studios are heavily invested in development. In fact, that's mostly what they do. Concept is king in Hollywood, so the studios are always on the lookout for what could be the next big thing. What properties or genres have performed well for the studio or for others over time? What deals have other studios inked? What emerging trends may stick? Games (Lara Croft), toys (Transformers), theme parks (*Pirates of the Caribbean*), books (*He's Just Not That into You*), and TV shows (*Get Smart*) all are potential sources for new products and (with a little luck) product lines.

IT shops do much the same thing. They look at new vendor offerings; they weigh which of their existing systems are reliable and which are problematic. Unfortunately, IT shops often lack the broad view, afforded by the portfolio model, that can be used to weld these insights into an effective development strategy.

Analyzing Present Value

Studio executives continually analyze their current production mix to maximize present value. This is a another prime component of a studio's ongoing mission. The theatrical release season is divided into four parts, two big and two small. The Summer season (beginning on Memorial Day) and the Christmas season (around Thanksgiving) are the big ones. Late Winter and Late Fall are the smaller ones. The key here is to balance the portfolio mix, to get the right combination of high concept and intimacy, drama and comedy, action and romance. Lots of studio planning goes into getting this mix right. As a result, lineups are never cast in concrete. In pursuit of this balance, some projects are pushed out to later dates, while others are put on the fast track.

It should be the same in the IT world. Senior executives need to understand where their operational architectures stand so they can anticipate appropriate responses to emerging or shifting business trends without the risk of introducing conflicting, overlapping, or superfluous solutions.

Leveraging Future Value

With any investment portfolio, it's important to focus not only on present value but on future value too. The same holds true for the studios: Their executives are continually looking for ways to leverage the value of their existing properties. To do this, they look for sequel opportunities. Sequels come with a good part of the planning and distribution thinking already in place, and they come to the table with a built-in audience. Fans of the first film are likely to buy tickets to the next. Another way to leverage value is through ancillary rights, spin-offs, TV remakes, and merchandizing. All of these avenues enhance a studio's return on investment and give a product a shelf life that is as long and profitable as possible.

Launching IT Portfolio Management

With portfolio management, IT shops can leverage value in the same way motion picture studios do. They can look at the shape of their current enterprise and adjust their IT applications suite as necessary to remove obsolescence and redundancy and to establish the right mix of functionality. They can then strategically shape the evolution of the enterprise toward established business objectives through the intelligent and informed selection of the right kinds of projects to push forward. Finally, this managed enterprise can then be used to identify opportunities for ongoing reuse and piggybacking, in terms of both design and operational throughput.

Three basic steps can be used to set an APM program in place in the IT shop: inventorying the applications portfolio, modeling the applications universe, and managing the portfolio.

Step 1: Inventory the Applications Portfolio

The big step in creating a portfolio management program (and sometimes it's a *really* big step) is to establish an inventory of application and system components and the relationships between them. For a large IT shop with extensive operations and multiple data centers, this task can seem quite daunting, especially if the shop's current documentation is not quite up to par. There's no practical way of avoiding it, however: The work just has to be done.

In building this inventory, it's a good idea to record the following core pieces of data about each component in the portfolio to help in maintaining the inventory and in pointing users to relevant pieces.

- **Application name**   The full name of the application, to uniquely identify the component from both the business and technical perspectives.

- **Business purpose**   This tag helps establish commonalities among systems and, through shared tags, the links and dependencies between them. It's an indicator of the business function the component performs. Redundancies and obsolescence can become quickly apparent when systems are tagged this way.

- **Business owners and stakeholders**   This identifies the business owners of the system (usually as a business unit or group) and also indicates which units or groups are its stakeholders. Stakeholders may be sponsors, direct users, and other people dependent on system operations.

- **Technical owners and stakeholders**   This identifies the technical owners of the system, those teams responsible for its ongoing uptime, performance, and maintenance.

- **Internal and external interfaces**   Here is where a major value of portfolio management comes into play. By identifying an application's interfaces (i.e., those within the environment and those that reach out of the environment) the organization can establish a picture of dependencies and efficiencies and evaluate the true scope when environmental changes are proposed.

- **Physical platforms/technical platforms**   This tag describes the technical foundation of the system in terms of hardware, software, and configuration components (with version histories). This information is valuable for addressing shifting strategic directions in the physical environment.

- **Operational history**   This is a brief operational history of the component, which is helpful in indicating its historical value, shelf life, and strategic fit.

- **Documentation repository**   Many—perhaps most—IT shops do not pay as much attention as they should to maintaining documentation. Portfolio management makes this a more visible activity in the organization. This tag indicates where the detailed technical documentation for the application resides.

Once this inventory has been established, it can now be modeled into a series of diagrams and images that represents the overall shape of the environment(s).

Step 2: Model the Applications Universe

With the physical inventory cataloged, the organization can proceed to create a logical model that reflects the layout and interconnectedness of the application and systems. Many kinds of models may be employed: communication models, process models, work flow models. Each organization will need to choose the type or combination of types that works best for it. The benefits begin to emerge when the models are joined to the physical catalog.

Models are typically created as graphic images picturing the shape of a system's components (logical or physical), as well as the relationship between these components. A communication model is chiefly used to depict one system's interactions with other systems, highlighting those points of connectivity at which communication is initiated. Process models present a different view. They map out the sequential or iterative activities that take place when a particular business process is run. Process models tend to focus on single-thread runs that may or may not cross over into other systems. Work flow models tend to combine human and systems interactions and thus are used to map out the dialog that is carried out when a certain activity is initiated. These types of models can be used singularly or in combination to establish a detailed picture of the interconnectedness of the systems that constitute a portfolio.

Step 3: Manage the Portfolio Through Governance and Guidelines

Steps 1 and 2 are the big steps in portfolio management. They require energy to set the complete catalog and models in place. Step 3 entails a lighter but longer-term commitment: ongoing management of the portfolio. This is a cultural commitment that focuses on value management. Representatives of the organization (usually high-level technology managers) work to minimize the total cost of ownership compared with derived value. This team of managers typically accomplishes this by acting as a strategic change control board, a body that periodically examines the portfolio in light of evolving business objectives, emerging business needs, and opportunities for improvement.

Active and committed attention by upper-level management to the portfolio will provide the following continuing benefits:

- **Management of application costs**   APM provides a basis for identifying opportunities for reuse and standardization. It also provides a mechanism for capturing histories of development and implementation costs, thereby allowing management to better predict budgets of similar projects.

- **Measurement of an application's business contribution**   APM provides the ability to measure a single application or system's contribution to business operations in comparison with portions of the entire portfolio.

- **Rationale for the applications portfolio**   APM provides a basis for describing the business mix provided by the portfolio as a response to the business missions of the organization.

- **Analysis of architectural fit**   APM provides an objective view of the enterprise framework so that additions, extensions, and modifications can be appropriately assessed in terms of architectural fit and technical viability.

■ **Identification of risk patterns**   APM provides a means for establishing a historical picture of application, system, and portfolio performance so that problem areas and risk patterns can be identified.

APM in the IT world shares many of the same drivers as portfolio management in Hollywood. In the same way that it helps the studio prioritize which projects it should concentrate on, APM helps IT shops assess the shapeability of its operating environments. Portfolio management also helps the studio avoid project overlaps, redundancies, and potential conflicts—and the same benefits are derived when IT shops possess a current and accurate picture of their own family of systems. Perhaps of greatest importance, portfolio management helps the studio with the practical, business side of production. The same is true for IT shops. APM helps IT shops better understand issues of scope, technology implementation, and planning parameters. It's a strategic practice with direct and tangible project management benefits.

Case in Point: Kohl's Department Stores

Headquartered in Menomonee Falls, Wisconsin, Kohl's has experienced impressive growth over the last few years. Its Information Services (IS) division has had to respond with an increasingly complex and sophisticated portfolio of business applications. This brought the need for effective portfolio management to the attention of senior IS management. Kohl's CIO, Jeff Marshall, recognizes its strategic value. "For any systems organization," he notes, "managing a diverse technology portfolio is just as important as a company managing its investment portfolios. There needs to be a tangible return on investment in both domains."

So Marshall's IS division began the process of mapping its portfolio—establishing the relationships that exist between and among applications. This mapping is primarily being used to help project teams understand more fully how their systems interface. Within the retail world, applications continually gather data, post data, pull data, exchange data, and promote data. In poorly documented environments, these interfaces, whose links can well be obscure, can easily remain hidden. Kohl's is using its growing set of integrated context models to identify for new projects those sets of interface considerations that may well need to be accounted for as projects move forward. The result being realized: fewer issues with unidentified scope, and fewer operational hiccups.

Second, Kohl's is leveraging this managed portfolio to help project teams identify opportunities for technology reuse. The portfolio provides the visibility needed to assess a project's particular needs against an existing base of functional capabilities. Thus, teams are able to identify opportunities to reuse, or leverage, these functionalities. Multiple benefits are being seen: shorter project cycle times, greater operational integration, and reduced costs, to cite a few.

Other organizations can realize these same benefits. Portfolio management can give you a firm handle on all your technology assets. It helps you better understand not only what you have but the value of what you have, and it helps you use that value to maximize the potential of your IT landscape. In the same way that Hollywood studios guard their properties, IT shops should guard their properties too, by leveraging them, extending them, capitalizing on their contributions, and using them as a basis for further development and growth.

For a Deeper Look...

- Bryan Maizlish and Robert Handler, *IT Portfolio Management: Unlocking the Business Value of Technology,* John Wiley & Sons, 2005

  This book delivers a very comprehensive discussion on the methods and techniques of IT portfolio management. Topics include the importance of balancing and aligning business objectives with the portfolio, how to generate maximum value from IT investments, and how to mitigate development and deployment risk. This is a current and accessible read.

- Jeffrey D. Kaplan, *Strategic IT Portfolio Management,* Jeffrey Kaplan Inc., 2005

  Kaplan's text focuses on how executive management can implement overall portfolio strategies to get the most out of IT investments. The book also presents tactical practices and methods that can be used to support the strategies. Topics include designing governance structures for appropriate decision making, promoting centralized control with decentralized execution, and fostering a culture of continuous improvement and strategic refinement.

- Anand Sanwal and Gary Crittenden, *Optimizing Corporate Portfolio Management: Aligning Investment Proposals with Organizational Strategy,* John Wiley & Sons, 2007

  This tome is not focused solely on IT portfolio management. It takes a broad view of corporate portfolio management (CPM) in general. Readers will be better able to understand how IT portfolio management can fit effectively under the umbrella of CPM. The book is full of practical advice and real-world examples. Great as an overview for IT portfolio management, enterprise portfolio management, and project portfolio management.

Chapter 3
Establish Green-Light Rules

The last chapter looked at how Hollywood studios keep a keen eye on their portfolios of entertainment properties. They want to leverage these properties in order to maximize profit positions. That's why the studios are so attracted to sequels, spin-offs, merchandising rights, and novelizations—these avenues open new income streams for existing products. At the same time, studios are always on the lookout for new properties with potential not only for strong box office performance but for strong ancillary life as well. So all new movie proposals are assessed against a set of criteria that include examining the current balance of the production mix with considerations of after-market options. New projects that best target both sides of this business strategy are given the green light to go into production.

This same strategy can be seen in the IT world, practiced as project portfolio management (PPM), introduced in the previous chapter. PPM is still an emerging trend. Most companies have yet to establish rules that govern the decision to implement new projects. But once in place, a method based on PPM can go a long way toward promoting project management success. With this tool, executives can see where money should be spent, why projects are or aren't necessary, and what resources may be needed for those projects that further business missions. Without it, project success can be doomed right from the start: Crazy, unviable projects are initiated; resources are unavailable; duplication goes unchecked; conflicts and incompatibilities go unrecognized until problems arise. This chapter looks at the studio practices used to assess and select the right projects to invest in—what production executives call the "green-light" process.

Inside the Hughes Hangar

Center Drive runs under the San Diego Freeway just west of Culver City. Along a south-side stretch of Center sits the now defunct Hughes Aircraft Company. Surrounded by a tall barbed-wire, chain-link fence, the site spreads for acres back from the highway into the brown sagebrush of the Playa Vista hills. As I drive down Center, I can make out, behind the fence, a series of two- and three-story faded pink stucco office buildings. Most look long abandoned; some are crumbling. The dominant feature of the complex, and the reason for its very existence, is the gigantic corrugated-metal building that dwarfs everything else in sight. It's so big it could easily swallow all of the office buildings at once, with room to spare, and maybe even the freeway. This is the famous aircraft hangar Howard Hughes erected in 1942 for one of his most ambitious projects, construction of the H-4—the Hercules—the world's largest airplane.

The H-4, dubbed the "Spruce Goose" by Hughes' detractors (in reference to the plane's building material), flew only once and then only briefly in 1947, but its birthplace remains active to this day. The hangar is being used now as a production facility for Steven Spielberg's DreamWorks studio. This is my destination. I'm here to see Pat Crowley, executive producer of the forthcoming DreamWorks action thriller, *Eagle Eye*.

Eagle Eye

Of all of the executives I met in Hollywood, Pat Crowley comes closest to being what I would call a producer's producer. He's a tall fellow, dressed casually, but with a commanding presence and a no-nonsense attitude about him. His track record is impressive. He's a former Executive Vice President of Production for the New Regency studio. His executive producer credits include *Sleepless in Seattle*, *Legends of the Fall*, and *Robocop II*. He produced *The Bourne Identity*, *The Bourne Supremacy*, and *The Bourne Ultimatum*. He's the kind of producer who's right at home with high-concept, big-budget projects. The picture he's constructing for Spielberg in the Hughes Hangar is no exception. It borrows the energy and frenetic pace of the Bourne series to tell the story of a young slacker and a single mom who get caught up in a political assassination plot. Estimated budget: $85 million.

I'm here to learn how movies get kicked into gear, how they move from concept to funding to production. From my own experience, this gate-keeping function seems largely absent in the IT world. New projects appear on an organization's radar almost as if by magic. Project initiation occurs as if mandated from on high, with little communication down the line regarding the reasons, imperatives, or driving forces behind the decision. More than a few of these projects arrive so ill-considered as to be almost unworkable. So I'm curious about how Hollywood makes the distinction between what somebody wants to produce and what actually gets produced.

"That's green lighting," Pat says. "Here's how it works."

Bearer of the Green Lantern

Green lighting is one of the rarest jobs in Hollywood. Only a handful of people at each studio have that power. (When Hollywood people mention that someone has "green-light power," they almost always lower their voices.) Green lighting is a restricted job because it sits so directly at the heart of business operations. A major studio might release 12 pictures in a year. An ability to pick well will certainly affect the studio's immediate financial performance and probably its future performance as well. The green light sets a project into motion.

I get a real appreciation for the importance of this gate-keeping function about an hour later, when Pat's assistant takes me on a tour of the hangar. Inside, crews are constructing two huge sets. One is an exact replica—to scale, it seems—of the House of Representatives assembly hall. Carpenter crews are hard at work laying in two-by-fours and half-inch plywood.

At the other end of the hangar is a near-finished set, a series of hallways in the CIA building that end in a large conference room. This set is just as solidly built.

Two huge sets are being finished and dressed to a minute level of detail. I ask Pat's assistant how they figure into the story. The House of Representatives assembly hall will be seen for about 2 minutes in the finished picture; the FBI set, for about 4 minutes. I don't know how much money I'm looking at, of course, as I walk around the hangar, but I know it's a *lot*. The size and complexity of movie making become immediately apparent. *Eagle Eye* represents a real and serious commitment by DreamWorks, and in choosing this project, DreamWorks no doubt left other offerings on the table. With good choices, over the course of a season the upside for a studio can be significant. That's the push behind the green-light process: Choose wisely to maximize the upside potential.

Technology's Unlocked Gate

In general, IT shops tend to lack a well-defined green-light method. Nor does the typical organization treat the shop's stable of ongoing projects as an entity to be regularly monitored. That's why many companies experience what they perceive as project management problems. Issues and roadblocks introduced at the macro level become obvious only at the micro level of the myriad tasks of implementing the project. Such lack of control, however, typically results from a *portfolio* management problem, which will in fact lead to compromised project management. When a portfolio (and all IT shops, no matter what the size, have one, whether defined or not) goes unmanaged, it becomes difficult to separate underperformers from high-reward investments. Redundancies and conflicts can be hard to detect. Spending may fall out of line with strategic objectives. Overall productivity may suffer.

The goal of a PPM solution, then, is to offer an efficient approach to analyzing and managing a portfolio of diverse projects so that the whole can be shaped to drive toward business goals and the parts can be managed for efficiencies and tactical applicability. IT shops have been slow to adopt PPM for many reasons. Here are four common ones:

- A lack of understanding across the enterprise about how IT can help achieve corporate goals through a managed portfolio of projects. (Even today, many business units think of IT only as a necessary evil.)

- Failure of many organizations to align strategic business objectives at the corporate level. In the absence of a synchronized mission, enterprise project value is hard to derive.

- The view from unenlightened management that redundancies, waste, failures, and shortfalls are local problems. In fact, such deficits rarely spring from poor decision making on the shop floor.

- The push of competing investments from diverse stakeholders, which fosters a "territorial protectorate" view of project selection.

Another aspect of the problem is that IT managers are routinely pressured to say "yes" to anyone who comes to them with a project proposal. In organizations in which IT is still seen as a "service" and its surrounding business units as "customers," this pressure can be worse. The result can be a direct and immediate adverse impact on the shop's ability to support its business missions.

It's when an organization begins to view IT as a partnership between business and technology that the possibility of PPM becomes real. Hollywood learned these lessons a long time ago. Moreover, it continually develops and refines its approaches for assessing project viabilities and adjusting work portfolios in response to strategic changes and market shifts.

The Green-Light Path in Hollywood

During another interview, a different producer related an interesting green-light story. James Cameron, the much-heralded producer-director of *Titanic*, is working on his next picture, a sci-fi action thriller titled *Avatar*. It's a big-budget space epic being backed by 20th Century Fox. The interesting part is that *Avatar* got the green light even when all of the major players acknowledged that the picture was currently impossible to make. At the time, the special effects demanded by the storyline could not be convincingly generated. Analysis of the project showed that the pace of development in the field of computer-generated imagery (CGI) was such that, by the time the project reached that phase of production, the technology would have arrived. Given that, along with the results of more routine analyses and Cameron's track record (*Titanic* being history's biggest all-time moneymaker), the studio decided to go ahead. Green lighting a project, then, in Hollywood is not science fiction. It's much closer to science. How the process tends to work is outlined next.

What's on the Slate?

Studios look to work a blend of the styles and genres they tend to do best. The right combination of comedy, drama, and action-adventure, big pictures and small pictures, will raise the likelihood of maximizing audience attraction and spread risk. So the studios continually assess what's on the slate alongside what's happening in the marketplace. They'll make adjustments accordingly, perhaps moving some pictures up and pushing others back.

What's the Property?

The first part of assessing a new property is to look at the property itself. An important aspect of the assessment is to make sure that it's not competing with something already on the slate and to make sure it's even the kind of picture the studio wants to make. So studio executives want to know what the story's about, what kind of characters it has, what makes it attractive. Because most studios tend to gravitate toward certain kinds of pictures targeting certain kinds of audiences, they want to determine up front if this is their kind of picture. Is it something they know how to do and have done well before? The studio's decision makers will want to feel comfortable with the property's content before they commit to assessing it further. But once it appears that project and studio may be a match for each other, the assessment can continue onward, to a look at the property's market potential.

What's the Potential?

The package potential of a new project is a primary green-light driver. It has an upfront and a backend component. The *upfront* component is an analysis of the property's initial attractiveness in light of what's currently hot in the marketplace: What's the hook? Does it come with a major star already interested? Does it ride the coattails of another success? The Disney studio, for example, had no problem green-lighting *Pirates of the Caribbean II* with a budget of $200 million, precisely because its package potential (the original's box office take, the return of Johnny Depp) was practically a given.

The *backend* component is a projection of box office returns. Pat explained that studios use complex computer modeling to map these projections. The system takes into account a host of package attributes, such as past genre performance, an actor's average box office draw over previous releases, current sales volumes, emerging trends, and so on. This body of data can be used to project how this kind of movie might perform. From that projection, the studio can decide if there's a prospect for a healthy ROI.

What's the After-Market?

Naturally, box office potential is a big green-light driver, but after-market potential often is just as important. For smaller projects, sometimes it's *more* important. After-market considerations include opportunities for income after a movie has been withdrawn from theaters, usually a few months after its initial release. International distribution, DVD sales, Internet downloads, and merchandising rights are all ways for a studio to continue making money from a project. Many times these income streams eclipse ticket sales, so they are heavily weighted in making green-light decisions.

That's the basis of Hollywood's green-light rules. If you're familiar with financial analysis, you'll recognize this concept as the basis for financial portfolio assessment. When considering a new investment, the studio assesses its current holdings, looks at the potential of return for the new project, and then decides if the move will complement the performance of the portfolio as a whole. It's a method that has proved effective for Hollywood (and Wall Street). And it's a method that can be put to the service of technology project management, helping to ensure that an IT shop takes on viable and mission-worthy software and systems projects. This point can be summarized as the third lesson of this book.

> **Lesson 3:** **Establish green-light rules** within your shop so that proposals for new projects can be strategically and consistently reviewed, assessed, and selected.

Let's look in brief at some ways in which this lesson may be applied in IT shops.

Project Portfolio Management for IT Organizations

Hollywood studios work to achieve a balanced portfolio of work in production. Each successful studio accomplishes this end by following its own customized green-light rules. And it follows up with careful production monitoring to ensure that a portfolio performs within its preset cost and schedule constraints.

In general, PPM in the world of IT operates the same way. It focuses on two work streams, each one serving as an oversight and control activity.

- PPM provides a gate that can be used to control what projects reach production.

- PPM serves as a source of up-line, centralized oversight that can initiate adjustments and refinements to the in-production portfolio.

The broad benefits that can emerge from both facets of this practice directly support project management success. They foster the selection of optimized initiatives, the effective utilization of available resources, and the coordination, management, and communication of operational change.

PPM Control Points

Recent research by Cooper, Edgett, and Klienschmidt reports an analysis that looked at a collection of successful technology organizations. The results found that the top-performing 20 percent of these companies all had established PPM methods that were consistently applied across each organization's various operating groups.[1] A deeper look at this tool shows that the inherent nature of such a program provides for a series of control points to help the shop better identify and control work that is important to organizational success.

But PPM can deliver the benefits of specific control points only when a shop commits the time and attention needed to set it properly into place. Some shops may be well positioned to move right away into PPM. Other shops—in which some of the necessary disciplines at the heart of successful PPM may be lacking—may find that they need first to shore up certain internal capabilities before moving forward.

Several control points of importance, depicted in Figure 3-1 as elements of a PPM program in an IT shop, are considered next.

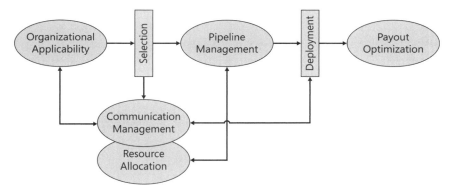

FIGURE 3-1 Interactions between PPM controls support project management in an IT shop.

Organizational Applicability

In a lot of IT shops, new projects are ushered in the door more by preference than by universal need. PPM is a way to determine early on if a project's purpose and focus have real applicability in the organization. It helps identify conflicts and redundancies, priorities and dependencies. The ultimate value of any project is expressed through a tangible ROI, which will come from providing a solution that enhances business operations. This is one of the strongest benefits of a well-managed PPM program: It works to unify what may be a disparate set of project requests into a cohesive whole, one pointed at established business missions.

Payout Optimization

PPM helps an organization filter from production those projects that are poorly aligned with business missions and IT capabilities. PPM can also help provide global monitoring activities, keeping an eye on projects in production and periodically verifying that these projects are

---

1   Robert G. Cooper, Scott J. Edgett, and Elko J. Kleinschmidt, "Optimizing the Stage-Gate Process", Part 2. Research Technology Management 45(5), 2002.

on course with respect to budget, schedule, and content. If warning signs of trouble appear, a properly designed PPM program can bring the project back into alignment with the enterprise's mission. If it appears to be too far gone, PPM can be used to postpone or even cancel it.

Resource Allocation

A company may have a seemingly unlimited number of IT projects percolating within its ranks, but it has only a limited set of IT resources. The company's people, facilities, equipment, and capacities available can accommodate only so much work. With too little work, these resources go idle; with overcommitment, the viability of individual efforts can become threatened. That's why resource leveling is such a key focus of both organizational management and project management. When it's not well practiced, resource allocations fail to capitalize on work potentials. The result is usually a combination of redundancy and waste. PPM can be used to address effective resource leveling. It's in a unique position to do so because it provides a broad-scope, high-level view of project activity.

Pipeline Management

Pipeline management is concerned with what is on its way into a production environment. Accordingly, pipeline management usually is given consideration rather late in a product's development life cycle, typically when implementation dates draw near. Unfortunately, such late awareness can lead to deployment and operational problems. In fact, a common complaint among operations and technical teams is that they are rarely given time or notice to prepare for new installs or configuration changes.

PPM can help alleviate that disconnect. It can bring deployment and operational considerations to the very front of the process, even making them part of the evaluation mix. In this way, projects that carry with them significant operational impacts can be readily identified and managed accordingly. It can also rebalance the project mix so that certain products move down the pipeline first, ones that may provide needed later support to others. Managing the pipeline in this way will help ensure that, by the time of implementation, downstream teams will have had adequate time to prepare to receive the product.

Communication Management

Communication management often is not included in the mix of PPM benefits, but I like to point it out simply because most, if not all, companies experience communication problems. PPM can contribute to effective communication in two important ways: It fosters commonality of agreement, and it promotes authority and direction. When communication streams move to and from the people managing the PPM program, they do so with the recognition of authority. Thus, this in-out exchange is also reliable; the organization at large understands the role and purpose of the evaluation board and recognizes the form and manner needed for communication with the board.

Beginning PPM in Your Shop

PPM is a great way to support project management success in the organization. It might even be seen as the beginning point for this success. By strategically managing the initiation of new projects, the tactical execution of those projects can become much more effective. Almost any IT shop, large or small, can benefit from some form of PPM program. Because all IT shops are different, however, dealing in various types of projects, no one way to set up a PPM program is possible. A look at how PPM has been implemented across a typical sampling of organizations will show that they typically share a set of basic elements. As borne out by my experience, five specific elements tend to be present in the most effective of these programs: a basic maturity in project management capability; presence of a baseline inventory; availability of an evaluation board; established evaluation criteria; and well-developed performance metrics.

Let's take a brief look at each of these basic attributes of organizations with successful PPM programs.

A Basic Maturity

Three manifestations of business readiness need to be in place for PPM to be effective. One is that the organization will know how to manage projects at the tactical or ground level. Springing from this ability, the organization will probably have some form of project management office in place, a point for the centralized focus of project activities. The last thing is a foundation for constructing a current and complete project portfolio. This could be a nascent spreadsheet or database, but the existence of such a foundation, in whatever form it takes, demonstrates the beginning move toward the larger strategy. Without this base in place, an organization may have a hard time adjusting to the discipline required of PPM.

A Baseline Inventory

The practical heart of any PPM program is the managed repository that holds the inventory of current organizational projects. For a PPM program to be in place, this inventory has to be created. That can be a tall order for many IT shops, especially those with little experience corralling disparate project initiatives, or larger shops, in which it's common to have hundreds of projects in the works. Nevertheless, the inventory process can become workable when broken down into its constituent parts. A good place to begin is by taking a look at the types of projects the organization engages in and deciding which of those it really needs in the portfolio. Perhaps only projects of a certain critical bent or size should be included, maybe at first just those that affect Sarbanes-Oxley compliance. A careful look at the mix will help in determining what kind of portfolio is needed to best manage the shop's work demands. Then it's necessary to design a way to type or categorize those projects that will indeed go into the repository. This will facilitate later management and reporting activities. From that point on, the repository can be used as the funnel through which all future project initiatives flow.

An Evaluation Board

A PPM program is typically governed by a chartered evaluation board. This board's member-ship usually comes from upper-level management, often a combination of IT management and business management. It's important that the management here be at a "senior" level. The board, after all, must have the authority to stop projects from entering the work pipe-line. Inclusion of lower levels of management or line workers, who may lack this authority, would tend to diminish the effectiveness of the board. It's also helpful to have senior mem-bers of the business represented on the board. They can provide a fresh perspective on proj-ect evaluation, as well as cementing a tone of consensus when project decisions are made.

The chief benefit such a board brings to the organization, derived from its main duties of meeting, assessing, and choosing, is that it fosters an enterprise-oriented decision-making framework. Both business missions and project objectives can be quickly compromised when work commitments are made in an uncoordinated or disconnected manner. The PPM evalu-ation board reduces this potential by centralizing the assessment of new work proposals, regulating a consistent way to conduct the assessments, and coordinating the dissemination of work decisions.

Evaluation Criteria

One of the strengths the PPM program can bring into an IT shop is a consistent approach to assessing and judging project proposals. To achieve this consistency, evaluation techniques need to be established, documented, and used. These evaluation criteria not only will drive the direction of the board but will also affect the format in which proposals are submitted. The criteria should be regarded as a tool both for the board and for all of IT and the business as well. The criteria should encapsulate the values that the organization holds with respect to its business missions. Knowing these criteria will help groups throughout the organization better plan and propose new project ideas.

Performance Metrics

The trickiest part of PPM may be establishing performance metrics, to serve as a way to evalu-ate the work in progress. As we've seen, the gating purpose of PPM is to ensure the adoption of viable, mission-supporting projects. Now the portfolio has to be *managed*. At its most ele-mental, this function drives the traditional project management concerns: Are the projects on budget, on schedule, and within spec? This is why PPM is such a great supporter of a project management methodology; that methodology is what it oversees. In support of this, then, the PPM evaluation board acts as a sort of "super project manager." If one part of the portfolio drifts off course, it may fall to the board to make adjustments based on criticalities and pri-orities. Such adjustments may consist of realigning resources, scheduling postponements or delays, or even canceling one effort in the interest of another. Individual project managers managing single projects will not have the degree of insight or oversight to make those kinds of choices and decisions. PPM, then, serves the organization as nothing more (or less) than project management at the top of the enterprise.

The green-light rules used by studios serve as the gate through which projects pass from development into the formal stages of production. Through the use of PPM, IT management can promote its own green-light approach, one that provides a new level of organizational oversight by introducing techniques for assessment, approval, and prioritization. When used in this way, a PPM program can deliver numerous benefits to the organization, including the heightened promotion of business missions, better coordination of resources, and reductions in redundancies and waste.

Case in Point: CalPERS of California

The California Public Employees' Retirement System (CalPERS) is a state organization that provides retirement and health benefits to 1.5 million public employees and retirees, and their families. Naturally, such a large organization requires the use of a diverse and extensive set of automation tools in order to see its mission through. The Information Technology Services Branch (ITSB) within CalPERS is responsible for all of those technology needs. These tools include systems analysis and design, programming, testing, implementation, and maintenance for its major computer systems. At any one time, dozens and dozens of ongoing projects may be in place, some big, some small, each pointed at a certain operational issue and each requiring its own focused set of money, time, and resources. To support this vast array, CalPERS's ITSB has made a serious commitment to PPM. The ITSB maintains a repository of all projects that last more than 30 days or 100 hours. CalPERS's IT managers then use a series of condition reports (with green, yellow, and red indicators) to monitor project progress. If a project looks to be veering off course—schedules slipping, resource levels climbing, spending rising—management can address the problem by adjusting the entire portfolio to accommodate the local need. Management performs this portfolio assessment regularly, across a series of life cycle milestones. Each milestone (such as plan approval or test completion) is linked to a performance target, and a key part of management's job (both project management and upper-level management) is to see that each project within the portfolio meets those targets. Accomplishing this goal also means that the portfolio itself should align with the CalPERS business mission. Using this management tool, CalPERS has demonstrated an ability to manage its portfolio not only toward the goal of maximizing operational value but also as a way to optimize budgets, timelines, resources, and facilities.

For a Deeper Look . . .

- Eduardo Miranda, *Running the Successful Hi-Tech Project Office,* Artech House, 2003

  I like this book because it begins from the interesting premise that most project failures are due to lack of resources and insufficient coordination across projects. It then goes on to describe how to design, implement, and run a project office geared to resource management and mission coordination.

- Gerald I. Kendall and Steven C. Rollins, *Advanced Project Portfolio Management and the PMO: Multiplying ROI at Warp Speed,* J. Ross Publishing, 2003

  This book covers the strategy, tactics, and processes that go into establishing a project management office, one designed to control project initiation and progress. The authors focus on four techniques to accomplish this goal: the use of Six Sigma as a performance measurement tool, the use of the theory of constraints to uncover throughput bottlenecks, the "4 × 4" method of strategic planning, and the critical-chain multiproject management approach.

- Parviz F. Rad and Ginger Levin, *Project Portfolio Management Tools & Techniques,* CRC, 2007

  This book is focused on how organizations—specifically research and development organizations, but the advice is general—can develop a formalized system that can be used to authorize the right projects and shun the wrong projects.

Chapter 4
Invest in a Solid Script

Technology development isn't really about building software, hardware, or systems. It's about creating business solutions through the automation of specialized business activities. In the absence of a business need or a business mission, there'd be little use for technology at all. The real focus of project management, then, isn't schedule and cost controls but realizing the business solution. See the mission through, and chances are—outright catastrophes aside—the project will be seen as a success. But bring it in exactly on schedule and exactly on budget with a somehow compromised (perhaps even useless) end product, and the effort, no matter how well managed, will be deemed marginal.

These considerations underscore the importance of working with sound requirements. Requirements describe the business mission of a project. They contain the purpose and scope of the project and the boundaries that shape it. They constitute the sole reason to have a project in the first place, so no project can move forward effectively without them (unless, of course, the project is there to create the requirements).

Most project managers and technology developers appreciate the value of a solid set of requirements. But not everyone in an organization may have access to this insight. As a result, project teams routinely deal with vague, poorly stated, incomplete, or conflicting requirements. When project work is based on a plan of such dubious merit, quality becomes unpredictable, and a host of all-too-familiar problems looms on the horizon: disconnected expectations, vague status reports, latticed architectures, soft testing, problematic integration, scope creep, and rework, rework, rework.

In any business, the project management office alone may not have the cultural sway to remove all impediments to requirements expression—the input of customers and external stakeholders is intricately tied to requirements development—but project managers can take steps to mitigate the situation. This chapter looks at some practices that support the sound development of requirements, practices that can be observed effectively at work in the motion picture industry. Motion picture projects work with requirements too. But on set, they're called the script.

The Package Drives the Script

I'm sitting in the glass-shielded office of Alan Blomquist, a producer for Parallel Entertainment, located on Wilshire Boulevard in the heart of Beverly Hills. The office overlooks a palm-lined avenue just down from Rodeo Drive. To reach the second story foyer, by private elevator, I had to be buzzed in by a private security guard whose main job, I took it, was to ferret out the script peddlers, story hawkers, and Big Ideas men who gravitate to successful production companies like this one. I was carrying a notebook and some loose-leaf papers. That's probably why the guard double-checked my ID and appointment time before hitting the Up button on the elevator control panel.

At the time, Parallel Entertainment happened to be riding a fresh wave of success. Among its other ventures, the company produced the ongoing "Blue Collar" comedy tour, then the hottest ticket on the circuit. The show features the well-known stand-ups Jeff Foxworthy, Bill Engvall, Ron White, and "Larry the Cable Guy." Larry the Cable Guy has become so popular that Parallel has developed a series of modestly budgeted movies for him to star in. Alan Blomquist, whose work includes *What's Eating Gilbert Grape?*, *The Cider House Rules*, and *Chocolat*, is overseeing this development.

That afternoon Alan was explaining the development process to me, and his points echoed the activities described by the other producers with whom I'd met. Because motion picture production is such an expensive business (even a little Larry the Cable Guy movie can cost $10 million), the potential for box office success must be built into the product up front. And although there is no magic formula for calculating the likelihood of that success, currently the best way to get there is with a solid script—what's often called a *bankable* script.

The parallel is easy to see (even more so when you're sitting in the offices of Parallel): The script contains the requirements the movie must fulfill, what IT people might call the business requirements and user requirements. Just like system or software requirements, the script, when properly shaped, realizes the business mission. For the upcoming Larry the Cable Guy movie (titled *Witless Protection*), the business mission was not some amorphous ambition such as "Make millions." (In the corporate and IT worlds, that would be like saying, "Make accounting run better.") It was a much more defined target: "Generate a 30 percent net return on production and marketing investments." That mission had been generated from a carefully engineered strategy that took into account the size of the Larry the Cable Guy fan base, the fixed costs embedded in film production, current distribution relationships, promotional opportunities, and a host of other hard-line business considerations. From that came the Numbers:

- Market analysis (past performance, fan base, extension base, genre support, and so forth), and from that . . .

- Gross sales projections (from domestic box office, international box office, cable, TV, DVD, and other sources), and from that . . .

- Net sales projections (less marketing, distributor fees, exhibitor fees, and the like), and from that . . .

- Gross profit (less production costs, point payouts, and other expenses), and from that . . .

- Net profit: the Number you can probably put in the bank.

All this before the first joke is put to paper.

Here's the great result (and one that IT people can borrow to help develop better require-ments): From that analysis comes a rational, practical, and trackable mission (in our example, to generate a 30 percent net return). That mission then becomes the basis for the script. A script can now be either identified and shaped or developed from scratch.

Aside from the CBA, which measures the potential worthiness of a potential project, there are additional characteristics of script development that can be directly applied to project man-agement in IT shops. We'll get to these later in the chapter, but right now let's take a quick look at the kinds of factors that shape the quality of requirements brought to the technology development teams, factors that may be in some ways unique to the IT domain.

The Business of Weak Requirements

Sometimes in the business world, our customers will come to us fully prepared to commu-nicate and work through what they need to see realized. In some kind of businesses, that's actually the case most of the time. And if that's the kind of shop you're in, feel free to ignore the advice in this chapter. It's been shaped to get you to where you already are (and maybe not even that far). In most business organizations, it's probably safe to say that customers come to IT shops not as prepared to work through requirements as the technology develop-ers would like. Is this laziness on the part of the customer? Is it an ambivalence to automa-tion? Is it due to a desire for territorial control?

I don't think it's really any of those, at least not to any significant degree. I think this percep-tion of un-preparedness or less-than-full preparedness stems from five traits that, in my ex-perience, seem to be common to a majority of business enterprises and IT shops. Let's take a quick look at these traits.

Speed-to-Market Business Pressures

A majority of IT shops in America are in-house operations that support commercial enter-prises, businesses that sell a product or a service in the marketplace. And in the business world, speed-to-market is a very real and valid consideration. The company that can be the first to get something out in front of its consumers stands a good chance of capturing a certain share of the market. That kind of competitive pressure can drive a company to begin initiatives even when the finer details have yet to be worked out. That can be risky, but the personality and rhythm of the marketplace can make it riskier to wait. And so technology shops often must work with business people who by default have to start projects whose true reach and scope haven't yet taken solid shape and will have to be delineated through

discovery later on. Such a starting point will invariably include a set of incomplete requirements, or at least requirements with a high degree of volatility. But the need to push ahead
remains, so project management must move forward in the best way it can.

Lack of Technological Appreciation

As IT experts, we know our domain, we know how it works, and we know what we need to
make it work. In the same way, the people we serve—our customers, both in-house and
otherwise—are business experts. They are masters of accounting, of shipping and receiving,
of customer service, of order provisioning, of sales projecting, and so on and so on. But even
though most business experts probably interact with technology on a daily basis and rely on
technological developments for the smoothness of their operations, they more than likely
are not IT savvy. Often our customers lack an understanding of what it takes to fully describe
a system, or of the importance of taking a certain amount of time up front to do so. Maybe
they just aren't interested in that facet of the enterprise, or have been exposed to weak
practices in the past, or perhaps we in IT have shielded them from an appropriate understanding. At the same time, we ourselves may lack an appreciation for the sophistication of
their business models, workflows, regulations, and interactions, so we may engage in a way
that is more willing to receive than to elicit. Both situations conspire to deliver incomplete
and weak requirements.

Lack of Commitment to Analysis

The mutual lack of appreciation just described—of technological needs and of business
needs—is also often evidenced in another trait: an organizational lack of commitment
to a proper analysis of business needs so that proper requirements can be developed.
Organizations, in their wish to see projects move forward (typically, as manifested by programmers banging out code), adopt a hurry-up-and-go attitude that maximizes execution
and minimizes preparation. Time for analyzing business needs, understanding business regi-
mens, and synthesizing business elements is often seen as a luxury and an unnecessary delay.
Accordingly, this period tends to be minimized. This astonishingly common tendency is not
always due to pressure applied from outside, by business units onto technology shops. Just
as often it comes from inside the shop, from technology managers wanting to get to what
they perceive as the "action stages" of a project.

Variations in Personal Expression

Here is one characteristic of requirements definition and development that, no matter what
tools may come our way, will probably remain with us always: Requirements remain exercises
in translation, based in some form of human language. That means they are forever at the

mercy of the expresser and of the interpreter, whether they're being written in the first place or simply studied. Although it's somewhat different in different organizations, the job of requirements definition usually falls to a business analyst. When the organization leaves this responsibility solely to the business analyst without providing tools such as standards and templates, requirements expression—the form and manner in which the requirements are documented—becomes highly variable and, in part, personality-based. When two or more analysts work on the same problem (perhaps in the absence of training on how to work synchronously), the diversity inherent in this approach can become magnified. This divergence leaves the door open to omissions, discontinuities, and ambiguities.

The Comfort of the Clacking

The fifth reason that organizational behavior can inadvertently promote weak or incomplete requirements is the idea (held by some) that progress is not under way in technology development unless keyboards are clacking: code being written, network diagrams being joined with bidirectional arrows, and CAD/CAM diagrams spinning away in three-dimensional hyperspace. In a way, this attitude is understandable. These are the visible products of development: lines of code, data flow diagrams, detailed schematics. To many eyes, everything flows either to or from these outputs—so why not get to them as quickly as possible?

Hurry-up-and-go pressures, speed-to-market imperatives, lack of understanding, lack of analysis, variation in expression—most shops have experienced one or more of these inherently negative forces, and some have suffered the whole lot. The net effect is that descriptions of requirements that are not really implementation ready may be forced on a project, with less than optimal results. Going forward with work anyway, without appreciating and accounting for the risk involved, invites scope creep, schedule slippage, and cost overruns—all because of poorly defined requirements.

Continuing the Parallels at Parallel Entertainment

Every action in Hollywood is born out of the opportunity to tell a story. Accordingly, the bankability of that story, the breadth of its appeal, is a paramount consideration, one that is inherent in the development stream of work.

In the world of corporate IT, in much the same way, business managers don't come to the table with a project idea unless they too have a story to tell, perhaps one of competitive advantage or streamlined operations or reduced costs. A business story that is considered compelling enough will turn into an IT project, for which that business story must be elaborated into a set of requirements. The protocols Alan explains for how a story is developed into a script ring just as true for IT as for Hollywood.

The Non-Negotiable Do's of Hollywood Script Development

Alan uses a proven business model for movie production. He works in a range that peaks out at about $30 million a project. Right now he's dealing in the $10 million range. That's really modest in an industry in which the average project comes in at around $65 million, but Alan's model shows its brains when you analyze its ROI. When all revenue sources are taken into account, a marketable $10 million movie is almost guaranteed to make money, maybe not hundreds of millions but enough millions to satisfy any business-savvy investor. We saw earlier how his team initially projected a viable investment for *Witless Protection* and how that projection shaped development of the script. The creative producers at 20th Century Fox, Buena Vista, New Line Cinema, and all of the independent production companies follow the same path.

They all follow five practices that IT people should probably pay attention to. Adopting and synthesizing these practices into daily work flows may well improve the ability of technology development teams to define IT requirements in ways that support realistic plans and performance expectations. Here they are in brief:

1. **Count the tickets (before they're printed).**   In other words, don't embark on a less-than-viable mission. Earlier in this chapter we looked at the use of CBAs to ascertain the potential viability and boundaries of movie projects. This preliminary understanding—"The numbers show we could sell about XX tickets"—helps establish an appropriate scope, one engineered to bring about a positive ROI.

2. **Build the script to sell the tickets.**   The right script must be developed for each project. The renowned screen writer Paul Schrader wrote the classic films *Taxi Driver*, *Raging Bull*, and *Affliction*, but his name was probably not in the hat when the producer of Jim Carrey's forthcoming comedy, *Yes Man*, was writer-shopping. Schrader tends to write in tones that probably would not take *Yes Man* in the direction Jim Carrey usually prefers. The script needs to be developed to the mission. Its elements should be directly traceable to the mission. Its whole purpose is to promote the mission. Get the right script in place, and the chance that the other success elements will materialize (star, budget, and so on) greatly increases.

3. **Allot time to write the right script.**   No sane producer is going to rush a script through just to get to the exciting part of being able to show it to Tom Hanks' agent. Peddling subpar material in Hollywood is professional suicide. Producers routinely give a writer (or a writing team) 12 weeks or so to get a first draft in place, a draft that wraps the business need with entertainment value. This commitment is not for the sake of art; it's for the sake of marketability. There may certainly be a whole series of rewrites and polishes, but a solid foundation—a solid baseline—is critical to the visible value of the project and its chances for further development.

4. **Follow the recognized script format.**   This is something of a down-line practice because although it is producer-endorsed, it is carried out by the writer. Look at any

handful of movie scripts—mix up the genres, mix up the writers—and you'll find that they all look amazingly alike. Same margins, same font, same use of slug lines, same page numbering, same page binding. This fixed format standardizes script analysis. Work breakdowns, scheduling, budgeting, and location needs all can be quickly ascertained through this format.

5. **Invest in proportion.**   The development phase of motion picture production is the least expensive of the five phases. Nevertheless, its importance is well appreciated. The decisions made at this stage will shape the future direction of the production, all the way down to how the movie will be promoted. That's why producers do not hesitate to invest in this phase. Proportionately, it's some of their smartest spending.

The Cardboard Box of Might-Have-Beens

Back in his office, Alan Blomquist brings out a cardboard box filled with scripts. "Here [at Parallel Entertainment] we have a closetful of these," he says. "Go over to DreamWorks, and they've got a floorful." This is a box full of might-have-beens, scripts that for one project or another and for one reason or another didn't prove workable. Either they came in complete but did not fit a current mission at Parallel, or they were commissioned for a specific project but missed the mark.

I was surprised at the level of objectivity Alan showed in his approach to this analysis. But the producers I spoke with at Paramount, Intermedia, Warner Bros., and elsewhere all exhibited this same objectivity. Most of all, they understand the size of the investment required for any project, in terms of dollars, people, time, and reputation. A bad project will suck up just as much of these as a good project, and probably more. So why not invest the time up front to make sure the foundation—the script—really is as solid as it can be?

And so the cardboard boxes stack up. But this accumulation of unused and unusable scripts is not a sign of failure. To the contrary, it is a symbol of success and evidence of business maturity. It's evidence that management is working up front to circumvent entry into projects that might prove culturally abject, management-adverse, or negatively profitable.

In any business, that's a symbol of management doing its proper job.

System Requirements as Technology's Script

The conventional wisdom in Hollywood says: If the script doesn't work, don't shoot it.

That same wisdom applies in corporate America. For technology projects, weak requirements, or the rush to work based on incomplete requirements, causes more problems than probably any other single situation. The ideal solution would be to insist on a fixed block of time for requirements development for each project, a non-negotiable phase dedicated solely to the creation of a solid set of requirements. But such a hard-line solution probably won't succeed in corporate America. (It doesn't even work that way in Hollywood. Writers are pressured just like other members of the creative and management teams.) But at the core of that ideal is a very realistic practice that IT people, and business management in general, can adopt. This practice constitutes the next lesson in this book:

> **Lesson 4:** **Ensure that ample time and resources are applied to the activities that make up requirements development.** Energy focused at this stage of the project will lead to sets of requirements that are more complete, reliable, and capable of delivering on the business mission.

Let's see how this might be realized efficiently in the IT world.

Addressing Requirements Development

The emphasis that Hollywood places on script development underscores the impact a script can have on a movie project. It's hard to make a good movie out of a bad script (and by "bad" here I mean mis-engineered), and it's hard to make money on a bad movie. The method of the Hollywood system sets quality gates around script development activities; the project will rarely move through these gates if the resulting pages don't align with the project's predefined business purpose.

Although IT shops often struggle with the practice of developing requirements, an interesting point is that the standards and bodies of knowledge regarded as representing the industry's method seem to echo the method of the Hollywood system. When you look at descriptions of the traditional or classic (waterfall) SDLC model, you see requirements development identified up front. When you look at a process improvement framework like CMMI, you see two process areas dedicated to requirements development and requirements management and other process areas (like configuration management) that support those two. The ISO 9001:2000 standard wraps its entire purpose around the proper management and realization of customer requirements. The PMI's PMBOK promotes requirements practices through its focus on project initiation, scope definition, scope verification, and scope control. Even a "flexible" management approach such as Agile promotes continuous refinement and analysis of requirements.

The difference between Hollywood's treatment of the script and IT's treatment of the requirements does not seem to stem from a gap in knowledge. We in the new technology industries pretty much recognize what those in the older motion picture industry have honed. The difference appears to be one of use. A-picture or B-picture, high concept or low concept, studio-backed or indie—no matter what the project, script development is a focused and concentrated effort. In American IT, owing in large part to the five business reasons cited earlier, the tendency is to whack at requirements definitions the way a farm worker whacks at sugar cane in a field: When enough stuff gets knocked down, the worker then moves forward. We IT people might always have to face that forward-march imperative, but we can make it work more to our advantage by committing to some basic practices that influence this process from the outside in.

Seven Productive Requirements Development Practices

The practices that Hollywood follows when it packages a motion picture project focus very early on the development of a sound, "bankable" script, one designed to promote a certain ROI. A look at management standards and frameworks that apply to technology industries reveals many of the same practices rendered in only slightly different form. The following seven practices are presented as being representative and reflective of both industries; each is an option you may wish to consider for your own IT shop (Figure 4-1).

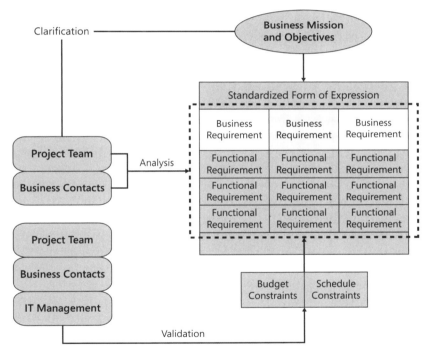

FIGURE 4-1 Requirements development benefits from a combined focus on the business, mission, the desired functionality, and the constraints of the project.

Practice 1: Orient Your Customers to Your Requirements Development Process

This practice presupposes that you have a requirements development process in place within your organization. In Hollywood, the method for identifying a storyline and developing a script is well known; from production company to production company, it's pretty much the same series of steps. (If a Warner Bros. producer tells the production chiefs that the script is in rewrite, they'll know exactly what that means.) In an IT shop, the responsibility to develop sound technology requirements requires appropriate emphasis and capability; these attributes are best embedded in the culture through some standardized procedures.

It's not enough, however, just to have the method in place, or for your people to understand it and be committed to it. It's just as important for your customers—including business users and organizational management—to understand the method, appreciate its contribution to quality, and be willing to participate in the process when they engage with you on projects. Now, as a project manager, you might not have the degree of influence required to win these stakeholders over that way, but you and your teams can set the tools in place so that this cooperative opportunity remains consistently available.

Practice 2: Establish the Business Mission

Earlier in this chapter we saw how a producer typically works through a CBA to quantify the viability of a proposed project. Out of this analysis will come a series of boundaries—usually sales and profit numbers—that the project, in order to be worth undertaking, must fall within. These constraints will further refine the analysis to identify the mission of the project. To support this mission, the creative team will then develop an appropriate script. A similar concept in the technology development world is the *vision statement*, a brief narrative encapsulation of a proposed project's business objectives. (See Karl Wiegers, *Software Requirements*, Second Edition, Microsoft Press, 2003, for guidance on vision statements.)

Sometimes the project development team does a good job with the vision statement, but more often the result is what might be called a soft vision, a description that is *qualitative* rather than quantitative. If managers in IT shops along with their customers could initially work through their own CBA (even a preliminary or predictive one), both parties would then be able to move forward with a shared initial purpose and mission description that can be used as the foundation for developing an appropriate and focused set of requirements. Such an analysis might describe the business impetus driving the idea; a solution approach, along with any possible alternatives; the benefits the business will receive in realizing the new functionality; and a rough order-of-magnitude estimate of cost. Using this as a common basis, the parties can then make a calculated decision regarding the merits of moving forward.

Practice 3: Commit to Analysis

With a business mission in place, business analysts can then begin the process of eliciting and documenting the requirements and then, after this, the functional requirements. Here is the point at which a true partnering between the business teams and the technology development teams should come into play. As I've mentioned, in the movie business, for a typical mainstream entertainment project, a production company will give a commissioned writer about 12 weeks to bring in a first draft of the script. After that, a series of rewrites and polishes may take place. There will be lots of reviews by lots of different people. Only when the script has been accepted as being in a workable condition—that is, close to its final form—does the subsequent work of production planning begin. The point is, Hollywood would never try to rush through or minimize this phase. It remains a fixed block within the studio production system.

IT shops could benefit by following suit, by committing through policy to always providing ample time to analyze the business mission and to deriving requirements that are complete and reliable, as well as practicable. Some organizations accomplish this goal by including a requirements development phase in the overall development life cycle. The duration and resource intensity of this phase may vary from project to project, but it should remain a non-negotiable component of work flow whose activities must be accounted for. Other teams may address this need by separating requirements development from other project activities, in essence pulling it out to be managed as its own project. Often that's a sensible and man-ageable approach.

Either option could work for your shop. The key is the commitment to a period of analysis. The approach to resist here—typically based on a deep-seated desire to hear programmers clacking away at keyboards (see Practice 7 coming up)—is to skip the analysis time altogether, or to shrink it to an inadequate minimum. Neglect of this important step almost always leads to suboptimal requirements that must be revisited repeatedly throughout the rest of the project.

Practice 4: Standardize a Form of Expression

Variety of expression in requirements definition probably is an attribute of the discipline of IT. After all, it's based on human language. But organizations can promote the development of requirements through use of some standardized samples, sets, forms, and templates. (See Stephen Withall, *Software Requirement Patterns*, Microsoft Press, 2007, for a book on exactly this subject.) The goal of these tools is to make the development and presentation of the requirements similar, no matter who has been working on them. Hollywood scripts show all the earmarks of this standardization process, no matter what type of picture is being made: romantic comedy, social drama, or alien invasion (or some combination!). All scripts use the same font size and the same margins. They use the same style of slug lines and name the initial appearance of characters in the same way. They run the same length: rarely under 90 pages and rarely over 120 pages. Title pages are in the same formats. Exactly two gold clips bind the pages together. Naturally, the content from script to script is not the same, but pre-sentation goes a long way toward cueing and protecting content. In fact, having some stan-dards and consistency in templates does not in any way compromise creative content.

When technology shops move in this direction toward standardization, they can reap the same benefits. Tools such as predefined categories of requirements considerations, templates for requirements documents, and checklists for quality and completeness help instantiate an organizational capability for requirements development, one that can shift with ease from team to team or customer to customer, in a consistent and repeatable manner. And when operations are consistent and repeatable, they can much more readily be improved.

Practice 5: Derive the Functional Requirements from Business Requirements

The people who make up the technical teams I've worked with in the past—analysts, designers, programmers—all have been very competent at their jobs. They can map out data flow diagrams that make sense, and they can write code that's clean and tight. Just tell them what you want, and they usually can give it to you. Establishing the functional requirements (as such outputs also are called) is not a trick for these professionals. Where the value of the requirements tends to fall short is in the link between the business mission and these functional descriptions. The problem most often is rooted in a gap in the business requirements that leads to missing or disjointed functional requirements.

This need for a clear link between business and functional requirements is why it's important to spend time specifically developing the business requirements, and to commit to working in partnership with the customer, who typically holds the business expertise. Many IT shops, however, tend to skimp here. Either they feel that it's the responsibility of the customer to come to the table with the business need fully defined, or their appreciation of requirements is weighted heavily toward the technical end. Either situation invites problems.

Let's say a writer for a Larry the Cable Guy movie turns in a script that, in Act II, calls for Larry's truck to become accidentally attached to a cargo plane, pulled into the air, released to slide down the nose of Thomas Jefferson on Mount Rushmore, splash into the Colorado River rapids, and plunge over a waterfall at the end. It's pretty obvious that the writer hasn't understood the business mission, either because he didn't have access to it or because he didn't pay attention to it.

Partnering with the customer—on whom the feasibility of this strategy, of course, will largely depend—is a sure way to bridge knowledge between the two domains. The technical team then has the opportunity to elicit business details to illuminate technical ones, details that the business folks may simply take for granted or details that imply the presence of links that the business folks can't confirm. At the same time, the business folks have the opportunity to clarify and reinforce the business mission for the technical teams. With this degree of clarity and opportunity for knowledge transfer in place, the likelihood that the functional requirements will prove valid and useful increases in proportion.

Practice 6: Balance the Requirements

Thoroughly establishing the business requirements before deriving the functional requirements will take your team a long way toward the point of actual production. Here's another tip to support this goal: Balance the requirements. That means balancing volume—the amount of functionality that needs to be produced in light of the budget and the schedule available to the project. In other words, if you have $10 million in the production budget, you probably can't shoot a 240-page script. This simple step brings two distinct advantages to any project. First, it harmonizes expectations across parties—customers, senior management, and your team share the same definition of scope. Second, it sets up a reasonable performance target. The project can be positioned for success early in a way that supports best practices at the same time that it addresses the core business mission of the initiative at hand.

Some managers I know would argue against this practice. Their opinion is that the best way to manage a team is to overcommit them, with the expectation that what they end up with will be close to an acceptable commitment. I don't much like this philosophy. It's a form of negative management, and it presupposes failure. When you're working with competent, well-intentioned professionals, that approach almost always leads to internal friction. (If you're not dealing with that caliber of people, go ahead and put this book down right now because your priorities have just shifted to human resources development.)

To balance the requirements, follow these general steps:

1. Make sure that all of your stakeholders are aware of the major project constraints: budget, schedule, resource levels, business needs.

2. Review the complete set of requirements with your clients and technical teams.

3. On the basis of this review, prioritize the requirements according to their alignment with business objectives.

4. Allocate an appropriate subset to the project, and then . . .

5. Provide for coordinated change control to adjust the scope as necessary across the life cycle of the project.

Practice 7: Link Requirements to an Early Test Strategy

The key word here is "early." That's not to say that project requirements won't change, but for most technology projects, the measure of success is going to hinge in large part on the results of test activities. When test planning is conducted late in the life cycle, the odds are increased that testing won't address all required functionality. But if project development teams take on this consideration early, when the business and functional requirements are being originally shaped, the chance that all of them will be properly accounted for—that is, represented in documentation—increases. There's another advantage here, one that contributes directly to scope, schedule, and budget control: Requirements development occurs chiefly at the start of a project. Testing occurs chiefly toward the end. Construction takes place in the middle. By book-ending construction with a firm scope up front and an organized confirmation on the back end, the building process can move forward with assurance, from a managed starting point to a managed destination. That's why it's advantageous to establish a test strategy early in the project life cycle. It provides a method to periodically validate what may be an evolving set of requirements before full efforts directed at construction begin.

Promoting the Investment in Requirements Development

The recommendations presented in this chapter are not "culture quakers." Adopting them probably will not shake an organization to its core. They are pretty simple, logical, and generally accepted in the IT world as a good way to do business. They also have a long track record of working very well for motion picture production. Looking to this industry for advice is not a stretch. Script development and script management—see Chapter 10—are closely related to requirements development and requirements management, and those script development and script management practices translate very effectively into the IT world.

The following case study offers a good example.

Case in Point: Athena Technologies

A navigational controls company in Warrenton, Virginia—Athena Technologies—practices just about every Hollywood technique described in this chapter for ensuring that a script for a project is developed to a workable and manageable form. Athena specializes in the design and engineering of navigation systems for unmanned aircraft. Because the company's product line sits at the heart of an aircraft and enables its full guidance and control, thoroughness and reliability of performance need to be given early and high priority. Athena understands this necessity, and the company's technical teams move from project to project using a requirements development and validation protocol that ensures predictable and workable end results.

To begin with, the company has established a series of documented procedures that guide the elicitation, documentation, review, and approval of requirements. These procedures are followed on all projects. The steps required to carry out these procedures are embedded into a master project schedule, ensuring that adequate time has been set aside for each step. In addition, although the company uses the RequisitePro requirements management tool, the teams also use a requirements document template that serves two purposes: It features preset sections that cue the team to think about a complete range of functionality, and it contains a set of typical requirements that usually go into this kind of product. Finally, the company works closely with its customer contacts during the requirements development phase, establishing in effect a partnership of understanding between the two parties. This collaborative partnership will be carried forward into design, production, and acceptance.

In view of its industry focus, it's not surprising that Athena is a process-centric company. The company follows Federal Aviation Administration (FAA) and U.S. Department of Defense guidelines. It also is a registered ISO 9001:2000 shop and has achieved CMMI Maturity

Level 3. An interesting point to ponder is which came first: compliance through sound practices or sound practices through compliance? In either case, Athena's people follow these practices methodically. They've refined them over time and they adjust and tailor them when needed, but they stand by the methodology as one that reflects Athena's values and priorities concerning predictability, reliability, quality, and performance.

Both in Hollywood and in corporate IT shops, these practices really do work well when they're conscientiously implemented. The interpretive challenges inherent in the discipline of requirements development probably will always be present, but project management can implement tools and techniques that make the discipline's related activities run as smoothly as practicable.

For a Deeper Look . . .

- Mike Cohn, *User Stories Applied: For Agile Software Development,* Addison-Wesley Professional, 2004

  User Stories Applied may be targeted to those using Agile's iterative techniques, but it's got a good take on the importance of requirements development and the necessity to involve various stakeholders in elicitation and definition activities. It puts appropriate emphasis on getting the requirements right as a prelude to getting the product right.

- Aybüke Aurum and Claes Wohlin, *Engineering and Managing Software Requirements*, Springer, 2005

  This book presents a heavy but thorough overview of the discipline. It provides overviews of current requirements models and techniques, discusses issues with market-driven requirements engineering and goal modeling, and presents statistics from practices in industrial projects.

- Elizabeth Hull, Kenneth Jackson, and Jeremy Dick, *Requirements Engineering,* Second Edition, Springer, 2004

  The text may be a little technical in parts, but *Requirements Engineering* includes some great material on the key elements that impact effective requirements development and management. It also features strong sections on the purpose and benefits of requirements traceability.

Chapter 5
Time Box the Projects

The kinds of stories we usually hear when people want to beat up on project management are the really big catastrophes: huge failures in large organizations that cost the stockholders (or taxpayers) billions of dollars. Actual statistics that tout outrageous overruns—schedule overages at 222 percent, say, or budget overruns at 330 percent—usually can be traced back to projects that had two traits in common: (1) big vision and (2) very little detail.

The irony is that this lethal combination is most often not the fault of project management, at least not at the line level. The culprit in such cases is higher-level management in allowing the intake of open-ended projects, projects that come in unbounded or unformed. That's a clear invitation to disaster. Without some realistic handle on scope, projects cannot be responsibly planned, sourced, or controlled. In my experience, this issue presents itself more than once in every enterprise. It's the Damocles sword that hangs over the head of all project managers and by default the IT shops they serve. Removing this one risk factor from project management's array of concerns might not remove 80 percent of IT challenges, but it might well reduce IT waste by 20 percent.

This chapter, then, addresses some techniques upper-level management and project management can use to set up projects for success early on. Most of these techniques are borrowed from the philosophies embedded in the iterative and specifically Agile development methodologies. But we'll look at their well-honed application in Hollywood, where they are put into practice every day as part of the studio production system.

Form, Format, and Formula

Eric Jones is an independent producer who has worked on prestige films like *Amistad* and small niche films like *House Party 4*. He was also production manager for *The Thorn Birds*, the most-watched TV miniseries in television history. I meet Eric at the Monte Cristo Club on Wilshire Boulevard for lunch to speak with him about form and format in Hollywood. I'm interested in this particular topic because of certain project management problems I have encountered in the IT world. These problems look to stem from an organization's lack of a production management strategy—that is, a way to right-size projects so that they align with resource availabilities and functional essentials. IT shops often commit to projects with poorly defined scopes, only to see these projects swell unexpectedly, swallowing money, time, and resources along the way. They are project management nightmares. It strikes me that movie projects might be prone to this same kind of swelling.

Eric tells me, yes, that kind of thing has been known to happen. *Heaven's Gate* and *Waterworld* are the two most frequently cited examples. By and large, however, that's not the case. He explains that the Hollywood system is designed to limit that kind of swelling, and it does so through the use of fixed forms and formats across the production life cycle. These forms and formats can be thought of as molds. Only so much can be poured into each, and each has been sized to hold a manageable amount. The creative, free-form aspects of movie making get all the press, but a closer look at this stage within the studio production system will show a very disciplined approach for aligning what a project should reach for with what it can grasp.

As I listen to Eric, I realize that I've heard of this approach before, explained in different terms. It sounds a lot like the iterative Agile methods of technology production, whereby scope is intentionally limited by a preset time box and a product is produced by integrating components created from multiple time box efforts. That's the idea in Hollywood, Eric confirms. Productions are controlled in large part by first limiting input at the start of each of the production phases. This ensures that a manageable amount of work is set before each team. Here are a few examples of the fixed formats Hollywood uses to limit the scope of projects.

- **The two-hour story**   The most obvious example of fixed form in Hollywood is probably a movie's running time. Most movies run about two hours. At one time, epics or major musicals could run much longer, but since the dawn of the multiplex, this type of show has virtually vanished. (The last studio release to have an intermission was Stanley Kubrick's *Barry Lyndon* in 1975.) Today the minimum length of a theatrical release is about 80 minutes, and the maximum is around 140 minutes. This two-hour limit is so widespread that studios routinely include it in production contracts. There are good business reasons for this limit: It's a way to gauge scope in the planning stages of production. It guides pacing and rhythm in the production phase. Later, it helps theaters maximize show times. And finally, and perhaps of most importance, market studies have shown that audiences in general prefer movies that run around two hours.

- **12-point Courier**   Scripts are another good example of how format is used in Hollywood. Scripts are important not just because they hold the story at the center of the production. They also are one of the chief tools used for production planning. Scripts are used to estimate running times. They serve as the basis for budgeting and scheduling. They cue the mood, tone, and overall design of the production. Accordingly, many different people must rely on the script. That's why scripts are *engineered* for production. So Hollywood has developed a fixed set of rules that govern how a script is formatted and presented. Dramatic instructions, scene shifts, font size, margins, use of capitalization—these elements have all been codified. As a result, all scripts look alike, down to the two clips holding the three-hole-punch paper together. This consistency delivers familiarity; it makes reading comprehension easier; it facilitates consistency in planning and estimation. It promotes production stability and coordinated creative realization.

- **The 45-day shoot**   The production phase of a project is also known as principal photography. It's in this phase that the bulk of the movie is made. Naturally, production is expensive—the most expensive phase in the process, and the most important from a product standpoint. So its time frame is locked down. A team will have a specified amount of time to shoot the movie. In Hollywood, a good average for principal photography is 45 days; smaller films might get somewhat less, larger films somewhat more, but the variance is rarely significant—45 days is about what it takes to shoot the typical two-hour movie. This production time box is carefully scheduled and budgeted in relationship to the script. And it's noted in the contracts of the key players and team members.

- **The release season**   At the macro level of production control is the release season, a set of big time boxes around which productions are planned and managed. This is deadline territory in Hollywood. Movies generally are slated for release into one of four seasons: Summer, Christmas, Early Fall, or Early Spring (there's more on this in Chapter 2, "Know Your Properties"). Completion targets are set for a studio's portfolio of new pictures, and as productions proceed, adjustments may be made accordingly. Because they tend to plan two years in advance, studios pay close attention to these delivery dates. Deadline slips can have significant impact on a studio's mix of new movies. The result can be redundancies and missed opportunities. Because these delivery dates are so crucial to market success, Hollywood's focus on control—introduced through release planning—rises to this highest level of business positioning.

These are just four examples of the way Hollywood uses fixed formats as part of its formula for production control. At the heart of each format is a deliberate, built-in limiting element that sets the material, whatever it may be, to a manageable level. This is evidenced throughout the production system and supports Hollywood's ability to bring its projects in on time, on budget, and to spec.

Part of the reason the world of IT has trouble getting the same results may be because technology shops do not, as a rule, push the idea of limitation through form or format. In fact, the opposite is often true. IT people have a disinclination to say "no" to any limitation. Let's take a look at some of the potential costs for IT shops that do *not* say "no," or at least, not so much.

IT Runaways and Throwaways

Form and format in the IT world are often found only in document templates. The idea that a production system would be intentionally structured to constrain the size of projects would no doubt strike many managers as antithetical. But that is precisely the recommendation in this chapter. Evidently, more and more IT managers are seeing value in this because lately, more and more IT shops, as my own observations indicate, are adopting some of the tenets and principles of the iterative Agile (and similar) development methods. These methods take an incremental look at technology product development, breaking up production into a series of iterative cycles of fixed duration in which manageable chunks of work are addressed. This approach brings distinct benefits to the organization: It tends to balance work loads with available resources. By focusing energies and attention on smaller pieces, it promotes quality. And through its shorter cycles, it allows for timely project management adjustments and repositioning.

Agile and iterative methods focus on limiting three aspects of technology product development: the amount of requirements accepted for a "build," the amount of time set aside for the build, and the size of the team producing the build. It's easy to see that with control over those elements, the job of managing deadlines, costs, and quality becomes much easier. What's surprising is how many IT shops make no effort at all to control any of these factors. What they do, often in the spirit of cooperation, enthusiasm, or fear, is to open wide the project intake gate and welcome anything that wanders in.

The Unlocked IT Gate

Chapter 3 looked at the subject of PPM and how that approach can be used in IT shops to strategically position incoming projects toward meeting general business goals and objectives. Part of that positioning involves screening new project proposals for relevance, value, and viability. That idea carries over here. When PPM is absent as a component of an organization's intake mechanisms, the in-house IT shop can find that it has been saddled with less than desirable projects. When the difficulties inherent in such projects are coupled with unbounded allocations of requirements, time, and people, real troubles can follow.

The threat seems obvious: nebulous projects that turn into runaway projects that turn into throwaway projects. Why, then, is this sequence fairly common in IT shops? As discussed next, four specific behavioral "symptoms" lend themselves to these kinds of projects: open release schedules, open entry criteria, short-view business mission support, and reactive project management controls.

Open Release Schedules

Release scheduling is a way to control what new systems or changes get rolled out into the production environment. Fixed schedules—say, once every quarter or twice a year—promote planning and preparation. Teams work with the understanding that there is a window of opportunity through which progress must pass, and if a project's work isn't ready on time, the team may have to wait for the next window to open. This is an effective technique, but many organizations use release scheduling more as a change control function than as a production control function. This allows production changes on a very frequent basis, almost as if the window were always open. Many shops don't use it at all. The result from a production standpoint is a reduced emphasis on planning and preparation, leading to a "we'll install it when it's ready" management view.

Open Entry Criteria

Many IT shops take on new project work without having the means to assess the complexity of the effort or the commitment that may be required to see it through. These shops sometimes conclude that those discoveries belong to the analysis teams after the project has been accepted. But this attitude often leads to those kinds of vague or overly ambitious projects that turn into runaways and throwaways. Without an assessment approach, the shop may be unwittingly setting itself up for resource, time, and technical commitments that could be better applied elsewhere.

Short-View Business Mission Support

The issue of short-view business mission support often arises from the preceding issue of open entry criteria. Out of a spirit of participation and cooperation, IT shops rarely say "no" to project requests. This is especially true in organizations that foster a customer service view of the business-IT relationship. No one wants to disappoint a customer. In actuality, a better view is probably to look on the relationship as an equal partnership. But without such a view or until shops adopt official intake and assessment mechanisms, projects will come in that are based on the particular (sometimes urgent) needs of individual groups. Without the right controls in place, controls that the business side should be aware of too, the chances that ill-defined projects will find a spot on the calendar will rise proportionately.

Reactive Project Management Controls

The fourth element that invites runaway projects appears when the shop's project management methods are *reactive* rather than proactive—when the project management style is to deal with a current symptom, rather than investigating and mitigating its cause. The temptation to manage in this style will be especially strong with large projects, in which the momentum that's been unleashed practically begs for continued forward motion. Reactive project management will spend its time making fine-point adjustments and tweaking detail. But without a solid view of the whole picture, it will be unable to anticipate when the whole itself, gradually and over time, demonstrates a significant drift from target. It's at that point the visible fallout will surface.

Those four elements invite problematic projects into an IT shop. When one or more are in place in any shop, that shop's ability to avoid doomed projects is diminished. This propensity, unfortunately, marks merely the beginning of the problems. Once it becomes apparent that the shop has hold of something unwieldy, it can expect to deal with a host of subsequent production issues.

The Classic Endgame

All of these conditions lead almost by default to the classic endgame scenario: compromised and failed projects. When IT shops take on unreal projects, ones with unreal scopes, unreal delivery dates, and unreal resource projections, trouble is inevitable. With these kinds of efforts, filled with unknowns, how (and whether) they can be managed to completion also must be classified as unknown. As a further complication, projects that balloon into big efforts and then morph into big problems are sure to attract big attention. Here is where project management most often gets its black eye, its bad rap, and where it's been labeled with those sky-is-falling statistics. The real fallout from these kinds of projects—the inevitable problems that can build to catastrophe—can be grouped into several distinct categories: unending scope discovery, mounting rework, perpetual development, resource quicksand, and, of course, schedule and budget overruns.

Unending Scope Discovery

In my experience, IT organizations often have problems constraining the requirements discovery period on their projects, even well-selected and well-defined projects. They don't want to close the door on their customers. They also feel an obligation to meet all possible customer expectations. But when that open-door attitude is brought to ill-scoped or poorly selected projects, the problems and issues it admits are compounded, magnified.

The desire to continue discovery, then, comes from a sense of obligation and also from a sense of necessity. In both instances, the original understanding of business and functional needs typically is only partially known. As more work is carried out on the project, new questions and gaps inevitably will arise. Subsequent investigations move the present level of detail to a new level, one that may reveal not only deeper paths still but broader ones as well, unexpected extensions and interactions that significantly add new considerations to the work. This can lead anew to fresh trails of discovery. When this ongoing discovery is not closely coordinated with design and development efforts, all three can quickly fall out of sync. This perpetuates even more discovery, and the cycle goes on.

Mounting Rework

If one factor could be reliably used to identify a project gone bad, it would probably be rework levels. The need for lots of rework is a sure indicator of real problems. What it demonstrates is simple: Somewhere, somehow, someone got something wrong. It's ironic that when an IT shop takes on a project whose scope is more than it can handle, rework tends to pop up all over the place, so the shop's work load actually increases even past the unmanageable point. Certainly, rework may be brought about by poor coding and other general mistakes, but such errors are more often the exception than the rule. The usual source is missing, incomplete, or conflicting requirements. With poorly scoped projects or overly ambitious attacks at otherwise well-characterized larger projects, teams tend to produce thin requirements.

A lack of scrutiny that probably let the project in the door in the first place can easily carry over into definitions of business objectives, business requirements, and technical requirements. When development moves forward from that point the stability of the work being produced can easily come into question. And as scope becomes clarified and amplified, it is common to discover that what was built earlier now has to be revisited—again.

Perpetual Development

Compounding issues with rework, ambiguously scoped projects tend to enter a stage of perpetual development. Design and development seem to go on forever, with no end in sight. Although an enormous amount of work may be in progress, very few discrete products seem to be emerging from all the activity. This low-level productivity is common with out-of-control projects. The original vagueness in scope leads naturally to vagueness in design, which spills over into inefficient coding. The product whose high-level identity was barely formed will be even less cleanly defined when viewed at the detail level. Separations and integration points remain unidentified; the parts that should constitute the whole never had a chance to be discovered. No wonder there is rarely anything to salvage from these efforts. At this stage, the smart move might be to put on the brakes, to step back and assess with fresh eyes—to bring about a renewed focus on mission and purpose. But many managers succumb to the temptation to simply get out of the woods. And they follow that temptation by beefing up technical teams so they can crank out even more code. That tactic rarely works. What it usually brings into the project is just more cycles of development, development, and development, typically with little benefit and much cost.

Resource Quicksand

Runaway projects can easily turn into virtual quicksand for the people involved. Original team members, faced with shallow results and stymied progress, may feel that they are stuck in an unending, unrewarding effort and may look for new assignments, either inside the company or out. Members may be pulled off other projects to bolster the one in trouble, thereby channeling resource problems across the enterprise. New help may be brought in quickly, but with little preparation and perhaps with little exposure to the project's business domains. The need of these helpers for orientation and acclimation may go unheeded, further slowing their ability to contribute. Such frenetic seat-filling usually has a detrimental effect. Teams begin to lose their focus; they fragment. Coordination and collaboration suffer. Worse, there's no easy resolution to the congestion. This kind of project can devolve into a pool of quicksand, sucking down the organization's best people and then gaping for more.

Schedule and Budget Overruns

When added together, the traits just described can amount to only one thing: overages. Rework combined with more work is going to require resource reinforcements, either in the number of people working or in the amounts of time the current folks put in. The result: schedule slippages, missed targets, and reset deadlines. Push that cycle through a few times, and project size begins to balloon. More money needs to be pumped into the project to support the change in scope. At this point, management may be faced with a dreaded decision: Is it better to cut losses now, with the understanding that there will be very little to show for it? Or is it better to continue on and try to make the best of a bad situation? Neither of these two choices provides a clean way out.

All of these conditions are hallmarks of unbridled projects. Their ability to run away with success, investments, and reputations is well known. Nevertheless, current practices in many IT shops continue to create these kinds of crisis-tinged scenarios. In such cases, the only way to address the problem is with some form of unequivocal "no": "No, we will not move forward; we will push at this no longer," or, "No, we will not stop working; we will see this thing through to the end."

IT shops could avoid many of these situations by using "no" much earlier, at a project's initiation. Hollywood achieves this control through the use of forms, formats, and formulas. These naturally limit the amount of work material accepted by a team and also balance the work with the team's ability to realize it as a high-quality product.

Limiting Through Form and Format

The ability to limit has direct application in IT shops. If IT shops have a difficult time saying "no," then they can at least say "yes" in a way that limits exposure to risky projects. And they can shape their production systems to drive them toward this end. In fact, such a shaping is right now becoming popular in many IT shops, derived from an application of specific iterative and Agile development techniques. From this idea of strategic limitation comes the fifth lesson of this book:

> **Lesson 5: Time box project work efforts** as a way to balance the amount of high-quality work that can be done with the level of available resources.

Let's look in brief at some ways this can be applied in IT shops.

Toward a Controlled Development Tempo

Many of the management attributes we've looked at in the Hollywood system ensure control over scope, costs, and schedules through the use of specific, time-proven practices, such as script analysis, preproduction planning, and the screening of dailies. But we've also now touched on a series of controls that have less to do with practices than with the form of the system itself. The studio production system comes embedded with a set of limiting factors that provide extended controls. These factors are evidenced in the kinds of forms and formats Hollywood uses to package a product and to keep that product to a manageable size.

Project managers can take specific steps to implement similar forms and formats to be used within the IT shop for control of project scope, budget, and schedule.

Iterative technology development promotes incremental production, by which a complex product is created over time through a series of small, manageable development cycles. Agile and Scrum are two popular forms of iterative development. Let's look at some of the techniques these methods use to control quality, scope, costs, and delivery dates. These techniques tend to mirror Hollywood's use of forms and formats to limit risk. And they have direct application in technology shops. The following four techniques, discussed in detail next, have special appeal to project managers wishing to avoid projects with ill-defined scopes or overambitious targets:

- Use of development "sprints" to limit the volume of work and the level of resource commitments

- Evolution of a product backlog used to house, prioritize, and allocate requirements

- Relationships with product owners that establish a partnership in the ongoing delivery of essential functionality

- Establishment of specialized teams with the experience to grow the product base over time

Build Around Development Sprints

A *sprint* is a development time box. It's a full life cycle that runs across a short period of time. This time frame is preset, defined in the organization's project management methodology. Scrum recommends that sprints last no longer than 30 days, but strict adherence to this rule is not the point. Rather, the focus here is on the value to be found in general timeline limitations. Because a sprint's project timeline is preset, business and technical teams can better determine just how much work can be reasonably accounted for in each cycle. That promotes requirements management and prioritization. And because the timelines are close-ended and short, projects have a harder time turning into runaways—a limit to just how far they can run has already been set in place.

Naturally, some considerations will require thinking through for shops that want to move from the use of work-driven, open-ended timelines to time-driven, close-ended work lines. For starters, it's important to determine the right-sized time box for the shop's types of projects. This will depend on factors such as current resource levels, project size, solution maturity, customer accessibility, and technical complexity. A sprint can be said to be sized right when its length allows for a "sustainable pace" of production—that is, little downtime and little overtime. The key is to keep the sprint as short as possible, given all those factors.

The idea behind the short sprints is to give teams the focus they need to develop and deliver high-quality components while working a manageable scope through fixed resources. For a particular shop, a sprint of 30 days may be right for most projects, although a few may call for a sprint of 120 days, for example.

Another step will be to convince the shop's customers that incremental, iterative development is the way to go. With customers used to "big bang" solutions, quite a bit of convincing may be required. But the advantages of time boxing are pretty easy to articulate. The use of sprints means that customers should be able to see a pattern of regular component delivery, with components built with a focus on reliability and dependability. They should also realize tighter controls over costs and better insight into work phase progress. On the other hand, they will need to recognize that the nature of incremental growth means that it's not possible to have everything at once (although what they really want may come sooner). That brings us to the next consideration.

Evolve a Managed Product Backlog

Sprints focus on the delivery of fixed sets of functionality over a fixed length of time. An appropriately sized and targeted group of requirements are selected for a sprint, and then the work commences. Completion of a sprint is usually seen not as the end of a project; it simply signals that it's time to move to the next set of requirements. The pool that these requirements are drawn from is called (in the Scrum methodology) the *product backlog*. This backlog can be seen as a baselined document (or repository) that represents the full scope of functionality desired for the complete solution. The product owners (described in the next section) manage and govern this baseline, and it is their job to select those requirements for each sprint. Of note, the product backlog can (and probably should) be developed independently of the sprint efforts. The backlog exists to feed the sprints. Once the backlog is empty, the product (and the project) can be said to be finished. But there is, at the same time, a critical dependency between the product backlog and the ongoing sprint. Because changes to already produced components can become part of a sprint's work scope, it's essential that the backlog be carefully managed by the product owners so that work products and requirements, over time and across changes, remain in sync.

Connect with the Product Owner

Iterative methods such as Agile and Scrum place special importance on establishing close relationships with the IT shop's business associates. In such methods, this relationship is viewed as a real partnership, one that works best through continuous contact, dialog, and feedback. The principal business role here, as it relates to the project team, is that of the product owner (or owners). Product owners are those people who represent the business, who usually report to the project sponsor, and who work with the project teams to realize the business solution. Accordingly, they are responsible for the product backlog, that set of requirements that represents the true scope of the project. Product owners are responsible for the maintenance and management of this backlog; they control what moves into the backlog and, more important, what moves out of the backlog and into the next sprint. In view of that responsibility, it's essential that the product owners work very closely with project management and technical management to determine the proper scope for each sprint. That's why it's beneficial to look at the relationship as a partnership. Ultimately, the product owner has the authority to make the call about *what* goes in. The project management and technical opinions are there to help influence how much of that "what" is finally chosen.

It's hard to apply time boxing effectively without the focused help of a product owner. This person provides the business-level participation needed to establish what is essential for a time box: an agreed-upon, limited scope. This person also provides the business continuity that carries the evolution of a product across multiple sprints.

Leverage Knowledge Teams

One important aspect of time boxing is the use of specialized and dedicated teams to run a project's sprints. Both of those qualities—specialized and dedicated—are important. *Specialization* contributes the degree of expertise and exposure the team will need to work on a continually evolving product. Because sprints build on each other and because they realize a growing set of business functionalities, progress and quality can be best ensured when the technical team members are comfortable working with the base technologies of the system and are at the same time familiar with the business foundations within the system. *Dedication* to the project provides the continuity necessary to move in a coordinated and focused manner from sprint to sprint, without the need for reestablishing team dynamics or redefining job roles. Together, specialization and dedication constitute the basis for a knowledge team. Qualified knowledge teams are better able to realize the short-track delivery goals inherent in iterative methods and at the same time maintain the grasp of a larger vision.

The use of knowledge teams has been shown to be very effective for system development. In my experience, when such teams are deployed in technology shops, the result has been stronger team dynamics, more effective communications, and enhanced production performances. Nevertheless, some shops are not apt to formulate teams this way. They may be used to the need for on-demand resource juggling, or they may need single resources to serve multiple purposes. Although it's possible to use semispecialized and semidedicated teams for iterative projects, that choice is not likely to come to the fore. Typically, once a shop makes the switch to iterative development, it will inevitably see the advantage of knowledge teams and move to identify them for those projects that will evolve through the use of focused sprints.

Benefits of the Time Box Approach

The use of iterative approaches, such as Agile, can help IT organizations manage the ultimate size and viability of their projects by imposing some elemental limitations, most often centered on project time frames. (The general shape of this approach is illustrated in Figure 5-1.) These limitations should not be seen as artificial. In most shops, they are very real. Resources, facilities, and missions are naturally limited. No shop can do everything it wants to do or everything it's asked to do. Problems come only when these limitations are not recognized, or are recognized but ignored. The quartet of major project management concerns—quality, cost, schedule, and resource control—can all be placed at risk when project attributes such as size, scope, and focus are undefined at the outset. The Agile approach of time boxing, combined with a focus on evolving requirements backlogs, can deliver a series of benefits that can have a positive impact on the ability of project management to control these areas. Five major benefits are recognized:

- Promoting a focus on essential functionality
- Nurturing the creation of practical schedules and dependable budgets
- Support for effective resource utilization
- Emphasis on the long-term view of IT and business missions
- Accommodating the project management framework

Let's take a quick look at each.

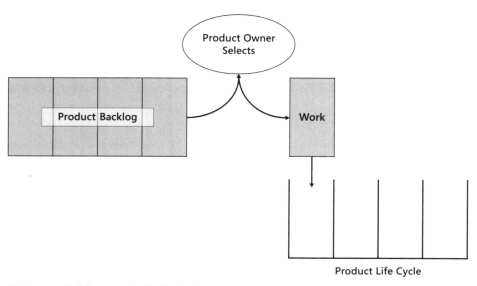

FIGURE 5-1 Building production limitations into your project management methodology can help control scope, ensure investments, and protect quality across the enterprise.

Promoting Focus and Prioritization

With projects based on a soft picture of scope, it's typical for customers, as they move with the project team deeper into the work, to begin asking for everything they can think of in terms of functionality. This broad reach for solutions is understandable: Customers may perceive their requests as part of their job, to provide their technology partners with a list of things to build. The problem this predicates is two-fold: It benignly encourages a steady intake of requirements, as if requirements discovery were expected to extend across the life of the project. At the same time, it encourages the unbounded submission of requirements: If it's on someone's wish list, it'll be tossed into the mix. Ultimately, the project team can end up with a large and widely diverse set of requirements, with untenable internal relationships and (perhaps worse) continually shifting shape and focus.

The use of the time box approach can help circumvent such situations before they arise. By setting a performance time frame as an integral characteristic of project scope, business and technology partners can focus on those business needs the solution should address. The limitation imposed by the time box can be used to free the team from worrying about superfluous functionality. In my experience, with the use of this approach, most people pretty much agree on the core requirements a solution must address. It's the like-to-haves that can lead to disagreement and loss of focus. When time boxing is set into place and communicated as a legitimate constraint, the various teams are able to focus on the primary mission at hand and identify those requirements pertinent to that mission. That core set can then be analyzed, validated, and prioritized by the stakeholders to form the basis for further project management planning, resource allocation, and benchmarking. And the like-to-haves can be saved to be prioritized later.

Nurturing Reliable Scheduling and Dependable Budgeting

Time boxing is also a great way to establish more reliable schedules and more dependable budgets. The reason is clear: It presets the size of the mold into which work can be poured. A well-designed time box approach is set up to reflect a balance between resources and project volumes. Furthermore, within that time box are contained those work phases identified as necessary to support the shop's project management methodology (to protect product quality). The box can then be used as one of project management's main tools for assessing and determining scope. From that determination can come resource needs and availabilities. In short, time boxing is a way to approximate scope, schedules, and budgets within a realistic, manageable framework. And the more realistic the schedule and the budget, the easier they are to control. They simply don't tend to vary as wildly as the unrealistic kind. This benefit is one that, in my experience, is quickly appreciated by both business stakeholders and technical management. After the first few cycles with time boxing, people appreciate its purpose and support its use. They are able to see how limitations in terms of scope and time frames support the steadfast and steady achievement of business and performance objectives.

Support of Effective Resource Utilization

The use of methods like time boxing, evolving product backlogs, and specialized teams will probably never remove all resource problems from the IT shop. Resource constraints will remain a reality—the ever-increasing demand for IT services guarantees it. Through the use of these Agile-like techniques, however, the ability to manage the resource demand crunch is enhanced. For starters, blind commitments can be avoided. When a shop takes on overambitious, vague, or ill-scoped projects, it runs the risk of locking down a team into an effort with no firm or agreed-upon end in sight. This confinement of resources makes it difficult to anticipate future availabilities and to plan appropriate allocations.

These Agile-like techniques also help avoid burnout. This common but seldom-addressed problem is the bane of project management. Dealing with massive or uncontrollable projects almost always leads to back-tracking, conflicts, and staff overtime (the chief cause of schedule and cost overruns). These can combine to directly influence employee retention. Chaotic and overblown projects can steadily tax the designers, analysts, and developers assigned to them. The rework, frustrations, and reputation hits these kinds of projects often rain down on team members may be enough to make them look for any nearby exit.

A very real advantage of the combination of scope control and time boxing is that it puts a ceiling on energy expenditures. It allows a project team to work at a sustainable pace over time and still deliver according to commitments. This trait is heavily emphasized by Agile proponents. Predictable, 8-hour workdays are seen as evidence of control and professionalism. Any project that has to abandon this predictability in favor of a production-at-all-costs approach is seen as a project in trouble. With the advantage of fixed schedule durations, workers will be less prone to feel trapped in a miasma of unrewarding work.

Fostering a Long-Term View of the IT Mission

Use of iterative methods touched on in this chapter can help promote a long-term view of IT and business mission success. A stronger emphasis on strategy over tactics can lead in turn to better decision making regarding new project work. Although this benefit may seem somewhat subjective in nature, it yields concrete results. When users and technical teams begin to experience how the iterative, incremental approach can support predictability, quality, and delivery, they tend to lose some of the make-or-break anxieties that typically accompany "big bang" and "do or die"–scaled projects. It then becomes easier to focus on the essentials—the business purpose of the solution and the best ways to realize that purpose. Most IT professionals will agree that many project problems stem from moving too quickly into areas not prepared to receive such motion. Hurry-up-and-go may appease stakeholders in the short term but opens the door for unnecessary risk and almost always causes problems later.

By embracing incremental progress, the organization communicates a different message. It says that it values prioritization and dependability over broad-based, blanket solutions; reliable progress toward goals rather than hit-or-miss tactics; and smooth operations over peaks and valleys of activity. This kind of long-term vision can become a valuable ally for an IT shop striving to realize its mission.

Accommodation of the Project Management Program Framework

This last advantage of the time box structure is one that supports a broader target: overall use of the project management system. This happens when the breakdown of the time box itself is designed to push specific portions of the system. When this tack is followed, executing the project from within the time box will ensure adherence to the system. Many project managers develop WBSs for their projects (see Chapter 6, "Strip Board the Script"). A WBS sequences those project activities required for production. Most schedules are based on a WBS. The use of the WBS then becomes an opportunity to embed important parts of the system in the process. The same opportunity exists in the time box approach. The time box holds the WBS; the WBS holds portions of the system.

As the time box cycles over and over from project to project, the organization typically becomes, almost by default, more familiar with and comfortable working within the system. Additionally, a process improvement advantage will emerge from this cyclical use. Project teams will be able to exercise the full range of components within the system much more readily than if they had been applied to long-term or open-ended efforts. As a result, it should be possible to gather a higher volume of performance and improvement data, to enable refinement of the system to better support organizational goals.

As noted at the beginning of this chapter, Hollywood's attraction to form and format lends support to its preference for production through the use of a system. IT professionals can look to this allegiance and see ways to address their own issues of scope, schedule, and budget control. One way is to recognize the value in an IT management technique that's been growing in popularity: the Agile practice of time boxing project durations around a fixed set of requirements pulled from a preapproved product backlog.

By choosing a subset of this backlog to fit within the volume of the time box, project managers can better ensure that scope will be fulfilled as promised, that schedules will be followed true to course, and that budget expenditures will fall within predictable ranges. Out of all of these efforts should come an enhanced ability to produce high-quality work and an increased capability to meet product production and delivery targets.

Case in Point: Time Boxing at Oatland Container Corp.

Oatland Container Corp. produces corrugated cardboard boxes and related packaging materials for the shipping and storage industries. If you've ever used one of those self-storage centers, chances are you've probably packed something into an Oatland box. Because of the demands of corporate growth, the company's Systems Division has seen its resources taxed to the point of strain. Recently it was faced with a growing series of project delays, problematic implementations, and a few embarrassing rollbacks. Management took a look at the situation and identified a host of organizational habits and factors as likely contributors to the troubles. Electing to tackle these issues a few at a time, management decided to focus on the unit's requirements elicitation and development processes. What it quickly found was that its business analysts had no set way to distinguish business objectives from business requirements, and business requirements from functional requirements, so they often inadvertently jumbled the three. The resulting confusion clouded early pictures of scope; major details got lost next to minor details. On top of this, the organization lacked well-managed operational documentation, so it had little reliable insight into system interfaces and dependencies. This further clouded the true picture of a project's scope and caused planning to fall short when it came to estimating actual amounts of work.

Out of this investigation, Oatland discovered its core issue. The Systems Division was having problems because it was taking on projects that were actually whole programs—in reality, series of interrelated projects. The scope issues had been keeping this revelation hidden until things had gone too far for them to turn around. The result: schedule and budget overruns, weak interconnections, and a loss of operational stability.

Oatland addressed the situation in two ways. First, management established and enforced requirements definition standards for its business analysts. Then management adopted the time box method for project allocation and set 3 months as the limit of a project life cycle. Ninety days is well past the recommended Agile limit of 30 days or so, but Oatland saw the promise in the general premise and made a commitment to working efforts that could fit within those bounds.

Together, the two approaches worked. It took about nine months for the Systems Division to see results, but when they began to arrive, they stayed. Scope issues became much clearer early on—so much so that management found that it was saying "no" to more projects than ever in the past, but now with good, verifiable reasons. The work it did take on was smaller but more focused and thus more amenable to end-to-end control. Interface issues dropped. Operational stability increased. Today Oatland is continuing its improvement efforts; those two moves did not solve all of its problems. But time boxing proved a reliable way to manage requirements and consequently scope, identify workable projects, and enhance delivery expectations.

For a Deeper Look . . .

- Craig Larman, *Agile and Iterative Development: A Manager's Guide,* Addison-Wesley Professional, 2004

  Larman's book features good advice on using time boxes in support of ongoing, iterative development. The text focuses on the management view and offers insights into ways in which an organization can adopt and sustain this type of development methodology.

- Ken Schwaber, *The Enterprise and Scrum,* Microsoft Press, 2007

  This book presents a good overview of how time boxes and product backlogs can be used together to achieve a controlled and manageable development pace across an IT organization. Also provided are good explanations of the roles and responsibilities of product owners.

Part II
Preproduction

Here we look at issues and topics that focus on how projects are planned and staffed and how sponsorship and commitments are obtained.

Chapter 6
Strip Board the Script

Many projects that fall into trouble do so because they were headed that way right from the start. Drifting schedules, budgets, and resource levels often indicate initial performance targets that were insufficiently stated to begin with. The drifting, then, is not so much a measure of moving off course as it is an indicator of correction toward a course reflecting the project's true nature. Projects get launched from such inauspicious beginnings for a variety of reasons. Preset deadlines and team sizes may be mandated from above. External business drivers may pressure premature action. But a chief and common reason for the drift, coming from within the shop, is planning that fails to use the requirements as a major tool for determining project parameters. The need for such reliance may seem obvious, yet it's surprising how often the details of the requirements are given short shrift when it comes to planning activities. Instead, management often places greater weight on intuition and past experience, on informed opinion, and on a sense of best-case possibilities. Although those forms of input are no doubt valuable, their contribution is proportionate only to their foundation in the requirements.

In view of the nature of estimation and the qualitative characteristics of project planning, the ability to pinpoint schedule, budget, and resource targets probably will remain elusive. And external and cultural pressures surely will always be factors to be dealt with. Specific planning techniques and practices, however, are available for use by project management to mitigate these conditions and to improve managers' ability to predict and articulate a project's true shape and size. This chapter reviews some of these techniques and practices, aimed at breaking down project requirements for optimal scheduling, budgeting, and resource allocation. In the movie-making business, this step in the preproduction process is recognized as being of prime importance. So let's begin with a quick look at how the studio production system derives project size from a close examination of the script.

The Time-Money Equation

As with most businesses, in Hollywood time is money, especially in view of the expensive nature of movie making. The more time spent on a production, the more costly it's going to get. So although Hollywood studios may appear to be extravagant in areas such as star salaries and executive perks, they all tend to be extremely stingy with time—because they've learned that's where it pays to be frugal.

Amy Kaufman knows about this necessity firsthand. She is a producer who has overseen a number of movies including the Jeff Bridges drama *The Door in the Floor* and the John Cusack romance, *Serendipity.* When I contacted her to discuss production planning, one of her first comments related to the task of scheduling. She mentioned that with all projects, one of the producer's first jobs was to "strip board the script." I thought she meant storyboarding. But as Amy explained, *strip boarding* is another process entirely. Today it is done on computer, but the name comes from the old practice of writing the scenes from a script out on a series of paper strips and then, after analysis, ordering those strips into an efficient shooting sequence. This carefully considered sequencing shapes the structure of the entire production and serves as the foundation for the production plans. Strip boarding is really an exercise in time management. It's all about compressing the duration of the production into the smallest time span practicable. The result: better cost and production controls down the line.

Strip Boarding the Script

This time management exercise will shape not only the budget but the actual shooting schedule, casting calls, crew calls, and all of the other details that make up a production effort. That's why it's done early in the game, while the unit is still in preproduction, and that's why it's assigned to a producer-level team member. It's a high-impact job that requires a well-practiced knowledge of production management techniques.

As mentioned earlier, the job of strip boarding is to analyze the script and then break it down into an economical shooting sequence. First, the script must be studied thoroughly with a view toward its structural composition. Then the individual scenes are identified; each is assessed for its production demands; and the scenes are then grouped and ordered. For example, a story's shift in locations is a primary strip boarding consideration. In my research, I was surprised to find how much of a production budget is dedicated to transportation, to moving people and equipment. Many producers I spoke to likened this undertaking to corralling a traveling carnival, or to fielding an army. Big trucks and lots of them are needed for the equipment, and because the endeavor also involves moving people, the trucks will be followed by catering and travel trailers and a host of other conveyances for on-the-road needs. With these potential challenges in mind, the producer's strip board seeks to minimize the need to move the production unit. Locations that can be reused or are close together are aligned on the strip board. As an adjunct to this strategy, the producer will also identify scenes that can be shot on a sound stage, which will park the whole company in one place for a while.

Another factor the producer will look at when working to order scenes is the availability of the main actors. If the production needs to accommodate certain actors' schedules, those scenes will be brought together on the strip board, even if this grouping means rearranging other scenes within the sequence. Weather is also considered. The producer tries to arrange scenes in a way that provides a degree of shooting flexibility. If an exterior planned for one day gets rained out, it would be nice to have an available standby, another scene that could be shot instead.

Lots of other considerations are involved in strip boarding. The fact that they can all be active at once, even competing against each other, makes this a complex exercise. Producers may spend weeks working on the strip board: drafting it, reviewing it with others, revising it. The goal always is to compress, to economize the shoot.

Order Through Understanding

Of necessity, strip boarding happens very early in preproduction. By its very nature, this highly intensive effort generates numerous advantages: Practical schedules can be developed. Reliable budget frameworks can be established. Key personnel can be accommodated. Moreover, from the act of scrutinizing the script so closely, the producers also acquire a complete, in-depth understanding of the story they wish to present. This understanding, which incorporates every detail of every scene, particularly in relation to other scenes and other details, represents the starting point for the control that will be needed across the rest of production. People are often surprised to learn that movies are not shot in story sequence—it seems like such a jumbled way to work. But practicality is key, and it's the strip board—and before that, the need to shape the production from the shape of the script—that drives this production approach.

Form Following Function in Technology Development

The power that comes from strip boarding is twofold; First, it sets a firm foundation upon which plans can be built; second, it gives managers a deep understanding of the project's script so that execution can be effectively controlled. These same two needs—for a foundation and an understanding—exist in IT shops today. Obtaining a firm understanding of the requirements should be a prerequisite to all planning activities. Yet more often than not—at least from my own experience across corporate IT—this step is skipped or, at best, minimized. Project managers tend to move directly into scheduling and budgeting activities without a thorough sorting or ordering of the work specifics. The bases they use instead are things like project life cycle phases, predelivered end dates, or preset budget parameters. The schedules, budgets, and management plans generated by this approach may appear on the surface to meet organizational objectives, but they often have little relationship to the realities of the work. This disconnect becomes a common source of project management problems.

That's not to say that the concept of strip boarding is not already reflected in the IT world. Indeed it is. A look at an established management framework like the PMI's PMBOK or the SEI's CMMI will show a series of "best practices" that deal with the creation of *work breakdown structures* (WBSs). Although this is a common term in most IT shops, its use is often

out of sync with its intended purpose. To many project managers, a WBS is simply the project schedule. Perhaps it has been "perked out" in MS Project or Primavera or any of the other
project scheduling systems available today. (And often that schedule is considered the entire
project management plan.) The way the project manager arrives at the schedule is typically
through what's been called "plate organization" (as in boiler plate). In plate organization,
chunks of work are grouped in generic categories, such as analysis, design, development,
testing, and so on. Most often, each plate category reflects an established step in the classical system development life cycle. The manager then prefigures the subtasks likely to support each plate. Out of this limited analysis emerges what might be called a one-dimensional
WBS: It reflects only one dimension of the project—the shape of the life cycle. At the same
time, it ignores the requirements, the source information that will by necessity dictate the
shape of the work.

Plate organization is so prevalent that it is often seen as a best practice in and of itself. But that
perception is an illusion. The result is not a work breakdown at all. It's just a *form* breakdown.
And when form does not follow function, a team can end up with a cantilevered project structure. In failing to reckon with the demands of the requirements, and to shape a work approach
that will best accommodate those demands, project management is ignoring the full dimension of considerations that such a commitment introduces. Here are several issues that typically
arise when an organization relies on plate organization as the sole way to create a WBS:

- **Mis-scaled schedules**   Schedules that arise from a plate-organized WBS will invariably
  have potentially serious flaws. Although they may be based on a convenient shape, and
  although that shape may account for the general activities that must be addressed in
  production, the lack of insight into product detail increases the risk for mis-scaling of
  time frames, either up or down, from the realities of actual production.

- **Miscalculated budgets**   When work details are not adequately accounted for and
  schedules have only a general affinity with reality, budgets will inevitably carry a high
  degree of predictive instability. In my experience, IT shops in which plate organization
  is the only WBS technique used rarely have confidence in their budgets. Anxiety about
  their accuracy and usefulness appears right at the start of project execution and carries
  through into subsequent phases. As a result, project managers feel forced to spend an
  inordinate amount of time focusing on budget control, often with consequent neglect
  of issues such as product quality and deliverability.

- **Inefficient resource allocations**   Plate organization typically specifies the need for
  analysts and developers and testers, and so on, for a project, but it's not very helpful
  in illuminating required team sizes or balancing resource levels. This approach treats a
  project as if it were shaped like a rectangle of time and phases, or perhaps like a stag-
  gered staircase. But the plate organization approach does not allow anticipation of the
  peaks and valleys that may run through these macro shapes at a micro level. Plate-
  organized schedules, then, are prone to the inefficient allocation of resources. It's tough
  to predict which personnel and other resources will be needed when and for how long.

- **Weak performance benchmarks**   Plate organization emphasizes the identification of generic benchmarks (plate categories). This categorization process may be fine in and of itself, but scheduling will later require that specific dates be tied to those benchmarks. The weak scheduling inherent in plate organization, however, means that management may have a difficult time assessing performance in terms of cause and effect. Are performance problems due to personnel issues or weak specifications, or do they perhaps stem from inaccurate benchmarks? It's hard to tell—so such problems are hard to manage.

- **Incompatible success criteria**   The four factors just described invariably combine to cloud the meaning of "project success." Because realistic expectations are not engineered early in the project life cycle, measures of success (or failure) lose concrete meaning as relevant outcomes are manifested toward the end.

Those are just some of the faults inherent in the one-dimensional views that can come from plate organization. A better approach is to borrow the Hollywood practice of strip boarding and engage in an enhanced WBS development activity, one that leverages plate organization with "source organization" to produce two-dimensional planning data. This goal constitutes the sixth lesson of this book:

> **Lesson 6:   Use source organization as a way to produce work breakdown structures** based on a logical sorting and ordering of the requirements.

The Two-Dimensional Work Breakdown Structure

The difference between plate organization and source organization is one of dimension. With a WBS created using the former, the shape of the development life cycle is basically spread in as practical a way as possible over a set span of time. This approach usually is based on only a general understanding of the requirements. Accordingly, plate organization tends to produce generic-looking schedules and project plans. In source organization, the approach to work breakdown is not so much *different* as it is *extended*, one that echoes Hollywood's use of strip boarding to drive a deeper understanding of work demands. Source organization begins with the plate format—important because it represents the framework of the project management system in place. Then the requirements are thoroughly assessed, sorted, and prioritized. This ordered output, set against the framework, becomes the foundation for all subsequent project planning activities, including budgeting and scheduling. The accuracy, reliability, and workability of all of these products will rise accordingly.

Creating a source-organized WBS entails two fundamental steps: (1) establishing an assessment team and (2) organizing the requirements.

Establish the Assessment Team

Probably the vast majority of technology projects are planned in isolation—if not total isolation, then at least substantial isolation. Project managers are given some fundamental constraints by higher-level management, together with some basic scope materials, and then asked to create a plan. The experienced project manager will actively seek expert opinion and input in this planning process, but if the culture doesn't promote strong interactions, fostering this approach from scratch may be difficult.

Source-organizing a WBS *demands* collaboration, however. So organizations using this approach will charge not just a project manager with the planning tasks but a dedicated support team as well. It is the makeup of this team that will bring value to the source-organizing activities. Management should appoint key project personnel in a mix that will represent the business characteristics of the project as well as the technical characteristics. The idea is to cover those viewpoints necessary to gain a complete understanding of the requirements, thereby garnering an effective ability to organize them.

Who should be included on the assessment team? That decision is up to the individual organization and the IT shop. But a full range of positions should be considered. A business analyst with a solid take on the business mission of the project would be a good choice. A technical architect responsible for the solution design could provide valuable integration insight. A programmer could spot opportunities for parsimonies and reuse. A tester could contribute suggestions for iterative builds and validation cycles. In short, almost any member of the project team could lend substantial input. The key is to establish the team, charge its members with the source organization mission, and then provide the time and resources needed to carry out the job. The team can then use a five-step process, presented next, to create the two-dimensional, source-organized WBS.

Organize the Requirements

Here's a familiar sequence with three basic requirements: (1) User inserts ATM card; (2) user enters PIN; (3) system prints receipt. It's easy to see how these three requirements for an ATM transaction can be organized into two groups: "Customer Entry" and "System Printing," with two requirements in the first group and one in the second. From this grouping, the relative weights of each can be evaluated, and possible durations assigned. One requirement can be prioritized over another. All three can be ordered into a work sequence that best accommodates the availability of UI experts and systems experts, if needed. And the working of those groups can be fitted into a project management framework in a way that maximizes development efficiencies. That's the whole idea behind source organization, and it's the key to turning out a well-designed, two-dimensional WBS.

This approach to creating a WBS is summarized in the following five steps.

1. **Prepare the framework.**   This is the plate-organizing step. It's an important step because it allows the project at hand to follow the flow of the company's project management system. This flow—the phases and mandatory steps required for development—needs to be wrapped as a framework around the project, like a kind of exoskeleton. This activity will produce the general shape of the emerging WBS.

2. **Understand the requirements.**   This is where the necessity of the assessment team becomes apparent. At this point, the members of the team study the project's requirements in order to thoroughly understand them. (This need is emphasized over and over again in the CMMI, ISO 9001, and PMBOK.) Firm, reliable project commitments can be established only when the team understands intimately what it's been enjoined to accomplish. Several avenues can be taken to arrive at this understanding: individual reviews, team meetings, and workshops. In addition to the strength in numbers afforded by a team approach, an important advantage is the availability of selective viewpoints from different specialists on the assessment team. It is the combination—the collaboration—of these viewpoints that will lead to a more complete understanding.

3. **Organize the requirements.**   Now the work of source organization really begins. And this is where the team's representative expertise makes its contribution. Once an understanding of the requirements has been achieved, the assessment team begins to allocate the requirements into related or complementary groups. Naturally, the type of categories or groups used will depend on the needs of each project or technology domain. But the idea remains the same whatever the project: to sort the requirements into groups that can be worked together. Once these relationships have been established—the desired depth of which again depends on the needs of the project—the team can prioritize the importance of the groups, sequencing them into chains of either dependence or production efficiencies.

4. **Sequence the requirements.**   Here the value of source organization is realized. Within the method framework established in step 1, the assessment team's expertise is leveraged to sequence the logical groupings of requirements into a preferred order of action. This order can be established through any number of considerations: technical complexity, resource availability, integration dependencies, requirements stability, and so on. Because the considerations can be many, and sometimes even competing, this step usually requires the most amount of concentrated work. But now the project's logical design begins to take shape. A management approach becomes clear. And a solid foundation emerges upon which schedules, budgets, and other plan components can be built.

5. **Assign the requirements.**   Step 4 is actually the last step in creating the WBS. This plan gives a breakdown of work that accommodates the phases of the production process (step 1). It recognizes the particular demands of the project (steps 2 and 3). And it shapes these demands into an ordered sequence that can be realized and managed by the project team (step 4). With this two-dimensional detail in place, expected durations and resource levels can now be assigned to the requirements; from these determinations, expected expenses can be derived. (For more on this topic, see Chapter 8, "Budget to the Board.")

Hollywood producers strip board their scripts in order to get a detailed picture of each project's initial scope and organizational demands. It's a routine practice in the motion picture industry, one that dates back easily to the 1930s and remains essential in preproduction work today. The world of IT has a similar need. For technology projects to be efficiently scheduled and accurately budgeted, project management must understand the business and system requirements that drive the project. The practice of source organization can promote this need in technology shops. It fosters the production of WBSs that reflect two key dimensions of project management: alignment with the project management system and the realization of functional delivery.

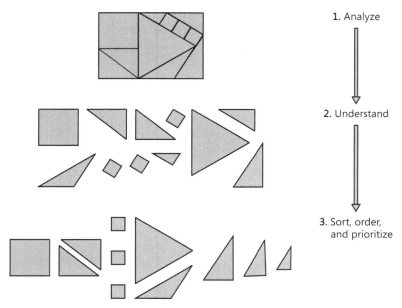

1. Analyze

2. Understand

3. Sort, order, and prioritize

FIGURE 6-1 The shape of the two-dimensional work breakdown structure.

Benefits of Source-Organized Work Breakdown Structures

The practice of producing source-organized WBSs may take some getting used to, especially in IT shops that traditionally rush through planning activities or historically prefer a generic, plate-organized WBS. But for the shop that embraces this practice, rewards are not long in coming. Many benefits are to be gained; several of the most tangible and distinct are listed next.

- **Organized scope**   WBSs, by default, organize work. Most of the time they do this in a very general way—by generic project phase, for example. But basing the layout of the WBS on the way in which requirement groups can be addressed will move the process from benign organization into proactive design. From there, activity breakdowns and sequencing can be taken to a finer level of detail, providing for a correspondingly finer level of control.

- **Aligned resources**   One of the toughest jobs of project management is resource planning. But that job gets easier when the shape of the WBS reflects the true shape of the work. Using this shape—based on the organization of the requirements—will allow optimal assignment of resources in response to work types, categories, and specialization.

- **Facilitated scheduling**   All WBSs serve as a foundation for the project schedule. But a WBS that's been built from an organization of the requirements has a firmer foundation to stand on. This gives project planners an edge in developing reliable, achievable schedules, by facilitating a greater level of *realistic* scheduling. The understanding that comes from the organizing activities provides the kind of insight needed to deliver more detailed decompositions of work over time. This more realistic appraisal in turn makes for stronger schedules.

- **Cleaner designs**   This fourth benefit leads naturally from the initial strip boarding activities and will carry value across the rest of the project life cycle. In the process of analyzing and organizing the requirements toward a workable WBS, the assessment team categorized, sorted, and sequenced the requirements. The shape that ensues can't help but approach the beginning of a solution design. With early characterization of even a very general shape for the structure, the project team's ability to strengthen and manage the design is set firmly in place.

As I learned from Amy Kaufman, the Hollywood practice of strip boarding springs from the producer's responsibility to establish workable budgets and schedules. And a proven way to begin both jobs is to analyze the script for patterns in scene use, location needs, casting requirements, and so on, and then order the shooting of the scenes in a way that effectively and efficiently leverages these patterns. From the results of this analysis and coordination process, reliable schedules and budget can be derived. The world of IT regularly deals with issues of realistic budgeting and scheduling. Some of these issues could be addressed by taking a tip from Hollywood. By creating WBSs based on a logical sorting and ordering of the requirements, the work patterns and groupings that emerge can be used to create more finely drawn schedules and stronger budgets—both of which lead to better project management.

Case in Point: Pryor Development Services

Pryor Development Services (PDS) provides software development and management services to companies in the gas and oil industries. The culture of these industries is one in which contractors traditionally work through firm fixed-price contracts, so for PDS to operate effectively (i.e., profitably), it needs the ability to schedule and cost its work accurately. PDS addresses this need in part through a three-step planning process. For *step one*, the company uses a technique it calls "task classification." When planning the development phase of a project, a focused PDS planning team, consisting of both managers and technical members, analyzes the requirements with the purpose of assigning them to particular task classes. These are not classes in the sense that might be applied to object-oriented design; they're much more general in nature. These classes sort the requirements according to the technical focus of each, as demanded by the particular project. For example, some requirements may be classified as UI tasks, others as Data Store tasks; some as Interface-to-X tasks, others as Interface-to-Y tasks; some as Local-Output, others as Remote-Output. Once this analysis is completed, the team ends up with the foundation for an ordered WBS, one that not only accounts for all the requirements but reflects relationships among requirements as well. In *step two*, the team uses past performance metrics as a basis for estimating the likely durations for each class. Project management then takes over for step three. Based on the skills needs of the project and the projected pool of available resources, the tasks are staffed and ordered and dates are assigned.

This three-step process serves PDS well. Because the task classes in use have been custom-defined by PDS over time, they readily reflect the technical domains that typically appear in its projects. So the "sorts" they produce are truly representative. Of note, the planning team is made up of a cross-section of project members, so the assessment and analysis results tend to be both more thoroughly reviewed and more likely to be backed by consensus. And because WBS segments are not datelined until resources have been considered, the resulting schedules are able to balance customer needs with the organization's ability to deliver.

What PDS is doing here is, in its own way, very close to the Hollywood practice of strip boarding the script. And what it delivers is very much the same: a clearer picture of scope, a greater ability to estimate, and firmer control of work commitments.

For a Deeper Look . . .

■ Project Management Institute, *Practice Standard for Work Breakdown Structures*, Second Edition, Project Management Institute, 2006

Yes, it's dry reading, but this hefty tome offers a complete look at the myriad issues surrounding activity identification, sequencing, duration estimation, schedule development, and schedule control. Full of worthy detail.

■ James P. Lewis, *Project Planning, Scheduling & Control*, Fourth Edition, McGraw-Hill, 2005

A good guidebook for project managers for over 15 years, Lewis' book addresses all of the key project management issues, including the core task of arranging work in logical order in view of projects requirements. This fourth edition has been revised, updated, and expanded.

■ Eric Uyttewaal, *Dynamic Scheduling with Microsoft Project 2002: The Book by and for Professionals*, Microsoft Press, 2003

This is more of a product, focusing on the purpose, use, and configuration of MS Project, but Uyttewaal manages to intersperse plenty of common-sense recommendations in this text, not only about how to best use Project but about how to best apply WBSs in support of overall mission objectives.

Chapter 7
Staff to the Genre

The overriding message of this book is that IT shops can enhance project success by establishing a project management system and following it, in much the same way that Hollywood follows the studio production system. When such a system is built around the management values of the IT shop, these values can be better controlled (and evidenced) from project to project. This emphasis on the system is well founded —but it's important at the same time to note the criticality of talent. *From my own observations, dogmatic separation of the two issues is not uncommon: One shop maintains that if the system's in place, people become interchangeable. Another insists that if it has good people, it has no need of a system. Neither viewpoint is based in reality. Good people work better when they work within a good system; they become free to innovate and create. And good systems can become better only through the shaping of talented people. This active appreciation of talent, the conscious push to bring in specially qualified people to work on project teams, has been long practiced in Hollywood. Part of this is due to the fact that Hollywood deals in genres—dramas, romantic comedies, westerns, all specialties of their own kinds. Over time, the studios have come to recognize that certain creative and technical professionals tend to perform better in one genre or another. So the studios and production companies carefully screen their candidates for experience and success with regard to these genres. The idea that a body-is-a-body-is-a-body is antithetical to thinking in Hollywood. And it should be that way in the world of IT. After all, IT deals with the same degrees of specialization: business specialties and technical specialties. People who are familiar and experienced with certain domains tend to be better able to contribute in those domains. Absent that experience and exposure, they may contribute less, or even slow a team's ability to meet its commitments. That's the subject of this chapter: the importance of talent and the role of project management in discerning and identifying that talent for its projects.*

The Central Role of Casting

Central Casting actually exists in Hollywood. It's a real talent agency, begun in 1926 to help studios fill their scenes with extras and day players. If a movie needed, for example, a French maître d', Central Casting could send over four or five of the right "type." If the part called for an Austrian ambassador, same thing. Today, Central Casting competes with a multitude of other talent agencies, but its mission is little changed. Every Hollywood movie needs its types—from tough bikers to ditzy waitresses—so it anchors a mini-industry primed to supply those types.

I learned about Central Casting from Steve Dunn. Steve is the Assistant Director (AD) for the romantic comedy *He's Just Not That into You,* and I visited him on the sound stage for that movie during the shooting of a party scene on an apartment set. The job of the 35 or so extras there was to mill around in the background, pretending to mix and chat, while two stars exchanged a few lines in the foreground. Coming into the interview, I thought Central Casting was maybe an industry joke, or a long-defunct operation. But no, Steve said—it's a going concern; his casting directors call on the company's agents time and time again. To illustrate, he pointed out Tall Girl with Long Hair. I looked across the stage. Standing on her mark next to the kitchen door was indeed a tall girl with long hair. There's a line in the script in which one of the stars mentions such a person in a side remark, so the crew had to ensure the presence of someone like that in the crowd. If necessary, someone could have called Central Casting and communicated those specs—"tall girl with long hair." The casting agents there would have gone to the talent database and run a query with those specs. Within an hour, the producers might be perusing a dozen headshots.

The real focus of our conversation is not on casting, however. It's on crew selection. As the AD, one of Steve's main duties is to coordinate the crew during the shoot so that the production rolls along as planned. He is in many ways the floor manager for the production. In that capacity, he's marshalled a broad array of talent behind the curtain. He's offered to share with me his insights into how movie crews are staffed. And in many ways the staffing process begins with producers looking for the right "type."

"Ninety Percent of the Job Is Casting"

That's what Steve quips when the director calls for a break on the set. It's a famous Hollywood maxim. Put the right people in the right roles, and audiences will respond. Miscast one critical part, and you could sink the whole project. That maxim applies to the acting talent, of course, but Steve mentions that it holds true in much the same way for a project's creative and technical talent. In previous chapters, we've seen how the rigors of the production system are in place to minimize risk, movie making being a complex and expensive business. One way to do that is to attach star power to a project. Another way is to attach "track" power—that is, hire production personnel who have a track record of delivering successful results with similar projects.

Any production crew is made up of a variety of craft specialties. A look at the major production departments will reveal an array of photographers, costume designers, stylists, electricians, carpenters, and on and on. All of these are very specialized jobs, more than a few of which can take years to master. Competency is crucial. One bad move—a dropped light, an out-of-focus lens—can set a production back perhaps a day or longer, at a cost that can top $200,000. That's why producers want to hire people who are proven practitioners of their trade. But this search for the right production specialists goes even further. The inclination in Hollywood is to "type staff" in the same way that it typecasts. Writers who have done good work with comedies get pitched comedy projects. Directors known for working well with big scopes and big casts get pitched epics. Cinematographers known for their ability to light for mood get pitched dark dramas and thrillers. And it goes down the line that way, even to the craft services vendor. It's all an attempt to design success in right from the start. The movie-making process is so expensive that it pays to invest it as many proven ingredients as possible. The right resources are one of those ingredients.

Working with the Right Types

A track record of past performance is important in Hollywood. So is a demonstrated affinity for a set of genres. At the same time, job competition is fierce. Because the motion picture is centered in Hollywood (60 percent of the population of Los Angeles works in some aspect of entertainment), the best come to Hollywood looking for work. And the vast majority of this work, perhaps as much as 95 percent, is contract work. Hollywood is a land of freelancers, all vying for a role on a limited number of productions. And that makes for another work trait that Hollywood crews need to demonstrate: the ability to cooperate. No matter how talented (within reason), a person who is known as a poor colleague or as unpleasant to deal with, or who lacks enthusiasm and motivation, will never land a job from among the limited number available. Producers want to hire people who are experienced, capable, affable, and motivated. And once they find those people, they tend to return to them time and again.

Hollywood, then, is very serious about resource management. From casting the right stars to signing the right director to choosing a prop master, the studios pay close attention to both past performance and present fit. This is not type casting in the blind sense of that word. It's more properly thought of as "right casting," and it directly relates to management's focus on success. When the people fit the project, the project's chance of success rises correspondingly.

Any Casting Is Not Right Casting

A project management system should carry the same weight in an IT shop that the studio system carries in Hollywood. Without such a system, the shop is left with only two traits to carry it through its mission, both personal in nature: skill and expertise. In a very real sense, these are shaky traits to build a business on, specifically because they rest in individual initiative and not in a broader organizational capability. But in the context of project management, these same traits, especially when they are set free within a system to operate to their full potential, can be major contributors to the success of a specific endeavor.

Here's a statistic of stunning significance: In 1996 the Abaca Labor Council studied workplace efficiencies and determined that experienced IT workers were 22 times more productive than their inexperienced counterparts. That translates to *2200 percent* greater productivity. And yet, impressive as that disparity is, many IT shops still tend to treat a body as a body, and technology projects are staffed as if the goal were simply to fill seats. Some project managers assign resources on the basis of job titles or roles, not specific experience or exposure. They assign by availability, not by design, perhaps under the assumption that the sound of keyboards clacking—whatever that clacking might turn out—is the sound of progress. I've seen this philosophy at work in company after company, especially those that are content with passive outsourcing and black box offshoring.

Today there is a real need to staff technology projects strategically—not just to fill positions but to fill them with the right people. Many of the issues typically attributed to weak project performance can be traced back to a weak focus on resource management. We've all seen the kinds of problems that arise when projects are staffed willy-nilly, when resources are considered more as interchangeable assets than strategic appointments. Here are just a few:

- **Unstable teams**   This is the classic symptom of an ill-staffed project. Once the project begins in earnest, staffing weaknesses will begin to show themselves in sluggish productivity. Management usually responds by changing team members, in and out. People are pulled off one important project and put on another. Others are assigned to make-work. Some do double duty. The result is the destabilization of teams; over time, this will lead to the fracturing of the harmonies and dynamics necessary for effective project execution.

- **Slow ramp-up times**   Staff a project with people who are unfamiliar with its technical or business domains, and you'll find that the team takes longer than desired getting up to productive speed. Certainly all projects entail a ramp-up period, but the hope is to make it as short as possible. Success depends on getting to the work at hand. When the project is used in part as on-the-job training, however, management will have to recognize that timelines, delivery milestones, and budget targets may all suffer.

- **Work discontinuities**   Skilled workers can produce high-quality products; unskilled workers, less so. When a team's skill balance is skewed the wrong way, the quality of work being produced will be unbalanced too. These discontinuities can lead to a host of problems: Individual components don't integrate well. Sleek units are paired with bloated units. Rework is needed to correct misdirected work. And on and on. If these problems continue unchecked, the product's very unity of purpose can quickly dissipate.

- **Unbalanced burdens**   Here's something else that happens within mismatched teams: The middling performers plod on, while the top performers absorb more and more of the burden. It's the classic hero syndrome. Project success shifts from a dependence on team performance to reliance on individual initiative. The heroes extend their areas of responsibility; they work overtime. When this happens, team unity will begin to fragment. Even in the midst of heroic efforts (or perhaps *because* of them), productivity, regressed here down to the local level, can only suffer.

- **Burnout**   The ultimate result of the misapplication or weak application of resources is staff burnout, a phenomenon that is more prevalent in IT shops than most of us would like to acknowledge. Time and time again I have seen good people leave promising positions because overtime and the frenetic pace were driving them to compromise quality of life. They were being sucked dry. No responsible organization wants to see this visited upon its work force. It's a sure sign that management has gone off track somewhere, and the really regrettable part of this problem is that it's the people on the front line who most often pay the price.

Most experienced IT professionals have seen those five issues at play more than once. They are common in our industry. But there is a better way, evident in the operation of mature shops: to treat resource management as an integral complement of project management. This approach is seen in the Hollywood system, too, as one that relies on the careful screening of people in order to assess previous experience, exposure, and success. That brings us to the lesson for this chapter:

> **Lesson 7: Employ a managed resource repository** as a tool to identify the relevant skills, experience, and availabilities needed to appropriately staff your IT projects.

Assign By Design

In Part I of this book, we looked at a couple of management approaches that help an IT organization shape its strategic direction. The first, APM (see Chapter 2, "Know Your Properties"), deals with a shop's ability to maximize project success by leveraging the current configuration of its operating environments. The second, PPM (see Chapter 3, "Establish Green-Light Rules"), deals with demand management, the shop's ability to evaluate and select appropriate projects based on allied business objectives. Now we come to the issue of resource management. As we have seen through Hollywood's example, resource management deals with the assigning the right resources—chiefly human resources—to a project development effort. This assignment includes consideration of the particular skills and knowledge sets required of each work domain. Many technology professionals consider APM, PPM, and resource management to be complementary sides of a common IT management triangle.

The theme of resource management, then, could be stated as "assign by design." A resource management program brings into an organization a set of capabilities that give management ongoing insight into the capabilities and availabilities of its workforce. This insight is then used to establish effective project teams. In this way, resource management, once in place, can be a significant contributor to project management success.

The process of setting such a program in place is not complex, but it will need attention and focus. In brief, the resource management program should account for six core steps or considerations.

1. Management's understanding of its project types and business missions;

2. The formation of a master resume repository;

3. Use of the repository for resource assignments;

4. Maintenance of resumes in the repository over time;

5. Strategic development and recruitment that reflects project and business mission needs; and

6. Cross-training to maximize depth in the knowledge base.

These steps trace a path toward effective resource management. So let's take a quick look at each.

Mission and Project Definition

At the base of resource management is a need for the shop to concretely understand its business missions and the project types the shop engages to realize those missions. (This same need is at the base of APM and PPM.) The resume repository that will emerge as a key part of the resource management program will in many ways express this understanding. Its design is a reflection of that understanding. So one of the first steps in shaping a program is to define those missions and describe the project types. This is typically evidenced through listing industry domains, business disciplines, customer types, technologies and tools, development specialties, and so on. The picture being painted here is one of organizational capability, one that captures the shop's current strengths, highlights its weaknesses, and illuminates a path for growth.

Repository Design

The core of any resource management program is its resume repository. Some organizations establish this as a human resources asset. Others set it up as a project management office asset. But regardless of who owns it, its purpose remains the same: to store resumes of the IT workforce so that project job roles can be appropriately assigned. The design of this repository will vary from shop to shop, of course, because the design will need to reflect the types of projects it engages in as well as the organization's general business missions (see section above). But most repositories are designed so that resources can be tagged with such identifiers as business domain expertise, technology tool proficiencies, educational disciplines, certifications, past company affiliations, and recognition and awards. The key is to design the repository so that its shape mirrors the kinds of demands the company's projects are required to fulfill. Once the design is complete, the next step in the set-up process is to build the repository and populate it with workforce resumes.

Centralized Resourcing

Creating the repository is core, but *using* the repository is key. And so this should become a matter of organizational policy. In order for resource management to realize its potential in a shop, the resume repository needs to become the chief tool used to screen for, identify, and assign team members to projects. Fortunately, this recognition is gaining wider and wider acceptance in more and more corporate IT shops. Off-the-shelf solutions like Microsoft's Project Server, with built-in repositories and query capabilities, make initiating resource management much simpler than ever before. Nevertheless, emphasis must be placed on the procedural use of the repository. Organizations used to making on-the-fly assignments will need to embrace the discipline of centralized, coordinated control.

Repository Maintenance

Maintaining the repository is another important consideration, mainly because ignoring it can quickly compromise a resource management program. For the repository to deliver maximum value, it must remain current over time. And so the organization needs to prompt the workforce to regularly update the resumes in the repository, preferably at predefined intervals. Many shops do this by rote at the end of every project, as part of lessons-learned sessions. Other shops include it as an activity in performance reviews. Still others schedule it as part of quarterly or seasonal assessments. But other avenues work just as well, and a specific maintenance approach can be selected according to the needs or convenience of the shop. The thing to avoid is letting updates slip and ending up with an outdated repository. Once the repository begins to lose its integrity as a true reflection of organizational capability, its ability to identify and establish well-designed teams suffers accordingly.

Development and Recruitment

The resume repository will naturally grow over time as current staff members add to their experiences and skill sets accordingly. But the growth of the repository should also come from external recruitment and tactical training plans—often-overlooked parts of resource management. As noted earlier, resource management needs to reflect an understanding of an organization's business mission and project types. This understanding comes into extended play in development and recruitment of staff. The idea is for the IT shop to shape its recruitment efforts so that they directly support knowledge and skill needs. Recruitment should be based in part on the current shape of the repository: What have we accounted for already? Where are our strengths? Conversely, where are we weak? What have we yet to fully account for? This strategic approach to recruitment is complemented with a training strategy that defines how internal growth and development can be fostered to further support shaping the repository in the appropriate way.

Cross-Training

Cross-training is a final consideration for a beginning resource management program. Cross-training is a risk reduction, opportunity-enhancement strategy. Through it, people are cross-trained in any mix of job roles and responsibilities, business disciplines, tools, and technologies. Risk is reduced because dependencies can be spread across multiple team members. Opportunities are enhanced because the likelihood of availability rises. Cross-training does call for a special commitment on the part of an IT shop, because it will require, at least at first, some reduction in workload bandwidth. The degree to which cross-training can be embraced, then, will vary from shop to shop. But to the degree it can be implemented, it will return the benefits in proportion.

Type casting is used in Hollywood to meet an expectation quickly, with minimal development: Frazzled hair plus tweed coat equals "eccentric professor." Sequinned dress and blond wig create "chanteuse." The look makes the part. And in much the same way, Hollywood employs type staffing. It wants to assemble members of a production crew who have proved effective at their jobs and have been successful with similar types of projects in the past. Studios pay as much attention to crew hiring as to casting; this emphasis is another element of risk reduction, of positioning a movie for success. When this same kind of care is brought to the staffing of IT projects, the same kinds of benefits ensue: The right experience and skill sets promote product creation through minimal development. Let's summarize with some other benefits. The concept of type staffing is illustrated in Figure 7-1.

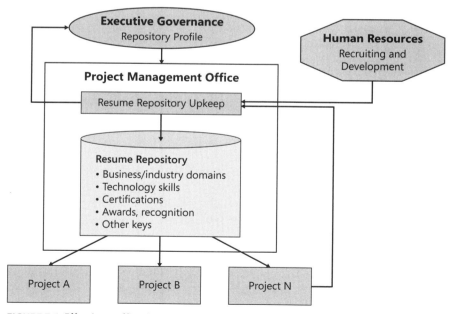

FIGURE 7-1 Effective staffing is a combination of internal development, external recruitment, and ongoing incentives.

Benefits of "Type Staffing"

Many IT shops have only a fixed pool of resources to draw from. And as in any organization, there will be strong players and weaker players in that pool. But the point of type staffing is not so much one of innate talent (nice as that is) as it is one of exposure or bent. If the project team can be staffed with the kinds of people who can demonstrate, in one way or another, an affinity for the type of work at hand, chances are that work will be accommodated in a more responsible and responsive manner. That's the real idea behind type staffing. Quickly then, here are four more specific benefits it can bring:

- **Provides coverage over technical and business challenges**   The big, and obvious, benefit to staffing your team with the right kinds of players is that you're better assured of surmounting the business and technical challenges that accompany most every IT project. Qualified people are able to get the job done. Inexperienced or other-experienced folk are going to need a period of acclimation and adjustment first in order to enter the contribution zone.

- **Enhances planning**   Much of the subject matter in this section of the book, the pre-production phase of the studio system, has dealt with the importance of planning. The practice of type staffing can make a contribution here. Experienced team players can be used not just to carry work load reliably but can be tapped to help plan that work-load path. Each such person possesses, to one extent or another, an expert opinion. And those opinions can be combined with management's to create plans better suited to exact but perhaps unseen project characteristics.

- **Facilitates efficiencies**   When you have good people on your team, you get the advantage not only of expedited performance but of past experience as well. In other words, you get their expert insight, their ability to deal with problems that they may have readily addressed in the past. Shortcuts, opportunities for reuse, and faster solutions can all come to light when your team is familiar with the territory and experienced in navigating the terrain.

- **Streamlines communications**   Here's an often underappreciated benefit of type staffing. When you bring people into a project team who are conversant in the business domains or technologies your project is addressing, you'll find that communication becomes streamlined: simpler, clearer, more effective. That's because these people come to the table with a common vocabulary already in place. Their expertise and familiarity can automatically give your project the kind of productivity boost that newcomers and under-skilled (or other-skilled) players simply don't possess.

With the break over on Sound Stage 2, Steve Dunn excuses himself and begins to call his teams back to the set. The camera crew gathers back around the camera. The First Assistant AD begins to assemble the 35 or so party extras back to their marks on the fake apartment floor. The gaffers begin to adjust lights. The grips move sand bags and flags. The script supervisor opens her shot list. Tall Girl with Long Hair reclaims her place next to the kitchen sink. The director comes out. Places, everybody . . . and back to business.

Case in Point: Athenati Integration Services

Based in the suburbs of Washington, DC, Athenati is a systems integration company that deals mainly in government contracting, particularly with the U.S. Department of Defense (DOD). In this regard, it has some special needs related to resource management. In order to win bids, the company must demonstrate through its proposals that it can staff project teams with qualified resources. And in the event of a win, the company must follow through with assignment of those resources. Because of the size of the company's resource pool—roughly 1200 people—and because its client base, although centered on the DOD, crosses a variety of disciplines, an especially crucial concern for Athenati is to maintain a current picture of the breadth and depth of its resources.

In late 2004, the company addressed this need through what it termed its "knowledge base" initiative. The idea behind the knowledge base was to establish a repository of skill sets linked to current employee resumes. It would then use this repository to strategically align resources with appropriate proposal opportunities and leverage it later to staff new contract work. Soliciting the help of its human resources department, the company anchored this initiative around two Microsoft products: SharePoint and Project Server. SharePoint was used as the entry point for resume submission and upkeep. This tool was used to identify a "super set" of corporate abilities, drawn from its job-type eligibilities. The repository was then populated with resumes, each one being keyed to its relevant ability categories. Project Server was used as a complement to the repository. It served as a centralized resource management tool and therefore was configured to help management assign and balance qualified resources based on availabilities.

The effort took about two years to gel, but once it did, upkeep of the repository became fairly straightforward. The company embedded a skills-update activity into its project close-out process. At the end of a work effort, team members would update their resumes with the particular skills they had demonstrated (within existing and potentially new categories) and also included any training they had undergone during that period. This update process fostered distributed management of the repository, enabling it to grow and remain current without needed heavy centralized control.

As a result of this initiative, Athenati today is able to quickly and flexibly position itself to address new business opportunities, knowing that it can put its best face forward. At the same time, it is able to capitalize on use of its current resources in ways that promote effective utilization and efficient realization of project objectives.

For a Deeper Look . . .

Here are some recent publications that can provide you with more information on how to help your organization implement practices that ally the assignment of project resources with a project's technology requirements.

- Anthony T. Cobb, *Leading Project Teams: An Introduction to the Basics of Project Management and Project Team Leadership*, Sage Publications, 2005

  Cobb offers good advice on how to organize project teams around prerequisite skill sets. He provides clear examples of how project managers can identify these skill sets early in project initiation and integrate them into subsequent planning and staff acqui-sition activities.

- James Williams, *Team Development for High Tech Project Managers*, Artech House Publishers, 2002

  This book directly addresses issues of team selection, development, and management for technology projects. It provides lots of case studies and real-world examples that illus-trate how resource pools can be established and maintained, and how project manage-ment can work to ensure that these pools are used in a project's early planning stages.

- Vijay K. Verma, *Managing the Project Team*, Project Management Institute, 1997

  Verma's book focuses on project management less in the IT domain than in the general business domain, but it provides valuable insight into methods and techniques that can be used to develop project teams in ways that tie directly to established business objectives.

Chapter 8
Budget to the Board

Budgeting is often done backwards on technology projects. Managers use deadline dates to backtrack durations, then expense resources over that time frame, and perhaps factor in some known ancillary cost; from there, a budget is born. Upper-level management will often evaluate this budget not on its reflection of scope but on its compatibility with the deadlines and the organization's spending thresholds. If it falls within those bounds, it's deemed worthy. In fact, however, budgets created this way are likely to be significantly over- or understated, with understating the more likely of the two. One reason why technology projects commonly overshoot spending projections is that this backwards approach to the budgeting process is encouraged from the outset. A far more realistic approach is to base budgets on data that have been derived from a careful analysis of requirements. This sequencing has proved itself useful across any number of industries. In Hollywood, it's unheard of to establish a production budget any other way. Why, then, do technology shops often opt for a different approach? And how might they do it better? These are the issues explored in this chapter. These considerations follow logically from Chapter 4, "Invest in a Solid Script," which looked at the value of investing in a solid script (the requirements); from Chapter 5, "Time Box the Projects," where the production life cycle was set; from Chapter 6, "Strip Board the Script," which looked at basing the shape of the schedule on the demands of the script; and from Chapter 7, "Staff to the Genre," which accounted for staffing requirements. Now we turn to a final planning parameter: deriving the budget.

Liberty Within Limits

Peter Macgregor-Scott is executive producer for the new Disney film, *Liberty*. *Liberty* is a big-scope action-adventure tale that kicks off when a band of rogue Russians, up to no good, disable U.S. military communication satellites. This strike virtually shuts down the nation's state-of-the-art Air Force, whose planes rely almost exclusively on those satellite feeds, even (it seems) for taking off. The United States responds by recruiting a salty pack of veteran airmen who must pilot a fleet of vintage, satellite-free war planes to save the day.

Peter and his team are staffed adjacent to the Buena Vista studio just off Alameda Drive. As I'm led along an upstairs corridor, I notice that the nameplates on each office door are capped with mouse ears. I'm taken to a large conference room, square and windowless with high walls. When the lights click on, I see that every available inch of wall space is covered with airplane material: pictures of airplanes, schematics of airplanes, close-ups of cockpit instrumentation, pages cut from encyclopedias. Hundreds of sheets of data, apparently grouped by plane model, hang in columns, some down to the floor—row after row after row.

Peter comes in and introduces himself and then takes me around the room. All of this, he explains, is part of early preproduction activities. He and his team are working to determine the look and feel of the movie, trying to gauge the right mix of hardware (his term for the airplanes) needed to tell the story in an exciting way. I comment on the degree of detail this research involves and compliment him on his apparent dedication to authenticity. Authenticity is certainly part of it, Peter admits, but he's driven by a much more practical reason: the budget. *Liberty* got the green light from Disney based on a ballpark estimate of about $90 million. Peter's job now is to put together a detailed production budget that will confirm the reliability of that initial estimate. If the numbers come close, things proceed. If what Peter comes up with overshoots budget limits by a less-than-comfortable margin, the studio chiefs will reconvene.

The Numbers Behind the Story

Peter emphasizes what other Hollywood executives have alluded to in all of my previous interviews: The budget is a movie project's strictest planning component. Once a budget has been accepted (and signed off on by all leading parties), the studio assumes that it is no longer dealing with soft approximations, that it now has a fixed-price contract in place, one designed to produce a professional product. Over the next 14 months or so, many adjustments will be made to the look, scope, and pace of *Liberty*, but very few such changes will touch the budget. In fact, most of the adjustments will be made to keep the budget intact. Schedules may be trimmed, the number of extras may be reduced, a scene here and there may be reworked—any or all of these modifications will be considered if it appears that the budget may be challenged.

Hollywood takes budgeting very seriously, a reasonable stance in view of the approximately $65 million required for even a run-of-the-mill project. Accordingly, producers go to great lengths to establish finely detailed and accurate budgets. Peter gives me a general overview of the budgeting process. It's a process that in and of itself can take a few months to complete, and one that requires its own brand of expertise. Here's a general breakdown of the considerations that go into establishing a motion picture budget.

■ **Script analysis**   As discussed in Chapter 4, for each new project, the script is thoroughly studied and analyzed, not only by the producers but by as many of the key technical team members as the producers can corral. This analysis culminates in the process of strip boarding. The strip board reveals (at close approximation) everything needed to bring each scene to life and also orders the scenes into a shooting sequence that can be practically and economically managed. "Budgeting to the board" is Hollywood slang for this tenet of movie making: All budgeting begins (and ultimately ends) with the script.

- **The shape of the system**   One of the reasons movie budgets rarely run over is the fact that the production system wraps a consistent shape around each project, with that shape dictating the flow of production activity (and thus costs) across the life of the project. Producers therefore always figure in preproduction costs, and they know what people and resources will be needed in that phase. It's the same with the production and post-production phases as well. The shape of the system also reflects the job roles that will be needed for each phase and the typical rates that will apply to different scales of technical talent. Combining the shape of the system with script analysis will begin to generate a very clear picture of project scope.

- **Prior experience**   Here is where the producers' expertise and experience come into play. By assessing the project, with all its unique demands, against similar projects worked on in the past, the producers are able to gauge likely costs. This review process goes further than that: Studios maintain whole libraries of budgets from previous projects, giving producers a full history of estimations to leverage. By referencing this array of data, they not only can more readily identify obvious costs but may uncover hidden or subtle costs that may be buried in the subtext of the story.

- **Experienced input and counsel**   A project may or may not have its key department heads hired at the point of budgeting. Nevertheless, the producers typically will reach out to as many experts as they can. The freelance nature of the business promotes even casual cooperation, so producers feel free calling other Hollywood professionals they know who may have worked on similar projects too. These professionals are queried about how they solved problems, or gained access, or found locations. They are invited to dialog and theorize. Producers understand that eventually a strong consensus will need to be built around the budget, so they actively work to get as many qualified people involved as possible.

- **Knowledge of established rates**   Knowledge of pay rates and compensation structures is another important facet of movie budgeting. Most crew members on a production team belong to a union or guild. Guild rates are not carved in stone, but they do provide a dependable basis for figuring personnel costs. For example, a key grip gets a straight time rate of (say) $26.98 for the first 8 hours of work, plus time and a half for up to 12 hours (double time after 12 hours). The average 12-hour day, then, will cost $377.72. Added to that will be the fixed union pension and health fees, the vacation and holiday benefit (.08 percent of rate), and payroll tax. And that's the cost for a key grip. The same formulas can be applied to compensation rates for all of the basic crew members.

- **Negotiation**   Finally, there is the power to negotiate. Everything is negotiable in Hollywood, and a good producer is always and foremost a good negotiator. From signing stars to renting a World War II–era P38 Mustang for a week, the producer must understand the give and take of bargaining in the pursuit of value.

Of course, the format of the budget itself can be considered as another aid to production management. For both big budget movies and small budget movies, the itemized budgets will look practically the same. Budget formats are highly standardized. The columns may have more zeros in one budget than in another, or one budget document may be 150 pages thick, whereas another is 70. But the content—the types of expense identified—will be very closely aligned. Here are the common expense items seen on just about every motion picture budget document:

Story rights	Set operations
Script	Special effects
Producer's unit	Set dressing
Direction	Property
Cast	Wardrobe
Travel and living—producers/directors	Makeup and hair
Travel and living—cast	Electrical
Residuals	Camera
Above-the-line fringe	Sound
Production staff	Transportation
Extra talent	Location expenses
Sound stage	Picture vehicle/animals
Production design	Film and lab
Set construction	Travel and living—crew
Editorial	Below-the-line fringe
Post-production film and lab	Titles and graphics
Optical effects	Stock footage
Music	Insurance
Post-production sound	General and administrative expenses

The steps we've just looked at—of analysis, input, and calculation—culminate in a *draft budget*. Studio executives will vet this draft, of course, perhaps suggesting modifications, perhaps not. But once the refinements are complete, the budget goes through a formal round of reviews and approval. Then it's time for all key parties to put their names to the contract. (For more on this topic, see Chapter 9, "Sign on the Dotted Line.")

The Mark of Professionalism

Two points from Peter's explanation are worthy of mention. The first is that budgeting is never done in isolation or without reference. The second is that the amount of detail that's explored is very deep. In fact, it's common for budget documents to run 100 pages or more. The attention to detail and the time such attention requires are very rarely given short shrift—the consequences are too pronounced. Of all a producer's duties, this is among the most important. Whole reputations are built on a person's ability to establish a bankable budget and then stick to it. It all starts with the script—with a thorough analysis of its range and demands. Add to that the shape of the production system, references to prior experience, input from other team members, and normative industry rates, and the studio now has the kinds of scope and depth perspectives that will generate a budget with meaning, one that truly reflects what the film will actually cost. The track record of this approach speaks for itself. The vast majority of movie productions come in with budget spread of around 6 percent. That translates to 99 to 105 percent of target.

Peter was only beginning the budgeting process for *Liberty* when I visited him, but I got a good feel for what both he and Disney expected of it. This process is time and resource intensive, and it takes an experienced leader to guide it. But the benefits that come from doing it properly are hard to argue with: thoroughness, consensus, and generation of a map to manage by, to be used in concert with the schedule.

The IT Budget and the Bottom Line

Budget fidelity is a different story in the world of corporate IT. Is there any other industry, sophisticated or not, that has the same problem with budgeting that we do? An IT project that runs 20 percent over budget is rarely considered to be compromised—chances are, it's heralded as a wild success! IT people frequently see budget overruns that hit 40, 70, even 140 percent. Many shops *automatically* inflate budgets in anticipation of overruns, having so little faith in the reliability of the original estimates. The problems that spring from weak budgeting can touch every facet of a project, and once they've surfaced, they usually do. What, then, is the source of this dissonance between projections and realities? Christopher Hawkins, a software crisis management consultant, has identified what he calls the top five budgeting pitfalls. My own experience wrestling with the budgeting process confirms that these are the big ones.

1. **Allowing nontechnical staffers to give estimates**   It's surprising how often managers, business sponsors, and other nontechnical folks are allowed to drive the budgeting process for technical projects. Perhaps organizations assume that budgeting is a "business thing," so business people—not computer people—should do it. But the estimations that make up a sound budget require a degree of technical knowledge that only technical people possess. Managers and stakeholders should certainly have the right to contribute to, review, and approve (or reject) a proposed budget. But expecting them

to be able to derive the estimates on their own is unfair to the business people and the technical folks alike.

2. **Being afraid to look in the mirror**   Most development shops avoid the unpleasant task of conducting postmortems on projects that have gone awry, that have experienced significant cost or schedule overruns. They do not analyze sources of mistakes, nor do they acknowledge that certain practices may need to be revisited and improved. This avoidance of any kind of introspection is a form of denial in which the shop resists learning from failure (one of business's best teachers). As a result, the shop exposes itself to the same problems again and again. Estimation and budgeting techniques that began weak remain weak.

3. **Underestimating design time and debugging time**   Budgets need to account for the "hidden" or "quiet" activities that go into development. Production is not just about gathering functional needs, coding, testing, and delivering; many support activities go hand in hand with those major ones. Without proper attention to such activities including design and debugging processes, the budgets that are built to cover them will rarely be adequate.

4. **Inadequate or unclear requirements**   This is a big reason why weak budgets get produced (and one already addressed in some detail in Chapter 4). It's simply not feasible to estimate the costs of a project when the size of that project remains unclear. And yet many IT managers feel pressured to kick projects into gear before the analysis teams have had the opportunity to pin down scope, or at least to establish a baseline view of that scope. Estimates produced from such a vague perception of the job at hand can be counted on only as guesses or perhaps hopeful wishes, or maybe even prayers.

5. **Taking too large a bite from the apple**   This is another scope-related issue (looked at in Chapter 5). When a development shop willingly takes on overscoped work, its ability to predict the demands of that work is diminished. The estimations, by necessity, must then fall back into the domain of guessing. Any value of the initial budgets will soon dissipate as the true project scope becomes clearer over time. This clarification will require another new, probably redundant round of budget analysis.[1]

In my experience, IT shops that lack an appropriate budgeting process in their project management systems can blunder into these five pitfalls repeatedly (some shops seem almost compelled to do so!). By contrast, the Hollywood system's budgeting process is well honed to avoid each of these pitfalls, not just implicitly but explicitly. This approach constitutes the eighth lesson of this book.

> **Lesson 8:** **Base budgets on a multifaceted analysis** of a project's requirements and characteristics.

---

[1] "The 5 Pitfalls of Estimating a Software Project," by Christopher Hawkins, July 1, 2004. Available at www.christopherhawkins.com (accessed April 8, 2008).

Budgeting Tips for Technology Projects

By adopting a similar multifaceted approach to estimation and cost projection, IT managers can establish a methodology that will promote the creation of more reliable budgets. For an IT shop that is fairly immature with respect to budget practices, this approach won't move mountains overnight. But it will provide a framework to use in developing a manageable, repeatable, and improvable budgeting process. Here, then, are seven tips for producing more effective budgets that IT managers may wish to include in their own framework. For a picture of how these seven might fit together in an overall budgeting process, see Figure 8-1.

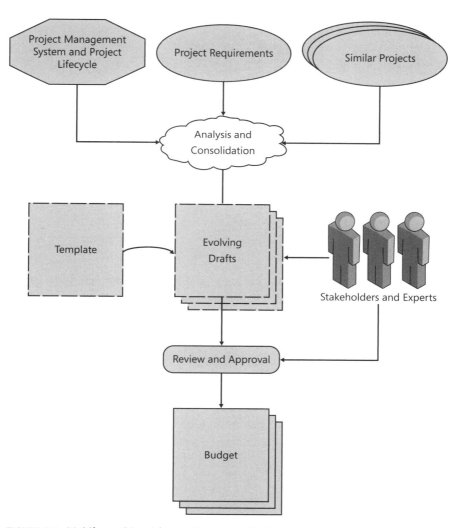

FIGURE 8-1: Multifaceted input for a well-designed budget.

1. **Invest in the process.**   Good budgets are the result of good work, and good work takes time. The organization needs to invest in the time and resources needed to see the process through. It's often helpful to think of the budgeting phase as a mini-project in and of itself. As a project, then, it will need a plan, people, tools, and management support. If these requirements are met, the numbers that come out of the process should reflect the scope and reach of the project in tangible, traceable ways.

2. **Begin with requirements analysis.**   A thorough analysis of the requirements is essential to effective budgeting. Chapter 6 looked at the development of a strategically sequenced WBS as an aid to realistic scheduling. This WBS, which emerged as the result of requirements analysis activities, can now play a vital role in determining costs. The WBS distributes the work into related groups—this solidifies scope. It highlights areas of technical challenge—this relates to resource density. And it ties to the schedule— this establishes durations. Once scope, resource densities, and durations are known, costs calculations can begin in earnest.

3. **Leverage the project life cycle.**   Two important points warrant mention here. First, because the project will flow through the shop's project management system (the theme of this book), the system's structure can be used to derive part of the cost structures. In other words, if moving through phases A, B, and C is recognized to produce products 1, 2, and 3, this knowledge can be used to derive much of the data needed to estimate those components. Second, it's helpful to include as part of this system a standardized budget template, one built to reflect the system. A look back at the line items from the Hollywood budget cited earlier in this chapter will show this idea at work. The template becomes, in effect, a checklist of considerations that planners and stakeholders can use to make sure their estimates cover the full range of project activities.

4. **Reference similar experience.**   Looking back on lessons learned, together with projected and actual numbers from similar projects, can provide an excellent starting point for delineating the budget needs of current work. Review of past projects that share commonalities in terms of industry focus, size, scope, technologies, and work products can provide the kinds of data and documentation that not only help set a budget in place but also clarify the rationale for why the numbers shake out the way they do. It's often possible to find much that can be reused or reframed for the current effort.

5. **Seek stakeholder input (and reviews).**   It's important to involve as many stakeholders as possible in determining estimates. Both business domain experts and technical experts should be included. Their experience and counsel can go a long way to discerning the true needs of a budget. The first step is to identify the appropriate stakeholders; then they are provided with the planning data amassed thus far (in steps 2, 3, and 4). Their opinions and assessments can be used to help consolidate a fiscal view of project scope. The benefit of stakeholder involvement is extended by keeping them in the process; their ongoing reviews and further comments concerning budget drafts can contribute to a gradual refinement process from which a workable, bankable budget emerges.

6. **Use parametric modeling.**   This is the technical form of budgeting that most people are at least somewhat familiar with. *Parametric modeling* is the use of estimation formulas as a way to derive variable costs. It's a fancy term, but there's no need to use complex or sophisticated formulas for it to add value to the budgeting process. Parametric modeling typically is used in techniques like source lines of code, function point analysis, and feature analysis. But it can also be applied with simpler concepts such as overhead costs, personnel rates, equipment, and facility charges. The addition of parametric modeling to the planning data developed in steps 2 through 5 makes an important contribution to the development of a very tractable budget.

7. **Negotiate the costs.**   Some costs associated with a development project are fixed, so there's not much that can be done about them. But it's important to recognize opportunities to identify and negotiate nonfixed costs. This is not a common IT practice, at least not in the direct realm of project management, and such opportunities may arise only sporadically on projects, but it's a consideration that can help drive budgets, even in a small way, to their optimal levels.

Each of these seven tips can be used alone or applied together to produce development budgets that are complete and practical and reflect the true scope and needs of a project.

Benefits of Multifaceted Budgeting

The budgeting approaches and tips presented in this chapter will certainly aid a project team in coming up with better estimates of project costs. Note, however, that the nature of estimating and budgeting probably will always ensure that the process remains an approximation. Budgets will rarely start off from precisely derived estimates. But a multifaceted approach does promote smoother control and firmer fiscal targets. Granted, it takes more time to budget to the board—that is, to base budget numbers not only on general project parameters but on a sharp appraisal of a WBS shaped from the requirements and other project characteristics. When project managers (through organizational support) are able to include these additional steps as a routine part of budgeting activities, they quickly find that the budgets they produce mirror actual expenses much more closely. This better approximation makes ongoing project management more effective, and it also provides the organization, from that point forward, with the ability to log more and more reliable budgets into a historical repository that can be used for improving and refining the budgeting process over time.

Listed next are three immediate benefits an IT shop can realize from this kind of budgeting.

- **Balanced customer and management expectations**   The whole idea of developing a budget, any budget, is to project spending commitments. The better the budget, the more manageable the commitments. A budget that is based on well-defined project traits is a budget that better reflects a project's full range of investment and performance considerations. This correlation will help establish a balance between the commitments required of IT management and those of the shop's customers.

- **More reliable ROIs** IT budgets that are produced solely from preset management constraints—one-stage budgets—lack a true picture of the work at hand, so they often prove unreliable over time (usually sooner than later). Multifaceted budgets, however, account for both management constraints and project constraints, so they carry a fuller picture of the work: of how well it's scoped, what challenges it may present, and what its realistic demands may be. This gives management teams the ability to better predict what ROI the organization might *realize* from the effort. As an added benefit, multifaceted budgeting can also be used to help identify upfront those kinds of mis-shaped projects—out of sync between cost and scope—that probably should be avoided, re-packaged, or even canceled.

- **Tighter cost controls** Multifaceted budgeting provides for tighter cost controls because it recognizes expenses at a finer, line-item level. It's *bottom-up* budgeting—and that gives a manager two advantages. First, top-sheet totals have been derived from aggregating incremental detail, so the totals have a solid basis in that detail and are thus more meaningful. Second, it allows control of the totals by management and reporting at the most basic possible level of detail. (Think of it as the "take care of the pennies to take care of the dollars" approach to budget control.) Such line-item detail can be used to predict and prevent budget variations of significant proportions.

Budgeting to the board, then, is the Hollywood way. It's an activity carried out by a producer or a production manager as a crucial step in the preproduction process. It sets the tone for the entire project as it moves forward. The budget in Hollywood becomes the final arbiter on decisions surrounding schedule, dash, and showbiz flash. Peter Macgregor-Scott's action film *Liberty*, because of its size and complexity, will require special attention to this preproduction component, and Peter may assign a team of specialists to turn out what may be in the end a 200-page budget. Today, many IT shops tend to take a slimmer approach. I've seen budgets for large multiphase IT projects that occupied a one-page spreadsheet. But technology managers who adopt at least some of the practices of multifaceted budgeting, as described in this chapter, will find that the results clearly support smoother cost tracking and progress assessments in all aspects of life cycle activity.

Case in Point: Westpoint-Taylor

Located west of Huntsville, Alabama, Westpoint-Taylor was (back in 1999) a small systems services shop that employed about 30 people. Small as it was, the company was riding a wave of wild success. Its people possessed an early expertise in Ajax techniques that they used to develop interactive Web applications quickly and with much finesse. They had a steadily growing client base, and because they were able to leverage their engineering proficiencies into a compact development toolkit, they could take on more and more work without necessarily adding staff. The company operated that way as a point of pride, using its energy and enthusiasm to carry it over periods of heavy demand. But problems soon arose—not from the technical quarter but from the project management quarter, as is typical for fast-growing companies experiencing such problems. Westpoint's main trouble surfaced initially as a customer satisfaction issue. The Web solutions it created usually worked well, but the company was quickly losing its ability to deliver on time and within budget. This difficulty pointed back to its internal project management practices. Westpoint's track record of innovation and achievement had bred a culture that valued discovery over prediction. As a result, its project management approach was less management in nature than it was mere administration, cleaning up the work trail rather than helping to pave it. So estimates were derived not from analyses of requirements (or even other concrete elements) but more from a project's attractions and challenges and management's intuition around them. Resources were assigned on the basis of pull and preference, not experience or exposure. Commitments often were made simply to ensure a contract's award. The fallout was unavoidable. Clients that valued delivery and cost commitments on an equal basis with quality began to go elsewhere. The competitors with more business maturity began to catch up to Westpoint's technical edge. Internal staff began to feel the wear of perpetually long work hours. Profits began to drop.

Luckily, or perhaps rightfully, the company's stellar technical reputation remained intact, and a very large federal avionics contractor (also in the Huntsville area), wishing to acquire Web service expertise, brought Westpoint-Taylor into its fold. A happy ending from a simple financial perspective, no doubt. But it's instructive to consider whether application of the company's zeal and talent for technology innovation to planning and managing the scope and budgets of its projects would have resulted in a more balanced, flexible, and long-lived enterprise.

For a Deeper Look . . .

- Richard Barrett, *Planning and Budgeting for the Agile Enterprise: A Driver-Based Budgeting Toolkit*, CIMA Publishing, 2007

   This book looks at budgeting mainly within shops that employ Agile development methods, but its advice and insights are general enough to apply to most shops. It emphasizes the importance of basing budgets on "driver parameters"—the schedule and requirements. It uses lots of illustrative case studies and work examples to make its points.

- John McManus, *Managing Stakeholders in Software Development Projects*, Butterworth-Heinemann, 2004

   I like this book's practitioner approach, and the focus it places on stakeholder involvement. The stakeholder angle highlights the linkage to budgeting based on requirements, particularly on the stakeholders' view of importance and prioritization regarding the requirements.

- Cyriac R. Roeding, Gert Purkert, Sandro K. Kindner, and Ralph Muller, *Secrets of Software Success: Management Insights from 100 Software Firms Around the World*, Harvard Business School Press, 1999

  This is a great overview, survey-type book containing general tips on project management success for technology shops. Among these tips are insights into how to budget projects appropriately, taking into account the known and unknown; how to integrate resource ad schedule needs with budget activities; and how to acquire budgetary agreements across stakeholder groups. Solid reading.

- Jonathan Arnowitz, Michael Arent, and Nevin Berger, *Effective Prototyping for Software Makers*, Morgan Kaufman, 2006

  It's the theme rather than the subject of this book that lends its value to this topic. The emphasis here is on prototyping, allowing the customer to envision a solution, from which a concrete plan to achieve it can be mapped. That view ties directly to the argument in this chapter that budgeting needs to be predicated on the solution—in this case, born from the requirements together with the plan of attack (the schedule) for realizing those requirements.

Chapter 9
Sign on the Dotted Line

The typical IT project reaches across three general stakeholder groups: project management (representing the project team), executive IT management (representing the IT mission at large), and the project sponsors (focused on the business aspects of the project). Problems can emerge when the expectations of one group fall out of sync with those of another of these groups. Part of the responsibility of project management, then, is to work to ensure that expectations of performance and perceptions of progress are shared across stakeholder groups. One of the best ways to accomplish this aim is to establish common agreements between the stakeholders early in the project life cycle, with special focus on the requirements and the project plans—mainly, the budget and the schedule. Surprisingly, this triumvirate of consensus is often overlooked. In many shops, projects begin by attacking technical details, in lieu of a commitment by the partners to a specific direction for that attack. Moreover, project work often commences in earnest although executive management has (or wants) only a high-level understanding of the commitments undertaken. It's no wonder, then, that expectations and perceptions can drift apart. Such discrepancies can be the beginning of many project management problems.

Hollywood faces a similar risk. Its projects have the same mix of stakeholders and the same essential work products: the script, the budget, and the schedule. But the risk has been long recognized in the movie business, so the studio production system accounts early on for the need to establish solid agreements. This chapter looks first at how the system approaches that need and then applies that approach to the corporate IT world. The point is to establish agreements between key stakeholders as a way to set in place a foundation for smooth coordination and collaboration across the project life cycle.

Contracts and Commitments

I met a failed producer in Hollywood—I'll call him Terry. When I contacted Terry through the Directors Guild of America, I assumed that because he was a member in good standing, he was probably pretty active in the industry.[1] I got a different impression when we first spoke on the phone—nothing explicit, just general negativity. I went ahead and arranged a meeting, thinking that some negative takes on the production system could be useful. But when we met at the Beverly Hills Wilshire, Terry wasn't interested in talking about the system. He

---

[1] The Directors Guild of America represents unit production managers, another name for producers.

wanted to talk about the prima donnas and backstabbers and incompetents he had to deal with as a line producer. He told me story after story involving one confrontation after the next. He had been fired from at least three projects, he said, but it wasn't his fault—he'd been working with crazy people. On a little prompting from me, he described the production teams he had been stuck with as follows: They demanded too much, appreciated too little, expected "yes" all the time, and wouldn't understand when something couldn't be done. Sure, he had rubbed people the wrong way, because he wasn't afraid to put his foot down. He had about had it with this business, he said, and wondered why I was looking for anything positive in it.

Terry seemed basically like a good guy. But on listening to his stories, I picked up on what may have been causing him to butt heads with others: He seemed to be continually disagreeing with agreements he had previously made. As a producer, he was fighting for budget changes over budgets he had developed. He was saying no to prop masters and costume designers when earlier discussions had indicated yes. In short, he was going back on his commitments—not because he was being intentionally dishonest, but because he believed that with each new analysis, his new decision was the right one to make. After several rounds of such honesty, some of the executives asked if he might leave.

Commitment is a big thing in Hollywood. In this land of contractors, few people can keep getting work without a proven ability to take their commitments seriously. A person who agrees to participate in a particular way on a project is expected to follow through professionally. At the same time, blind adherence to a previous commitment (especially in the face of evidence pointing to a need for change) is discouraged. Much of preproduction time is devoted to bringing teams together to review and discuss potential production decisions. The agreements that come out of these reviews and discussions are taken seriously—they are used to fund production. Because a production team is made up of a heterogeneous collection of specialized talent, it's essential to foster an explicit appreciation of commitment and follow through for each and every movie project. In Hollywood, this explicit appreciation takes the form of a contract, and everyone involved in the project will sign it. Let's take a quick look at the three main groups that need to commit to a production's vision.

- **The producer's unit**   This is the management arm of the team: the executive producers, the unit producers, the production managers. They will sign contracts with the studio to fulfill certain job roles. They will also be required to sign off on the major production artifacts: the script, the budget, and the schedule. Specific attention to these aspects of the production process makes sense. This team, after all, was largely responsible for setting those artifacts into place. The studio wants to know that they have no hesitation in promising to deliver on these artifacts.

- **The creative talent**   This group consists of the cast and the creative leads—the director, the cinematographer, the composer, and so on. These people are charged with reviewing the script, understanding what their roles will be in its realization, and acknowledging the time and costs that will be allocated to those roles. They will sign contracts with the producers to demonstrate this agreement. In most cases, the producers can be pretty confident that mutual expectations will be met, because they will have sought out these leads early in the planning process, getting their input into the shape of the script, the budget, and the schedule.

- **The crew**   Hollywood crews—from the script supervisor to the gaffers to the grips— are made up mainly of guild and union members. These team members sign contracts too, but such agreements tend to be more general and task-specific. These agreements do not usually require script reviews or broad budget approvals. But they do acknowl- edge—and thus cement—time and cost requirements for the tasks required of the various members of this group.

No production will proceed until all three groups have agreed to these fundamental param- eters of the project. The agreements imply a two-fold promise:

1. Commitment to professional performance: participation, contribution, and collaboration

2. Commitment to responsible performance: delivery within scope, budget, and schedule parameters

Note, however, that these commitments do not mean that nothing can change. Change is common on every movie project. But the commitments serve as a foundation for smooth change management. Once the agreements are in place and production begins, the teams will meet regularly to discuss the project parameters. How is shooting going? Are we get- ting the scenes we need? What are expenses like? How's the schedule? All of the department heads will contribute to these discussions. In fact, it's bad form not to. If adjustments need to be made, then they will be made, with the original commitments being used as the baseline against which those adjustments take shape.

That's the essence of signing on the dotted line in Hollywood. On the surface, such agree- ments may seem like just a lot of paperwork, or as a way to get green M&Ms delivered to the star's trailer every morning. But a formal contract is much more. Out of it comes not just a set of individual agreements but a commonality of agreement among parties, and a form of commitment that can be used to shape performance expectations across the life of the production.

Stakeholder Involvement for IT Projects

In Hollywood, the producer's unit, the creative talent, and the movie crew are the three es- sential stakeholder groups, all more or less dependent on one another. In IT shops, that same dependency exists among the project team, IT management, and the business spon- sors: They all are key stakeholders; they each have a stake in the outcome of the project. Removing any one from the framework of the project would open up management and communication holes. Nevertheless, many development organizations work with only a loose partnership set among these parties. Most often, it's the business sponsors who seem to fade into the background. Sometimes it's upper-level IT management. In my own experience, it's striking how often this approach seems to be the preferred way to build the product. The project team may feel that others are just going to get in the way. Upper-management IT executives may feel that they shouldn't be concerned with details. The business sponsors may figure that they have real work to do and shouldn't be bothered with technical concerns. So each of the groups goes its own way.

Of course, the opposite approach is the preferred path. In fact, many project management professionals cite stakeholder involvement as key to project success. In almost any other industry, that's a given. The housing business is a prime example: When a landowner, a banker, and a general contractor come together to build a home, attention from all three is sure to be constant. The landowner will want to make sure the house is going up as designed. The contractor will want to make sure the work crews are making effective progress. And the bank will be releasing monies only when certain construction benchmarks and inspections have been met. That type of involvement is never seen as meddling or as micromanaging—on the contrary, it's encouraged as responsible participation. Surely an IT project, whose costs can easily surpass those of building a house, should be given the same kind of attention from its stakeholders.

Balance Through Involvement

A look at poplar technology management frameworks—CMMI, the PMBOK, ISO 9001, or Six Sigma—will show that each places a special emphasis on stakeholder involvement. Such involvement is viewed as an integral and essential management practice. At the center of stakeholder involvement sit two requisites: input and feedback. Stakeholders are needed to provide expert input into such considerations as functionality, budgets, schedules, and other key work products. This expertise may take the form of business advice, technical advice, or management advice. That advice will contribute much to the successful shape of a project. Continued involvement during the life cycle of the project is essential. Periodic feedback from stakeholders on overall progress and on certain products will be needed as they come together. This feedback will ensure that all parties are moving in sync. Foster a string association here, and synchronicity remains tight. Skip it, and three distinct risks are introduced: soft communications, mismatched expectations, and weak change control. These are discussed next.

1. **Soft communications**   Loose stakeholder associations mean ineffective or incomplete communications. Key people do not exchange information at the level they should. Frequency suffers as well as depth. Commonalities of understanding start to diverge. Original visions and directives may dissipate. Assumptions begin to replace agreements. A likely result is that expectations regarding project specificities may begin to differ among the stakeholders.

2. **Mismatched expectations**   When stakeholder involvement is low or nonexistent, different teams will inevitably adopt different expectations—about performance or progress or status or feature sets. And when the stakeholders eventually come together (as they must, at least at the end of a project), they may have very different interpretations of and reactions to what they see. This mismatch is a common project management issue that leads to unforeseen disagreements. The result often is difficulty with change control.

3. **Weak change control**   Without regular stakeholder involvement, project change control becomes problematic. The result will be diminished controls over scope, budgets, and schedules. These items will always require some adjustments from time to time, no matter what the project. But effective and intelligent assessment of such change cannot take place if key decision makers are left out of the process, or if they enter into the process with a less-than-current understanding of the issues at hand.

In combination, these three inadequacies lead inexorably to less than optimal outcomes (all too familiar to some of us): confused project teams, dissatisfied customers, and disenchanted executive management.

Hollywood Lesson

To avoid the pitfalls of weak stakeholder involvement, we need only look back to the Hollywood system for a solution. The routine of spelling out responsibilities and expectations in written documents, the active seeking out of expert advice early in preproduction, and the use of regular production status meetings all can be borrowed and adapted for IT. This approach constitutes the ninth lesson of this book:

> **Lesson 9:** **Establish a stakeholder framework for your projects,** one designed specifically to support early commitment and ongoing feedback.

Let's look now at ways to establish this framework.

Facilitating Stakeholder Involvement

Two crucial roles for a project's stakeholders, then, are early input and regular feedback. How can these activities be facilitated within an organization? For some shops, this in-house recruitment can represent a big change, especially if management and business partners have hitherto shown little interest in being involved. The key is to communicate the necessity of this involvement not from a project level but from an executive level, and to then wed it to the shop's definition of project success. At the project level, initiating stakeholder involvement is a little easier, mainly because it becomes a tactical job at that point. As discussed next, a combination of two broad techniques can be used to push this agenda forward: identifying the right stakeholders and then proactively managing their involvement.

Identifying Stakeholders

For each project, there can be many stakeholders, as well as many different types of stakeholders. By definition, a *stakeholder* is any party that has an interest in the outcome of the project. This could be an explicit, direct interest or an implicit, tangential one. One of the keys to project management success, then, is identifying the right set of stakeholders for the project at hand. The whole purpose of involving stakeholders is to gain their ongoing support so that the project gains and retains the momentum it needs to reach its goals. Certain people will be able to contribute to this purpose more than others. Those are the folks whose involvement should be specifically targeted.

Stakeholders can be grouped according to their relationship to your project. Typically, they may play any of five key roles:

- **Sponsors**   These are those stakeholders who typically fund the project. They may or not be users of the product, but they have ultimate authority over the development effort, and their expectations are the ones that need to be chiefly addressed.

- **Targets**   These stakeholders are usually related to the sponsor. They will be the direct users of the product being developed. They usually have heavy influence with the sponsors and may be a vital source of input and feedback to the project team. They are also very often a main source of project change requests (sometimes channeled through sponsors, sometimes not).

- **Agents**   These are the members of the project team (including project management). They are the ones charged with designing and developing the product. As stakeholders, they provide a source for primary communications, and they drive general stakeholder involvement. From these agents come progress reports, performance reports, and solicitations for work products reviews.

- **Partners**   These stakeholders support the agents. They usually are members of upper-level IT management. They provide the agents with the facilities, tools, and executive support required by the project. The partners often have an already established relationship with the sponsors.

- **Advocates**   Advocates can be thought of as peripheral stakeholders. They usually have no direct authority to influence the project, but they may have a tangential stake in the project's outcome, so they may be able to influence the actions and perceptions of the sponsors and the targets.

Early on in initiation, it's important to take a look at the project's scope. Scope is a great pointer to stakeholder groups. What business need is being addressed? Who will use the product? What business units will be impacted by the work? Who is the funding party? How big is the project? How visible is the project? Answering these questions can help establish a chart of those persons and groups within the organization that the project manager may wish to reach out to. They may respond; they may not. But it's important from a project management standpoint that they at least be given the opportunity to respond. If stakeholder involvement is encouraged by organizational executives, collecting the groups needed for this effort should be feasible.

Once key stakeholders have been identified, careful planning and management will make their involvement as convenient and productive as possible.. This is illustrated in Figure 9-1.

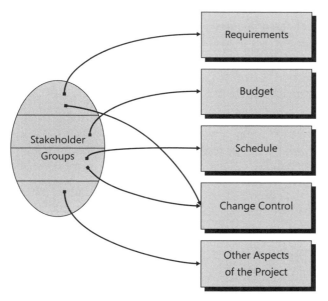

FIGURE 9-1 Various stakeholder groups can provide vital input and feedback across the project life cycle.

Involving Stakeholders

Identifying the right stakeholders will marshal a set of resources that can go a long way to ensuring project efficiencies and effectiveness. But identifying them is just the first step. The real key is to get the right people involved and keep them involved. Let's look now at a set of activities project management can undertake to help ensure stakeholder involvement across the life of the project.

Plan Stakeholder Touch Points

How much stakeholder involvement is needed? As a general rule, the more involvement, the better. The exact level, of course, will depend on singularities in each development shop.

It's important to account for specific touch points as a project gets under way. These touch points represent project artifacts and procedures that typically have a direct impact on realizing the project's business mission. They possess much more value when key stakeholders are directly involved in their creation and management. Seven of these common touch points are listed next.

- **The requirements**   Documented requirements establish the business scope and feature sets the project will address. In many ways, it represents the voice of the customer. Because the requirements constitute the team's interpretation of what the stakeholders want and need, it's essential that they help set these requirements in place and confirm the final, workable form.

- **The budget**   The project's stakeholders will have to make an investment in order for the project to reach fulfillment. This is usually an investment of money, but it can also be time, resources, or any number of other elements. The project team and the stakeholders will need to agree on the size and extent of that investment. And both parties will need to monitor that investment as it potentially evolves over time.

- **The schedule**   The schedule will set major performance expectations for the project: start dates, end dates, and milestones. Schedules are very often driven by external business drivers with very real dependencies often attached to them. The schedule that will govern the project will need stakeholder buy-in in light of these external drivers.

- **The communication plan**   Aside from the budget and the schedule, a project may incorporate multiple plans (quality plans, scope control plans, and so on.). But a key plan to share with stakeholders is the one that will be used to describe and manage their involvement in the project. This is the communication plan. This plan defines at what points stakeholders will be asked to participate in project activities, such as document content contributions and documents reviews and approvals.

- **The change control process**   Here is a critical touch point. The change control process defines how requests for change are introduced, assessed, and managed over the course of the project. Some changes will undoubtedly come from the project team (the agents), but a majority come from the other stakeholders. For change to be controlled smoothly, the stakeholders need to be aware of the process and be prepared to participate in it.

- **The verification plan**   Verification activities confirm that the functionality in the end product traces back to the originating requirements. How verification is effected will go a long way toward demonstrating that the customer's specifications have been met. That's why it's important to seek their input and feedback in planning these activities. These stakeholders should be comfortable up front with the verification approach so that they have confidence in the test results.

■   **The validation plan**   This is important in terms of final acceptance and agreements regarding suitability. The validation plan defines how the product will be tested in a real-world, production-like environment. Get the environment wrong, and the tests may not confirm true product performance. When stakeholders help shape the design of the validation plan, the project team is better assured that the tests conducted will be accepted by all parties as having value and merit.

Seek Early Input

The seven artifacts just described should hold special interest for an IT project's stakeholders. It may be possible to identify more, but these seven tend to have a direct bearing on how a product is shaped and delivered for business purposes. Most of these artifacts will be developed by members of the project team; project managers, business analysts, test managers, and so on. A two-phase creation process is the usual sequence: First they are drafted; then they are reviewed for approval. Here we deal with the first step. The project team should seek out the project's stakeholders during the initial drafting stage to ensure the content of the documents represents the views of the stakeholders (their needs, expertise, and insights). If these views are incorporated in the appropriate documents early in the project life cycle, odds are that acceptance and smooth management will follow. Of greater importance, the applicable value of the document will be maximized.

Seek Periodic Feedback

Key stakeholders should be included with those parties who have the authority to approve key project artifacts. Sometimes this approval is needed for legal reasons: The business can't move forward without it. But it's more often useful for reasons of confirmation and comfort. When stakeholders have the opportunity to review work in progress, to comment on specifics and suggest (where necessary) revisions, the project team implements the appropriate response: It can incorporate recommendations to make the artifacts stronger, or it can explain why certain limitations may be necessary. Either way, the work moves incrementally forward and, with it, a continued and shared understanding among parties.

Demonstrate Agreement

As is evident in the title of this chapter, "Sign on the Dotted Line," demonstrating agreement among stakeholders is important. It's evidence that everyone is indeed in accord regarding expectations for the endeavor. This evidence can take many forms. Often it calls for formal signatures, ink on paper. But other ways can be just as valid: e-mail exchanges, electronic signatures, whatever is acceptable within an organization's culture. The point is to take a specific action that says continue on, proceed with the work—an action that yields concrete and visible documentation.

Sustain Commitment

Early input is designed to achieve agreement. Periodic feedback is intended to sustain agreement. In Hollywood, when a script has been finally approved, it is placed under strict version control. Any new pages that are then released are color coded blue, yellow, or pink, signifying successive versions. This color code system is a visual cue of change and currency. The counterpart in the world of IT is the use of baselines. Stakeholder commitment can be sustained only through the careful control of the documents they have hitherto reviewed and approved. These documents can be protected through the use of some form of configuration management. Identifying these key documents and then protecting the integrity of their content will help ensure that the bases for all stakeholder agreements remain intact.

Control Change

Perhaps the strongest advantage to be gained from stakeholder involvement is coordinated change control. Unmanaged change can wreck a project—in fact, it has a well-known history of doing so. At the same time, change will always be a given. A significant part of this change is likely to come from those stakeholders that are focused on the business missions contained in the work. If these stakeholders have not stayed current with the shape of the work or on evolving project parameters, they can quickly introduce change requests that conflict with the project's capability to address them. If stakeholders and team members work closely together, however, they will share common understandings that will promote the intelligent assessment of change and its impact on essential project goals.

An important point is that stakeholders should be regarded as important extensions of the project team. They can make the same kinds of substantial contributions to project success that come from the team's most technically adept and experienced members. It's essential to identify the right stakeholders, actively seek their early input, and promote ongoing feedback over the life of the project. This approach will help ensure that project visions and expectations remain in sync among all parties, from the technical folks clear across to the business folks.

Benefits of Stakeholder Agreement

Happy stakeholders can make the difference between a rewarding project and a miserable one. When project teams practice the techniques just described for the process of confirming agreement, stakeholders tend to be the happier kind. The tangible benefits that can come from these practices are many and varied; here are four especially important ones.

- **Firm success criteria**   Project success begins by defining what success means for the project and its stakeholders (the project team included). When stakeholders can come together early on and agree on the important operating parameters for the project, the chance for success (or compromise) to be realized equally across all parties will rise accordingly. These criteria may be any blend of schedule, budget, scope, quality, or the like; that blend will naturally vary from project to project, organization to organization. Through active stakeholder involvement, those criteria not only can be set into place at the outset but can then serve as a means of tracking and measuring performance.

- **Allied performance expectations**   Multiple stakeholders may potentially be involved in any one project. It's important for all of them to share a common view of how things will proceed, of the directions that will be set for going forward. They should also share a common vision regarding the major tasks and deliverables that will mark project progress and performance. Development of this shared vision can best be achieved by actively involving stakeholders in these activities, in the development and review of the work products, and in periodic status reporting.

- **Fuller communications**   Communication is the whole idea behind stakeholder involvement. When people pop sporadically in and out of project activity, it's hard to keep a smooth stream of communication going. But when stakeholders have participated in defining major benchmarks and achieving key milestones, sharing the same general view of status as the rest of the team, communication that is fuller and more open is more easily attained.

- **Coordinated change**   As alluded to earlier in the chapter, keeping stakeholders involved in project activities and up to date on project progress will promote cooperation needed for introducing and managing change. If baselines are used to manage the products they helped produce, they should be able to clearly see their needs reflected in the products. Accordingly, they should be more attuned to assessing and approving any alterations to these needs.

Hollywood has long used formal contracts to establish agreements and commitments among key personnel hired onto a motion picture project. Complementing this approach, the studio production system then promotes ongoing feedback and analysis from these parties to ensure that the production's goals are being met. The same can be achieved in the world of IT, perhaps with less emphasis on the formal dotted line. By actively identifying stakeholders, seeking their early input, and encouraging their ongoing feedback, common expectations and mutual agreements between technical and business teams can be established and maintained.

Case in Point: Kohl's Department Stores Revisited

The IS division within Kohl's Department Stores recently established an enterprise requirements management program. The purpose of the program is to provide standards across growing IS teams that will help govern how business and system requirements are defined, presented, and managed. Part of this program is a stakeholder framework. The stakeholder framework identifies which organizational groups need to be included in requirements elicitation, which ones need to be involved in document inspections, and which will be required to approve final requirements. At the start of each new project, the framework document is filled in with specific names and contact information. Those stakeholders then form the foundation of the project's communication plan. Project teams work to produce a set of four requirements documents, and whenever the point comes in which these are being developed, reviewed, or approved, the project teams communicate by means of the framework.

Use of the stakeholder framework delivered benefits almost immediately. For starters, the project teams found that they were now much better able to pin down scope. The framework prompted them proactively to place early scope definitions in front of those groups best able to assess the appropriateness and completeness of these early views. Second, the teams found that the framework—used as a cue for managing peer reviews and inspections—promoted feedback all along the life cycle. This feedback helped identify issues and conflicts before they had time to mature into serious problems. Thus, evolving work products tend to be of high quality, resulting in end products of still higher quality. Finally, Kohl's management has seen a stronger sense of community and participation when projects are first initiated. The effectiveness of intergroup cooperation and collaboration has likewise been enhanced.

Kohl's stakeholder framework represents just one way in which an organization can foster the involvement of key groups and persons who have a stake in a project's outcome. There are many other avenues an IT shop can take to reach the same goal: relevant input and regular feedback aimed at producing a usable, high-quality product.

For a Deeper Look . . .

- Jean Tabaka, *Collaboration Explained: Facilitation Skills for Software Project Leaders*, Addison-Wesley Professional, 2006

    Tabaka looks at stakeholder collaboration from several perspectives, with emphasis on preparing teams to collaborate, building collaborative cultures, defining collaboration roles and agendas, and using collaboration to plan and estimate projects.

- Carl Kessler and John Sweitzer, *Outside-in Software Development: A Practical Approach to Building Successful Stakeholder-Based Products*, IBM Press, 2007

    This book focuses on building value-add products by understanding project stakeholders and the organizational and business context they operate in. It includes discussions on identifying the short- and long-term stakeholder goals a project will satisfy, effectively mapping project expectations to outcomes, and continuously enhancing alignment with stakeholder goals.

- Yuk Kuen Wong, *Modern Software Review: Techniques and Technologies*, IRM Press, 2006

    Wong's text focuses mainly on software defect prevention but offers good advice on how to apply reviews and inspections to those iterative artifacts (including estimates and plans) that culminate in a workable product.

Part III
Production

In this section we look at the kinds of topics that influence how projects are monitored, tracked, and controlled, and how progress is reported on.

Chapter 10
Stick to the Script

In the world of technology development, scope creep has probably caused more projects to spin out of control than any other single problem or issue. Scope creep occurs when requirements fall into an uncontrolled state of flux—existing ones change, new ones slip in, and others become obsolete. When it does, the project manager's ability to manage schedule, costs, and product quality is greatly diminished. Yet scope creep remains an all-too-common problem in corporate IT shops. In fact, many organizations simply accept it as part-and-parcel with the job and are resigned to deal with its fallout, rather than addressing its underlying cause. But the cause itself is no mystery: Scope creep stems from a loose and unstructured approach to stakeholder interactions, one that inadvertently yet directly promotes ongoing shifts in focus, mission, and purpose. This organizational trait may be the most common management complaint cited by project managers, probably because it can come from any corner and its potential for disruption is great.

To reduce the risk and impact of scope creep, organizations can implement some light and flexible procedures to control the need for change. To this end, this chapter looks at the importance of requirements management. Let's begin by looking at the counterpart to requirements management used in motion picture production: script control.

The Script as Bible

Conducting the initial research for this book, I spoke with more than 20 motion picture professionals. Some were studio executives at places like Warner Bros., 20th Century Fox, and Paramount. Some were executive producers who ran their own production companies. Others were unit production managers and first assistant directors, those on-the-set managers who make sure each production moves according to plan.

Some of these folks dealt at the high end of the business by routinely overseeing $100 million projects. Others worked on a more modest scale, with pictures costing $5 million to $10 million. One of the themes of this book is that this diverse group of professionals shares the exact same approach to management, whether the picture is a blockbuster or a low-budget knock-off. During our discussions, each and every one of these professionals emphasized—in one form or another but most often in exactly the same words—a cardinal rule of movie making: "The script is the Bible."

As set forth in Chapter 1, "Know the System," Chapter 3, "Establish Green-Light Rules," and especially Chapter 4, "Invest in a Solid Script," movie production centers on the script.

Schedules and budgets are derived from it; stars sign up to the project on the basis of their reading of it; and locations, sets, costumes, and special effects are all designed in accordance with the requirements of the script. The job of the crew is ultimately to shoot the script. The schedule, the budget, and the script are the three foundational elements of motion picture management, and of these three, the script forms the bedrock.

With exceedingly few exceptions, movies do not get into production without some form of a completed script in place. Proceeding without a script is antithetical to Hollywood production methodology. A story is the catalyst for every focused attempt at initiating a project.

So the saying "The script is the Bible" is not an empty platitude in Hollywood (a town known for more than its fair share of empty platitudes). It's taken seriously by everyone along the production line—from the studio finance office, to the producers, director, and stars, right down to the gaffers, grips, and production assistants.

Of course, this isn't to say that the script won't change. Invariably, the script *will* change—that's unavoidable. Many producers say that change is part of the creative process. Directors, performers, and designers may come up with a bundle of new ideas once pro forma production is in full swing. Most of those people were probably hired because of their ability to innovate—so crimping that imaginative energy may not be productive. But just as the term *show business* is equal parts "show" and "business," so follows professional conduct on the set. Inspiration may be a catalyst for change, but Information is always its arbiter.

Here's an example: Ascendant Media was about halfway into principal photography on a modern-day western about a gang of rustlers preying on the wild mustang population of Nevada. A key round-up scene starring a herd of trained horses was scheduled to be shot in a week at a state-owned sanctuary close to the Utah border. The location manager, however, while scouting some scenes for second-unit "beauty shots," discovered that the production company could secure a permit to shoot for a week in a breathtaking canyon further north near Idaho. The location manager, armed with fee information and photographs, pitched it to the director. The director liked it and pitched it to the producer. The department heads then got together and looked at what this change would require. They assessed location accessibility, likely weather conditions, pack-up and travel time (crew and talent and horses), local facilities, the cost of the permit, the effort to return to the next planned location, the chance to absorb some costs in future consolidation, and so on. In short, they analyzed the opportunity in detail, while continually weighing the expense against the added dramatic punch the new location would bring. In the end, the numbers proved manageable, and the production unit approved the change.

Those kinds of changes pop up on every movie project, often in big ways, often in small ways, but always often. That's why the producer's unit—the team responsible for the management of the production—typically moves with the company wherever it goes while production is in process.

Because change opens the door for cost and schedule overruns, changes are never made willy-nilly. Even when productions go script change–crazy and it looks like the inmates have taken over the asylum, informed consent is still the rule of the day.

Here's another example: Francis Ford Coppola's 1979 masterpiece, *Apocalypse Now*, is a film whose script was never fully completed. (I'm not sure if, to this day, a definitive final draft even exists.) Storylines and plot elements were being envisioned even while the picture was being edited. People in the business thought Coppola was crazy. The picture kept getting bigger and bigger. Coppola had contracted for creative control, but few studio executives at United Artists (UA) believed he *was* in creative control. Coppola himself doubted it a lot of the time, but for the 14 months that *Apocalypse Now* was in production in the Philippines, shaky executives at UA were kept in the loop on every fresh vision, approach, or turn the picture took. They analyzed every new idea and request coming in from the mid-Pacific and consistently, if reluctantly, approved them, going back to the coffers time and time again for more money.

Coppola had creative control, but UA retained business control. Had Coppola decided to go his own way on the picture, to forgo the communication path while on the studio's ticket, the studio would have simply shut him down. In fact, well into production, when it became obvious that the script (and therefore the scope, schedule, budget, and vision of the movie) was far from being locked down, UA sent writer John Milius to rein Coppola back in line. Milius went. When he came back, he enthusiastically explained why a movie originally budgeted at $12 million would be twice as good with an additional infusion of $24 million.

UA executives relented; that far into the commitment, they almost had to. Seen in hindsight, it was a gamble that paid off. *Apocalypse Now* made almost $100 million in its opening release. The point, however, is not that creative anarchy can or should be forgiven if the project is a success. And it's not whether any of the project's stakeholders—Coppola, Milius, or UA—were right. The point is that, right or wrong, they were *all in agreement*. The decisions regarding the script (and the impact waves those decisions sent out) were made through communication and consultation across teams, not after the fact but well before, and not without a thorough understanding of both sides of each decision—the upside and the downside—by all parties.

The vast majority of movie productions never approach such script creep calamities. Changes that are more typical and routine include a shift in location (say, café to library), adjusting a dialog line (to the preference of the performer), or a revision to use of a prop ("It'd be funnier with a seven-layer cake . . ."). But these run-of-the-mill changes still receive a robust and appropriate level of scrutiny. Line changes are almost always okayed without much discussion because no production impact is involved. But other changes get the full assessment. Schedule and cost impacts are discussed down to the detail: Who will provide it? How long will we have to wait? How long will it take to execute? Will it cause any down-line bottlenecks? If the answers indicate a quick accommodation, the response is something like "Great idea, C.B. Pure genius. Let's do it." And if they don't: "Great idea, C.B. Let's see if we can fit it in later. For now, we better run with what's on the page."

The Requirements as Contract

Most IT professionals who have developed systems and software, managed technology organizations, or consulted on management practices would probably acknowledge that the avenues for change in corporate America are not nearly as well paved as they are in Hollywood. On some projects, customers have been known to walk in the door with new idea after new idea, no matter what phase the project may be in. And when that main door appears to be closed, they find a back door: They call in a favor or pressure a manager. Likewise, system architects may mislead the customer because of a desire to work with a new tool or exciting piece of technology; they twist the requirements to a preferred agenda.

Most of the time, scope creep appears in a much more benign manner. Lots of times, project execution begins without a clear sense of what the requirements ought to be; the project team starts with a vague destination and accepts that things will be worked out from there. Maybe the customer comes up with a steady supply of new requirements because the technology people have never clarified the bounds within which they create systems, or the need to work through a requirements development phase, iterative though it may be. Maybe the IT shop supports a culture that emphasizes end results over managed means. Maybe the project team feels stretched too thin to afford the time it takes to proactively engage with the customer. Or maybe the customer has no real interest in engaging with the project team.

There are all kinds of reasons for scope creep, and its effects can make for a frustrating situation to be in. It robs project managers of the central element they need to control: the shape of the work. And when the shape of the work cannot be controlled—that is, when it cannot be pre-realized through plans and resource allocations—project activities begin to become scattered and commonality of vision is lost. Groups separate into teams, teams into individuals. When a project reaches that state, rework, poor quality, schedule slippage, and cost overruns are never far behind.

That's what scope creep can do—that's what it *does* do. But the idea inherent in the phrase "the scope is changing" is not a bad thing. In fact, technology shops would do well to promote change as good. (Sometimes seven-layer cakes *are* funnier than two-layer cakes.) The action to avoid is the "creeping" part of scope creep, in the form of unsolicited, undocumented, and nonvalidated requirements, ones that seem to tiptoe in on little cat feet or float down from the air vents on slips of paper. It's that kind of uncontrolled change that causes the problems. So the key is for executives and project managers alike to be aware of change, to recognize that change is inevitable, and to manage it as an elemental characteristic of project evolution. It's the same as script control.

Technology projects rely on scripts just like motion picture projects do. In the IT domain, the equivalent of the script is the requirements documents. Often two kinds of these documents exist for a project: a *business requirements document*, which describes the business needs that the solution (product or system) must address, and a *system requirements document*, which describes the technical functionality the solution must accommodate to realize the business mission. Most experienced project managers understand two basic needs related to these documents: first, the need to document a requirements baseline, and second, the need to establish mechanisms for smooth change control of that baseline.

The importance of the baseline is clear. It serves as an agreed-on starting point for project work. The key concept here is agreement. For a baseline to have any value, it needs to have the endorsement of the project's key stakeholders: the customers, senior management, and key members of the technical team. In the absence of a commitment from any one of those parties, the requirements remain nothing more than a collection of potential promises, so it's helpful, and even advisable for technology shops and their customers to regard the requirements baseline as a form of contract between parties. It's the general blueprint for what the shop will build; it's the script that will be translated to the screen.

The importance of change control, if not apparent at the outset, will quickly show its value as a project builds momentum. The reason is simple: As noted earlier, the requirements (just like movie scripts) are guaranteed to change. Some changes will be small, some will be big—but if avenues do not exist for the orderly evolution of business and technical requirements over time, through communication and consultation, the purpose, focus, and integrated shape of the requirements may quickly disintegrate. Again, it's a good idea for a development project to have in place a policy or procedure supported by senior management that describes how change will be introduced, assessed, approved, and integrated into ongoing project work.

Let's go back for a minute to the set of New Line Cinema's upcoming romantic comedy, *He's Just Not That into You*.

Hollywood-Style Change Control

Baselining the script and tracking script changes are both *de jure* and *de rigueur* Hollywood practices. Because the production process is expensive and work-intensive (12-hour days are the rule), producers are concerned primarily with schedule and budget affinity. They can trust the "theater" of the piece to the creative team; the director, writer, stars, and designers will see that aspect of the mission through. But the management oversight that that mission is wrapped in falls into the producer's domain. (Project managers will quickly recognize this domain.) That's why the producer moves with the production crew. That's why Michael Beugg, executive producer of *He's Just Not That into You*, was on his cell phone at 8 o'clock on a Thursday night talking to Kris Kristofferson's agent.

A Bump on the Head

Kris Kristofferson has a featured role in *He's Just Not That into You*, and he was scheduled to shoot a dialog scene on a Los Angeles Center Studios sound stage on Friday. But he had just banged his head on a weight bar while working out in the Ritz Carlton's exercise room. Nothing too serious, but his forehead was bruised and, at the moment, somewhat swollen. He didn't think he'd be ready to shoot on Friday. Could they give him a day for the swelling to go down?

That's a common kind of change request on a movie set. Michael said he would see what he could do. He contacted the director and the first assistant, and together they discussed the next day's call sheet. They looked at what could be moved up from Saturday, and it turned out that both days called for work on the same set. The extras on call for Saturday could be brought in tomorrow instead, and Kris's scene could be pushed to Saturday.

They also called the makeup artist. Could she be sure to bring some masking makeup to the set in case Kris's bruise needed to be covered?

Then another call to the Ritz Carlton to extend Kris's stay.

Steven Dunn, the first assistant, prepped a new call sheet and arranged for its distribution out to the department heads. The situation was under control. Michael got back to Kris's agent, let him know the game plan, and that was that. The schedule was still on course, with a slight increase in cost that could probably be made up later on. That was routine in Michael's role of executive producer, and in Steve's job as well. Notification, assessment, redirection, replanning—these are the components of change control on a Hollywood set.

Following the Script

Two basic kinds of scope creep occur in Hollywood: Either the script has to be changed, or how something is presented in the script has to be changed. Adding a new ending is an example of the former. Changing the location of the ending is an example of the latter.

So much planning and preparation go into movie production that change is frowned on, but it is recognized as a fact of life. So over the course of its 100-year history, Hollywood has built up an infrastructure that handles change directly and efficiently. Here are the elements that support change management (and work to avoid scope creep) when a movie is in production:

- **Final Draft tool**   Here is an idea actually borrowed from the technology industry. Final Draft is a version-control tool for movie scripts. (There are other products like it, but Final Draft is the current standard.) When a final draft of the script is approved, this product locks it down. No one can make changes to it without proper authorization.

From this locked version, the production unit will issue daily call sheets, which describe immediately upcoming work.

- **Script supervisor**   With the final draft in hand, the script supervisor tracks production progress and makes sure that everything in the script is being shot as scripted.

- **Creative team**   The creative team includes the director, the writer, the stars, and the various designers. These are the core players whose work will tend to be most affected by a change request. It is their responses that will shape adjustments to the cost and schedule. Accordingly, the producer is very conscientious about keeping these people informed about new change requests and seeking their input on the proper ways to respond.

- **Management team**   The management team includes the producer, the unit production manager, the first assistant director, the production supervisor (accountant), and other support members. These people need to be managing response to change. They are the team that assesses the proposed alternatives; examines cost, schedule, and other impacts; and then pushes for the most desirable option. They work intimately with the creative team so that the final decision supports, to as great an extent as possible, both the creative and the business missions of the project.

- **Production chief**   The production chief is the studio executive who oversees the movie from the highest level of management. Although not overly concerned with day-to-day operations (although he or she does get weekly cost and progress reports), the production chief will get involved with changes when the best available alternatives require significant changes to the budget, the schedule, the tone of the film, or any combination of those. After all, it's the studio that has commissioned the work to begin with, so it's the studio that has final approval of any deviations from the original plan. But producers bring in the production chief only under those circumstances in which the production unexpectedly must deal with big change.

Technology Interpretation

Incomplete requirements, weak requirements, poorly described and misinterpreted requirements—these all lead to changes in scope on technology projects. In some instances, not enough time or energy initially may be dedicated to requirements investigation and development activities, as described in Chapter 4. Most of the time, however, such change is simply a characteristic of product development. Requirements change; they have always changed and they will always change. A point worthy of emphasis is that change is not the culprit here. It is change creeping in—unseen, unnoticed—that becomes the culprit. Hollywood has learned to deal with that kind of change. Its production system has institutionalized a method that avoids scope creep through communication, assessment, and commonality of priorities. Technology shops, on the other hand, are not as unified in their approach to scope creep. Some deal with it one way, others a different way. But it's possible to take something from the movie examples cited earlier: Whatever method is elected to employ, if it's based on some form of notification, assessment, decision, and communication, then it will probably deliver benefits that enhance ability to manage scope. This is the essence of the next lesson of the book:

 Lesson 10: **Establish a change request/approval procedure** that can be used by all relevant stakeholders on a project to submit requests for change, assess the impact of the request, and act to either table the request or integrate it into current project plans.

Moving Toward Improvement

Thus far in this chapter, we've seen the problems that can arise when changes to a project go unchecked. In the motion picture industry, these changes stem from reinterpretation of the script: new camera moves, new line readings, new locations or sets, different props, and so on. In the technology industries, these changes stem from reanalysis of the requirements: additions of new functionality, modifications to feature sets, removal of obsolete or unneeded components. In both industries, if such change, necessary though it may be, is poorly monitored or managed, less than optimal outcomes can be expected. Hollywood addresses this management need through its time-proven production system: Script supervisors monitor script execution, changes are discussed and approved by all relevant parties, and budgets and schedules are updated to reflect the change. Corporate IT has begun to move in a similar direction. Appropriate change control and proper configuration management are becoming focal points in more and more IT shops.

The Discipline of Requirements Management

Most project managers seem to share the general feeling that change control could be better handled in the IT workspace. Many IT people recognize ways in which change control could be introduced. The subject is not foreign to the technology industry. In fact, three of industry's best-known management or improvement frameworks discuss the purpose and activities of change control in some detail. Here's a quick summary:

- **The PMI's PMBOK**   The PMBOK defines management techniques for requirements control in two major areas (and many more implied areas). The first occurs under Project Scope Management. Here a set of component processes are described that enable the appropriate initiation of the project, as well as the appropriate definition, verification, and control of scope changes. The second area occurs under Project Integration Management. Here the component process, Integrated Change Control, is introduced; this facilitates the recognition and management of change across all relevant teams and project parties.

- **CMMI**   The CMMI process describes two areas that address the importance of change control for requirements: Requirements Management and Configuration Management. In each of these, goals and practices are defined to help teams establish mechanisms to review and approve requirements documents, establish official baselines of requirements documents, track requirements changes over time, and control how baselines are updated to reflect approved requests.

- **ISO 9001:2000**   9001 establishes up front the criticality of ensuring the realization of the customer requirements. Then, in Section 7 of the standard, requirements are set forth that describe the need for control of requirements specifications, the importance of baselining requirements and design documents requirements, and the need for "preservation of product" to establish change histories.

Nevertheless, the problem persists, to one degree or another—mainly because most IT shops lack an established change control or change management procedure. Hollywood manages change so well because the paths of change review and approval have been embedded into the production system. There are no back doors to this system, so nothing can creep in unnoticed. Corporate IT shops can improve their abilities related to change control by borrowing from the Hollywood model: by embedding practices for the review, analysis, and approval of change requests, and by committing to these practices so that they eventually become integrated into the organization's culture.

These practices need not be complex. They can start off simple and light and then grow as needed through lessons learned, as described next.

A Simple Requirements Control Procedure

Controlling the requirements sounds like a big job, and certainly in some shops and for some projects, doing so will, by necessity, be a big job. But for most projects, it doesn't have to be. A simple procedure can be set into place that will enhance project management's ability to manage change and subsequently enhance fidelity to commitments regarding scope, cost, schedule, and quality of the project. Here's an example of just such a simple procedure:

1. **Share the idea with key stakeholders.**   The keys to successful change management are communication and common understanding. A good first step, then, is for the requestor to share the idea for the change with the key stakeholders most likely to be impacted or affected by the change. Usually the best way to do this is to document the change. Change request forms are the typical tool employed here, but it's not absolutely necessary that the idea be written up in detail. Some types of technology shops—such as those that deal mainly with smaller projects or those that are committed to the Agile method of product development—tend to rely more on face-to-face meetings than on formal documentation. Either approach will work well if the central charge is carried out: to share the idea with key stakeholders.

2. **Assess the impact of the change.**   Assessing the impact of the change is necessary to determine the value the change may potentially bring to the project. Assessing the impact of a change can take many forms: how long it might take, how much it might cost, how many components it might touch, what teams will need to address it. The factors considered will not be the same for all shops. Each shop should select those factors that mean the most to them. But the idea of standardizing on some common set is a good one. It helps ensure that assessments can be consistently conducted in an equitable way for all changes, no matter where they come from.

3. **Determine the relative importance of the change.**   The assessment should deliver a set of results that will help to determine the relative importance of the change. This analysis should yield some kind of weighting or score. Under a certain threshold, perhaps the change is tabled or denied. Above that threshold, maybe it's approved. At the same time, a set of other change requests, similarly scored, may require consideration. If it's not possible to act on the whole volume at once, it will be necessary to examine the change requests side by side and prioritize them. This will help ensure that high-value changes are acted on first.

4. **Decide on a course of action.**   Now it's time to decide what to do. Throw out some change requests, set some aside to work on or consider later, and approve others for inclusion in project work. This works best when it is a group decision, collectively arrived at from group input and analysis. Once the course of action is decided, work can be jointly refocused and moved forward in coordinated harmony.

5. **But first re-baseline the requirements documents.**   Incorporate the change, and make the new document available to the people who will need it. This step is important even for small shops or those that use Agile (or RAD, Spiral, or other) software. The requirements need to be kept current in documented form, both as a reference for external parties (management and customers) and as a way to establish an audit trail of change across project life cycles.

6. **Implement the change.**   Now everyone can move forward. Plans can be updated (with new costs, new components, new schedules, and so on), and the change can be mapped into current project work activities.

Project management can do three additional things to make a light procedure like this work for the shop's projects. First, share it with the customer before the project begins or very early on in project initiation. (Better yet, create it with customer input.) Second, get senior management to endorse the procedure. Visible executive commitment goes a long way toward encouraging down-line support. And third, use the procedure not just for big change requests or certain phases in the project but for all change requests across all phases. For both internal teams and customers, this will demonstrate a commitment to orderly change management and will also show (if the procedure thus created is appropriate for the organization's culture) that the procedure is really not a burden to support and that it really does improve efficiencies and commonality of vision.

An experienced Hollywood production crew could hardly ask for more.

Tracking the Scope

Part of the responsibility of project management is resource management—allocating a team appropriate for the project work and developing that team to perform for the particular project. One aspect of this development should include orienting the team to the needs of requirements management and change control. A look at the Hollywood model reveals a useful pattern that fits well with the traditional makeup of a technical team. Here's a brief list of roles and tools that a project manager can shape to ensure that scope creep presents minimal problems for the project at hand.

- **Business analysts**   Just as a movie set employs a script supervisor to ensure that the work is shot as scripted, so too can a technology team use a person to own or oversee the requirements. Usually this person is a business analyst. The chief role of the business analyst is to work with customers and stakeholders to define the business requirements and the functional requirements. Through this process, the business analyst often becomes a technical expert in the scope and content of the requirements. So it's often useful to extend the business analyst's role to include working to version-control requirements baselines, participating in change activities, and ensuring that requirements are being incorporated into project work products.

- **Requirements management tools**   Baseline control of the requirements does not require the use of an automated tool, but some form of document control or configuration management system can bring distinct benefits. There are many such tools to choose from (Requisite Pro, Doors, and CyberDoc). These tools feature embedded processes that help manage how requirements are described, recorded, changed, and tracked. If such a tool is available in the organization, the project manager should consider using it through proper configuration and appointing someone on the team to manage its use.

- **Technical team**   In movie production, the creative team members (director, writer, talent, designers) all participate in change discussions. The same should probably hold true for the project's technical team members. At the outset of the project (perhaps as part of project kickoff), it may be useful to cue these technical folks regarding the importance of change control and the need to solicit their opinions and input across the project's full life cycle. The goal is bring them in as active participants in this aspect of project management, not as a sideline job but as one integral to the technical shape of their work.

- **Project manager**   It's also important for the project manager to appreciate his or her role in controlling scope creep and managing change. Just as the producer is the one to ultimately okay changes in storyline, costs, and schedule shifts, so the project manager is the one who is ultimately accountable for the project's managed performance. Go into the project with this responsibility in mind and with the appreciation that change management—and coordinating this across teams—is a major part of effective project management.

- **Change control board**   Some organizations establish change control boards to assess and monitor change requests across projects. Such boards are like the studio executives who need to be brought in when certain changes have the potential to significantly affect scope, costs, and schedules. Change control boards can be helpful to a technology team for a couple of reasons. First, they provide an objective view on the change requests, and second, they provide a procedural avenue that supports a modulated approach to request submission, assessment, and action choices. If an organization employs a change control board, its members should be aligned early on with the focus and needs of the project, the board's approach to change management should be honored, and it should be actively engaged when the need for change arises. The typical shape of a basic change control process is illustrated in Figure 10-1.

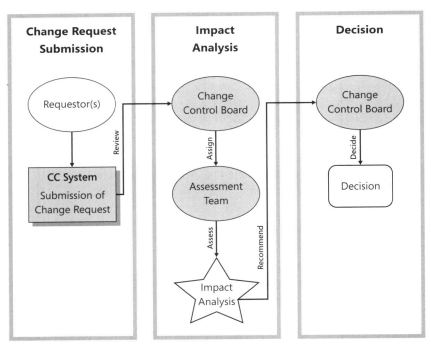

FIGURE 10-1 A change control (CC) process is effective for the proper control of evolving requirements.

Case in Point: The Fall of Indus

A dramatic case in point, observed firsthand, was the demise of a software company as a consequence of rampant scope creep. The year was 1999. The company was Indus International, which developed and sold software systems for asset management–intensive industries: oil refineries, automotive plants, steel mills. The company had been in trouble for about a year. Sales had been declining, and the competitive edge of its product line had been lost. Indus's parent company had decided on an aggressive market recoup strategy, pumping millions into an all-out product line revamp initiative. I was brought in as a consultant to help implement process controls across the organization. The parent company wanted to use CMMI as a management framework to help modulate the burn rate on those millions. The hope was that through process would come increased accountability and focus. Unfortunately, things didn't work out that way.

It's not that the company was adverse to process; most of Indus's technology managers thought that some degree of process could help coordinate workflows. But the pressure of declining sales and corporate disappointment put such "amorphous" strategic initiatives low on the totem pole. At the top was an unbridled desire for action—in any direction, even in all directions.

This impetus for action, in fact, was what caused the fall of Indus. A drive for change within the enterprise to become anything other than what it was prompted an unmitigated disconnect between the software development teams, the company's sales force, and its executive management. The sales team, wanting to lead the turnaround, actively courted the company's clients, and as sales forces are poised to do, they eagerly solicited ideas about new features that would make their product more attractive. They brought back these ideas en masse and with enthusiasm to the development folks. Executive management, anxious to demonstrate a no-holds-barred commitment to any success avenue, resisted any impulse to put a cap on all of these great ideas. The ideas flooded in. Development management, aware that things were in bad shape and not wanting to be the culprits who said no to success, let the waters breach the dam.

But no one coordinated, no one assessed, and no one prioritized.

But the teams doing the real work couldn't keep up. Product scope was in a constant state of flux. Code integration suffered, test cycles ran over and over again, documentation fell out of sync. Release dates slipped, teams worked late into the nights, and the money disappeared. After three financial quarters at this hectic pace, no saleable product resulted from all of this effort.

Finally, enough was enough: The parent company laid off the work force, closed the doors, and sold the company's assets to a competitor. That effectively ended the scope creep.

For a Deeper Look . . .

- Suzanne Robertson and James C. Robertson, *Mastering the Requirements Process*, Second Edition, Addison-Wesley, 2006

  This book is based mainly on the authors' own requirements process model, Volere, which describes a good step-by-step guide for eliciting and gathering business and system requirements. The book complements this with good advice on the importance of establishing requirements baselines and employing coordinated requirements change control. It also has good material on the importance of identifying the right stakeholders and the proper use of quality gates.

- Soren Lauesen, *Software Requirements: Styles & Techniques*, Addison-Wesley, 2002

  Lauesen focuses on the art of defining and managing sets of requirements and doing so according to the particular culture at hand. The author describes different types of requirements styles and discusses potential best uses of each. There are good sections on aligning requirements with business needs and on using requirements sets as a baseline for quality checks. The author also provides the reader with 20 techniques that can be used to more effectively elicit requirements from users.

Chapter 11
Work to the Call Sheets

As IT project managers, most of us know plenty about tracking. Daily we have to track schedules, budgets, and resources; plans and communications; and stakeholders and supervisors. But we're often not very good at tracking the work—that is, the production of the technical components of that thing we are building. And the more technical the project is, the less we tend to look at the work. After all, project managers are usually not technical types, so should they be expected to oversee technical jobs? The "pure management" part of the project management job is big enough on its own, so isn't it better to delegate technical task management to technical leads? Anyway, doesn't project management's poking its nose into raw development border on micro-management? These are valid questions only when it's recognized that the answer to each is "no." Although appointing a project manager as the sole *arbiter of technical quality probably is not advisable, the project manager nevertheless has an essential role in technical management. In fact, in most mature IT shops, project managers can be found actively managing the identification and distribution of technical tasks. This aspect of management is not done in isolation, of course; rather, ,it's a responsibility that falls squarely into the project management domain. What do these mature shops do that the others don't? It's not a technical capability that sets them apart—it's a* managerial *one, and has to do with what the PMI's PMBOK defines as the adoption and use of a* work authorization system (WAS). *This chapter explores the use of work authorizations as a way for project management to retain a firm handle on project work activities, especially in relation to both the WBS and the technical demands of the project. Let's start with a look at how Hollywood uses its own system of work authorizations, referred to as* call sheets.

Yes Man

Marty Ewing is the executive producer of the Jim Carrey comedy *Yes Man*. *Yes Man* is a story about a man who decides that for a year he'll say yes to every invitation he receives. On the day Marty has set aside for our interview, the crew is shooting on location at the Blue Moon café in West LA. A couple of side streets have been roped off, and police are redirecting traffic around the strip of stores that buffer the Blue Moon. When I arrive at about 10 o'clock that morning, the production is in full force. Thick cables run across the ground seemingly in every direction. Lights and reflectors stand tall on heavy metal tripods. Grip trucks full of more equipment wait out back. A sound crew strings microphone cables against an interior wall of the café. Another crew huddles around the camera. Activity bustles all around me, but it's not at all chaotic or rushed. A lot of different jobs are going on all at the same time, but a certain harmony seems to prevail. All of the crew members look like they know just what they're doing.

I'm told Marty is half a block away in his trailer. His assistant leads me over to a large parking lot that has been virtually taken over by trailers: trailers for each cast member, for the director and his team, for key department heads like makeup and wardrobe, and for the producer's own team. Marty's is not so much a getaway as it is a compact office: small conference table, sofa, filing cabinets, flat panel TV screen. When I come in, he's just finishing a meeting with one of his chief reports, the first assistant director. After introductions, he takes me back to the Blue Moon for a view of the set. He knows I'm interested in the techniques of production management, so as he leads me around, he points out here and there what everyone is doing. I make a rough count of about 75 people and maybe 5 van-line–sized equipment trucks. Quite a setup, I comment. Marty says that an entry and exit shot is what's scheduled. Just an entry and an exit? I want to ask about this when Jim Carrey arrives with a modest entourage. Marty asks me if I'd like to hang out and observe and then excuses himself. I stand back and watch the crew at work. What happens over the next two hours is this: Jim Carrey walks into the café; Jim Carrey walks out of the café. Over and over again.

Here's how Marty will explain it later: In movie production, nothing is left to chance. Even spontaneity is planned. Production is so expensive that no one wants to rely on luck, inspiration, synchronicity, or serendipity for professional results. That's the reason, he says, for all the people and all the trucks. Even though a relatively minor part of the movie was being shot that day, he had a managerial obligation to treat it with the same thoroughness a more complex scene might call for. After all, if a producer took a lighter approach and it resulted in, say, a one-day delay, that could potentially cost the production a hundred thousand dollars. To the uninformed observer, productions may seem big, sometimes even extravagant, but they're that way because any other way is just too dicey. That obligation, Marty says, dictates a large part of his job: planning and coordinating these production teams so that everything comes together, in big ways and small ones. He refers back to his meeting with the first assistant director. They had been discussing the next day's call sheet. The call sheet, it turns out, is a key management tool that breaks down the production schedule into very specific points of activity. Prepared day by day, it organizes the work the cast and crew will be expected to achieve on the day's shoot.

In Hollywood, every production day on the set begins and ends with call sheets. A call sheet can be thought of as a work order. It provides a listing of everyone—cast and crew—who's due on the set for the next day's work and documents what they'll be doing. Handed out at the end of the day, they are used the next morning to confirm that everybody's present and that things are ready to go. The detail on each call sheet is pretty impressive. It accounts for hundreds of different people and jobs. It pinpoints different times of arrival, notes when certain actors should be in makeup, identifies specific props that will be needed, and shows what parts of the script (down to the eighth of a page) will be shot. There is even an estimated lunch count provided for craft services. The productions I was privy to in researching this book—*Yes Man*, *He's Just Not That into You*, *Proud Mary*, and *Witless Protection*—all used call sheets as a key management tool. And from production to production, the call sheets all looked pretty much alike. The assistant director produces them (perhaps with help from the script supervisor and the producer); the crew works from them; and the producer manages, in large part, by them.

A counterpart to call sheets in the field of technology development can be found in the PMBOK's recommendations regarding work authorizations and the use of a WAS. As tools of project management, work authorizations are used to initiate specific development activities, and the WAS is used to track the status of outstanding authorizations. Work authorizations, then, function in the same way as described for call sheets: They manage the distribution of work and track the state of this work over time.

Tracking the Work in IT

Call sheets are very detailed breakdowns of work that has to get done daily on a movie shoot. The value they bring is that nothing is left to chance and nothing gets lost. IT projects could benefit from a similar approach because it is not uncommon for development teams to face complex, broadly scoped projects, in which things do often go missing. The 2006 Standish Group study of IT project performance found that about 40 percent of software projects were "compromised," meaning in part that users did not receive components of functionality they had bargained for.[1] Surely lots of reasons may contribute to that missing functionality, but one that shouldn't be ignored—even though it's embarrassing—is a simple one: Someone forgot to do it.

It's easy, though, to understand why. Look at the breadth of activities that have to go into a development effort: requirements definition, analysis, design, coding, reviews, multiple forms of testing, documentation, support preparation, and so on. Then look at the depth of those activities. Databases need to be accounted for, along with operating platforms, system and user interfaces, reports, data management and storage rules, and on and on. The result is a mountain of work that's both mighty high and mighty wide. Often, project management's view is limited only to management tools such as the schedule, the budget, and the requirements documents. At the same time, the technical teams typically are nose down in the micro detail of the solution, often unaware of how all the separate, specialized activities will eventually hook together. In these kinds of environments, things are bound to get lost or forgotten, because three important views of the work have been lost (or, more accurately, never achieved).

---

1   Available at www.standishgroup.com/quarterly_reports/index.php (accessed April 8, 2008).

First, *clarity of assignment* is lacking. In other words, tangible, finite knowledge of who is working on what is not available. Project management may know the broad areas that are being addressed, but technology solutions are not realized through broad strokes. Second, *visibility of the work* also tends to be lost. Project management may see that lots of work is going on but lacks the ability to distinguish discrete parts in the wash of activity. As a result, it's very difficult to determine the amount of progress truly achieved versus the backlog of work remaining. Finally, *accommodation of the work* becomes impossible. In these kinds of environments, project management simply has a hard time setting down a benchmark from which a current production position can be assessed—that is, a position known to the kind of detail that lends itself to confident prediction. When the work itself is not visible, then it becomes difficult to judge whether all the work is being accommodated. The inevitable drawback: Not all of the work has been accommodated, even though most of the resources may have been expended.

Such situations make project managers uncomfortable—technical team members, too, and executive management. But the alternative open to them often makes them just as uncomfortable. Hollywood's use of call sheets is an approach that's well suited to application in the technology development domain. The PMI has been offering a similar tool for use in IT shops for years now. The PMI promotes this approach through the use of work authorizations, which can be thought of as task orders or work requests. Work authorizations assign project work at a manageable, incremental level in order to track and accommodate all of the functionality required for a given solution. The essence of this approach, used by Hollywood and recommended by the PMI, constitutes the next lesson of this book.

> **Lesson 11:** **Establish a work authorization system** to manage incremental tasks in a manner that supports accommodation of all project work.

The view here is at the incremental level, at the task level, most often a technical level. But it's here that the real work of a project gets done. Let's take a deeper look.

Incrementing the Solution

The subject of this chapter is how a WAS can be used to help effectively plan for and monitor incremental project work, in very much the same way that Hollywood uses call sheets to manage its production crews and schedules. The terms "work authorizations" and "work authorization system" come directly from the PMI and can be found in the PMBOK. Here's how the current PMBOK Guide describes the terms.[2]

---

[2] Project Management Institute, *A Guide to the Project Management Body of Knowledge*, Third Edition, PMBOK Guides, 2004.

[The] Work Authorization System (WAS) is a subsystem of the overall project management system. It is a collection of formal documented procedures that defines how project work will be authorized (committed) to ensure that the work is done by the identified organization, at the right time, and in the proper sequence. It includes the steps, documents, tracking system, and defined approval levels needed to issue work authorizations.

So the PMI, it turns out, is a fan of call sheets, too. The key traits of the system are that it is formalized (documented) and official (recognized as having authority). After that, the shape of the system can be just about anything appropriate to the types and sizes of projects for a specific IT shop. Its design is pretty much up to the individual shop, as noted by Rudd McGary[3]:

PMBOK suggests that determining whether to use a formal work authorization system is a question of balancing cost against use. If putting a formal system in place will take too long or will actually be a cost that the project must support, there certainly will be times when verbal authorization will be used. Verbal authorization is used most often in smaller projects where a formal work authorization system may be too costly or complex to install.

Basically, a WAS is in place to issue work requests, or task orders. It is typically seen as an extension of the project schedule, which often carries within it a work breakdown structure. The work authorizations take the task lines in the WBS and may further delineate them, breaking them down into smaller, directly assignable tasks. The core of any WAS is a task catalog. This is the master list of tasks that will need to be assigned over the course of the project. The job of project management is to reference the catalog, assign tasks to the right people, monitor their progress, and then follow up with further assignments until the contents of the catalog have all been accounted for.

For project managers to whom the idea of a WAS sounds appealing, who think it may hold promise as an aid to better project management, here are ten steps to consider including in the system.

1. **Think independence.**   WASs are *not* in place to promote micro-management, although some people see them that way. They are instead a tool for organizing work and accounting for its completion. More informed views probably see these systems as promoting independence combined with visibility, two desirable cultural traits. So in designing the system, the notion of independence should be kept in mind. The flow of the system (as described in the following steps) works best when it provides for the strategic issuing of work, followed by the freedom to attend to it coupled with periodic checkups.

2. **Start with the WBS.**   The project's WBS is an excellent organizing mechanism. It identifies all of the major tasks a project will need to address and attempts to place them

---

3   Rudd McGary, *Passing the PMP® Exam: How to Take It and Pass It*, Prentice-Hall, 2005.

in a logical order (for more on this topic, see Chapter 6, "Strip Board the Script"). Many project managers use the WBS as the foundation for creating the schedule. It should also serve as the foundation for the WAS's catalog of tasks that will be managed. The following chart presents five points of detail that should be considered in establishing this catalog.

Project tasks that need to be completed	Look to the WBS, and from it, extract—or derive as necessary—the catalog of tasks that will need to be addressed for the particular phase of the project you are managing.
Sequence for completing required tasks	Sort and order the tasks into groups or families, linking related ones and ordering dependent ones.
Documents and/or deliverables that need to be developed	Identify what deliverables (outputs, work products) will be required for each task, and document them.
Methods of tracking project progress	Define how project management and members of the project team will track the progress of outstanding work authorizations: points of contact and review, methods of status reporting.
Required approvals for authorizing work	Authorizations have authority only when they come from the recognized leaders. Identify who these people are for each kind of authorization to be used, and then provide avenues for their review and approval of the forms.

These points are put into practice in the subsequent steps.

3. **Use a recognized form.**   Some type of authorization form needs to be established for the WAS. It can be electronic or paper, whatever suits the team best. But one standardized format should be chosen so that it becomes recognizable across the team as an official and familiar form for assigning work. Following are some common data points to include on the authorization form developed for this purpose.

Project-identifying data	General project-identifying data, such as project name, project manager, department, business sponsor, and so on
Task name	The name of the task being assigned (usually taken from the WBS)
Task description	A description of the work that needs to be done, with as much detail as necessary for the owner to proceed effectively.

Related tasks	Other tasks that may have dependencies linked to this present task
Owners	The names of the team members who will be responsible for executing the work
Contributors	The names of the team members (or other stakeholders) who will contribute to the work
Start date	An estimated start date for the work
End date	An estimated end date for the work
Deliverable	A brief description of the main deliverable that will result from the effort
Verification method	A brief description of the acceptance criteria that will be used to evaluate the suitability of the deliverable

4. **Align complementary tasks.**   When the work catalog has been established with the help of the project team (see step 6), take time to sort and organize the work into logical or connected units. Keep in mind factors such as dependencies, level of effort, technical focus, criticality, and so on. The shape the catalog takes does not have to exactly jibe with the schedule so long as the end result of one does not negatively affect the other. The goal here is an appropriately prioritized order of work, so that one session of authorizations will naturally lead to subsequent sessions.

5. **Assign based on qualifications.**   In Chapter 7, "Staff to the Genre," we saw the importance of staffing a project team with skilled, qualified people. The practice of throwing bodies at a job (although it sounds silly, it is nevertheless common in the IT business) is rarely effective. The value of a WAS can be enhanced when it is filtered through a careful assessment of available resources. That is, assign tasks from the catalog with an appreciation of who is available to receive them. Certain tasks that may have high importance but require skill sets that are otherwise committed might be better left until later. Project management should work with members of the technical team to ensure that the right work is assigned to the right people. (There's more on this in the next step.)

6. **Shape the work with the help of the team.**   The purpose of the WAS is to manage a catalog of project work so that piece by piece, its contents move from a status of pending to a status of complete. Because this work is technical, project management should engage the help of the team—or at least the team leads—in identifying and organizing the distribution of this work (as covered in steps 2 to 5). The team members can provide the technical insight so that the assignments make good sense not only from the standpoint of the project's overall parameters (schedule, budgets, and so on) but also from the standpoint of technical and development efficiencies.

7. **Monitor.**   All project managers know the value of status meetings. With this step, the value of status meetings can be more fully realized. Here's a common current deficit: People attend status meetings to find out how things are going, project managers included. Work authorizations constitute a great mechanism to know how things *should* be going; status meetings can then serve to verify that understanding. The outstanding authorizations can form the basis of each meeting agenda. Linking the authorizations to status meetings is not absolutely necessary, however; it's merely a convenience to do so. The real point is to monitor the progress of each authorization to ensure that the work at the incremental level is proceeding as planned. If it is not, adjustments can be made. If it is, then a reasonable assumption is that the larger project goals and objectives are probably being met as well.

8. **Verify.**   When the task lead is ready to turn in the finished work, make sure there are acceptance criteria against which the quality of the work can be weighed. Then conduct a formal inspection process to apply these criteria to the work. Naturally these criteria and the procedural steps used must align with the type of work produced. System code will require a different approach from, say, a technical design. But the intent with regard to both is the same: not to close out a particular authorization until the team can confirm that the work is suitable for movement farther along in the production process. Sometimes this may call for formal testing, sometimes for a peer review. Select the approach that best matches the kinds and varieties of items being built.

9. **Measure.**   This is a small step but an important one. Its value will show itself in future projects. Here the project manager records the performance of the task not in terms of product quality (what was built during that task) but in terms of management quality (how well it was planned). The project manager typically will note measures such as planned duration versus actual duration, planned resources versus actual resources, size of the deliverable, and so on—in short, the kinds of measures used to indicate project performance as a whole. With accumulation of these measures over time, they can be relied on as a basis for future project planning and task allocation activities.

10. **Repeat.**   Follow the cycle around again. With that set of tasks completed and verified, get back together with the technical leads and return to the work catalog. Examine it against the project's current status and determine which new assignments should now be made. Bring them down, create the proper work authorizations, issue them, and move forward. On moving through this process, cycle after cycle, the catalog will grow smaller over time as verified deliverables accumulate. That's as good a marker of project progress as one could hope to have.

These ten steps outline an approach that can be used to implement a WAS in the IT shop. A couple of noteworthy points: The WAS need not be complex; its purpose and intent are very straightforward. But in order for its value to be realized, the system will have to be followed. Project management will need to use it as the central tool for assigning, tracking, and verifying work tasks. So the system will have to be strategically managed; the way work is grouped, ordered, and parceled out must be in close harmony with the functional, schedule, and budgetary parameters of the project. For project managers, however, this is not a new consideration. So implementing some type of WAS may feel like a logical and natural extension of general project management duties. Implementing an effective one will take any project a long way toward a successful outcome.

Benefits of a Work Authorization System

As noted earlier, the project manager can choose to implement a WAS that is robust and broad or can select one that is light and streamlined. Both can make project management efforts more effective, precise, and timely. Three key benefits, summarized next, can be realized through the conscientious use of a WAS, no matter what its shape or size.

- **Clarity of assignment** Use of a WAS will help make clear who is engaged in what work across the project life cycle. Through committed use, this clarity will be realized at three points. Inside the team, members will understand how tasks have been distributed; therefore, each will be better able to integrate and communicate with other relevant teammates. The customer will have access to information that demonstrates task-level control over the project; this information can be used to support status and progress reports, as well as to demonstrate the impact of change. Project management will be better able to manage performance in relation to specific schedule, budget, and resource targets through insight into incremental accomplishments set against a backlog of work.

- **Visibility of the work** Backlogs of work that remain invisible to many project stakeholders can begin to seem overwhelming after a while. A WAS can help reduce that concern. It makes work visible, and once it's visible it becomes less daunting. The system does this on the front end by providing a catalog of tasks derived from the WBS that will need to be parceled out. Scope becomes visible to all. It maintains this visibility through explicit assignation of the work to identified parties. Project managers, customers, and technical team members all can follow the work if they wish as each component passes through the production process.

- **Accommodation of the work** If it's not clear who is handling the work and the work itself is not visible, then it becomes difficult to judge whether all the work is being accommodated. Invisible, unassigned work can easily fall through the cracks. Adoption of a WAS helps prevent such adverse outcomes. Through task visibility and clarity of appointment, project management can ensure that all the work is being accounted for, that it is indeed being assigned and addressed. Moreover, project management will be able to report this status in concrete, tangible terms, on as regular a basis as may be needed by different stakeholders.

Clarity, visibility, and accommodation: These three traits may define the ultimate job of project management. Ensuring that all three are present on a project will significantly reduce the risk of schedules drifting, budgets inflating, and scope creeping. Just as call sheets marshal the forces of a production crew to address the work at hand, IT shops can use WASs to manage the identification, dissemination, and tracking of specific development tasks.

Case in Point: Palter-Taft Technologies

Palter-Taft Technologies (PTT) designs and manufactures navigation controls for specialized avionic systems. A big part of that work is developing software and then configuring it within hardware components. In some ways, PTT may have an advantage over typical corporate IT shops. The configurability of its product line is limited to some extent. On the other hand, the complexity and sophistication of its development demands—how to guide multimillion-dollar airplanes in flight—mandate broad control over every detail of the work. PTT's project management methodology is designed to help with that charge. One tool of the method is the use of work authorization forms (WAFs) as a way to describe and authorize particular work tasks across a project's life cycle. The company has adopted many of the project management recommendations found in the PMI's PMBOK; this is where the idea for using WAFs came from.

PTT's project managers assign WAFs on a biweekly basis. They get together with the technical team leads, look at what work has been accomplished, assess what work needs to be addressed, and determine which resources are most suited to these current needs. They then create authorizations for the tasks they can fit into the current work and resource windows, trying to set each at about two weeks' worth of effort. Once agreed upon, the WAFs are assigned to specific team members, and the members are left free to work them through. The project managers will then use the WAFs as the starting point for their status meetings. Progress on the WAFs traces directly to progress on the project and serves as a bellwether for schedule, budget, and resource performance. The company has been using WAFs for about two years now and reports that this form of work management has been of significant help in tracking incremental progress and meeting more general delivery schedules. WAFs form the basis for mapping out work and for tracking the fulfillment of that work. PTT's project management methodology promotes this; the work authorizations serve as one technique to make sure the work goes as planned and within the parameters planned for it.

For a Deeper Look . . .

- Gregory T. Haugan, *Effective Work Breakdown Structures*, Project Management Institute, 2001

  Haugan offers insight into how to apply the WBS to different types of projects and use it throughout the project life cycle to plan, control and communicate. The book includes WBS principles, structural checklists, and example action steps. At 120 pages, it's a concise, compact guide.

- Richard Whitehead, *Leading a Software Development Team: A Developer's Guide to Successfully Leading People & Projects*, Addison-Wesley, 2001

  Whitehead takes a question-and-answer approach to team management and activity tracking. The book features a lot of information on how project managers can foster efficiencies, overcome problems, lead toward specific goals, and make good decisions—all aimed at getting a project out on time.

- Ursula Kuehn, *Integrated Cost and Schedule Control in Project Management*, Management Concepts, 2006

  This book contains a very detailed look at how empirical controls can be used to manage cost and schedule performance in an integrated manner. Includes sections on defining scope, establishing work packages, addressing risk, and tracking progress. Complete and thorough.

Chapter 12
Ante Up the Completion Bond

Whenever an organization invests in a production system, it must also invest in maintenance of that system. In the IT world, this responsibility falls within the domain of quality assurance—which often is misinterpreted to mean testing in a general sense, although that is more accurately termed quality control. *Quality assurance takes a broader view: It's a form of testing that takes place across the production process, verifying process components as well as product components to better ensure that the final output will meet original specifications. This in-progress testing most often takes the form of quality audits; consequently, many project managers are hesitant to fully embrace quality assurance. They feel that it's an intrusion into their work methods, that they are being judged. Companies that set up their quality oversight programs in a way that requires program auditors to serve as judges or spies have the wrong perspective on the purpose and use of such programs. As emphasized throughout this chapter, the intent of quality assurance is not to be intrusive but to be supportive—to help project teams stay on process, and to provide guidance should they begin to drift off track. Project management will then welcome quality assurance auditors as organization lieutenants charged with helping each team meet its mission objectives.*

Essentially the same approach is used in Hollywood, where it's been working well for decades. For major studio productions, studio executives monitor progress against a production's weekly production reports. They use this form of audit— objectively comparing actual against planned values—as a way to determine if things are moving along smoothly. If they're not, the studio will certainly send someone down to find out what's happening and set things back on track—one way or another. This form of auditing is even stricter with independent production companies. These companies are required to put up a completion bond for each project, and if they fail to make progress according to plan, the bond company has the right to come in and take over the project.

As an introduction to the process of quality assurance, let's take a quick look at how a completion bond works.

Gospel Hill

Every year, each of the six major studios in Hollywood produces its own slate of pictures. Most movies, however, are made by independents—production companies that are in business to find properties, produce them, and then strike deals with the majors to release them. One of those independents is 8th Street Films, which specializes in producing small to midrange pictures designed for very specific audiences—not always the same audience, but always a particular audience. (*The Californians*, *Kids in America*, and *Once Upon a Wedding* are 8th Street productions.) The company's president, Scott Rosenfelt, has just released *Gospel Hill*, a drama starring Angela Bassett and Danny Glover that Scott personally produced. The budget, about $5 million, is well below the Hollywood average of $65 million, but it's still a lot of money. Today I'm discussing that investment with Scott at a small coffee shop in Fisherman's Village on the beach end of Marina del Rey. I get how a studio like Warner Bros. can fund a small picture by leveraging the success of bigger ones, but I wonder how these much smaller companies are able to bring it off. Where do they go when they want to lay hands on $20 million?

Scott outlines the funding process for me, noting that the independents rely mainly on *equity partners*, companies and individuals willing to invest in a production for a large share of the revenues. It takes time to make these kinds of contacts; as Scott observes, the world of equity partners is a small one. You need a good package to pitch, and you need a track record of doing good work. If those two are in place, and the partners have heard of you and your company, you've got a shot at getting your picture funded. *Gospel Hill* had all of these ingredients: a solid story, a committed production team, and a well-known cast already interested in the project. So the financing was not too difficult to achieve.

But there's a catch, Scott says: the completion bond (although later he'll explain that that's not really a catch at all but in fact an aid). Scott explains that equity partners will not just turn over millions in investment dollars clean to a studio—big or small—without some form of guarantee that the picture will indeed get made, and get made according to the script. That's where a completion bond company comes in. The bond company sells a form of insurance—the bond. The bond guarantees that if a production runs over schedule or over budget, the bond company will cover the extra costs needed to see it through. In Hollywood, independent production companies are required by their investor pools to cover each production with such a completion bond. There are no guarantees of box office success, so the investors want at least a guarantee that the product will be completed to compete for box office success.

That's a nice form of insurance, I comment. It's more than that, Scott says—it's a form of partnership. The bond company is more than an insurer; it's also an auditor. One of its jobs is to guarantee that the project or any of its components doesn't get off track, so it keeps a close eye on things, making sure the producer and the team stay on process, follow documented plans, and produce professional output.

The counterpart of this process in the IT world, using ISO, CMMI, and the PMBOK, is readily identified: quality auditing.

Protecting the Investment

Just as there are many independent production companies in Hollywood, there are also many completion bond companies. Some of the major ones are Film Finances Inc., The Motion Picture Bond Company, and International Film Guarantors (IFG). IFG, for example, has put up completion bonds for such mainstream films as *8 Seconds*, *Air Force One*, *Austin Powers: The Spy Who Shagged Me*, and *Mrs. Doubtfire*. As one of the larger of these companies, IFG is actually able to bond projects budgeted up to $200 million. But whether the focus is on big projects or small projects, the decision to bond is never casual. When approached with a bond request, the companies all tend to move along five common steps.

1. **Analyzing the package**   The first thing the bond company wants to study is the production package. This includes the script, the schedule, the location plan, resumes of key personnel, and current financing commitments. From this initial analysis, the company gets an impression of how well prepared the production team is. If the package is solid, consideration continues. But if the preparation at this stage is subpar, a red flag goes up. The company may want the package revised or may decide to may bow out altogether.

2. **Assessing the team**   If the package looks professional and viable, the next step is for the involved parties to meet. The production leads and representatives of the bond company come together to discuss the project and its specific opportunities and risks. The bond company is looking to garner a deeper appreciation for the solidity of the project and to feel comfortable that the production leads have the experience and capabilities to shepherd the project through production. This assessment often entails multiple meetings and negotiations until a decision can be reached.

3. **Contracting for the bond**   When the bond company buys into the project, it sets a coverage fee (usually about 3 percent of the production budget) and prepares specific legal agreements that spell out the rights the company will have as overseer on the project. These rights almost always include the power to cosign on draw-downs (budget payouts), to recommend key personnel, and to intervene with its own personnel should project performance become problematic.

4. **Monitoring production**   Here's the big job of the bond company, its chief responsibility. Once the bond is in place, production is free to kick into gear. From that point, in protecting its investment, the company will regularly monitor production process. It will study production reports and analyze cost reports. As necessary, representatives will meet with production personnel to get further updates. The objective is to ensure that the team is operating within its plans; that it is conscious of and following its commitments; and that it is adhering to recognized production principles (the system) as a matter of professional course.

5. **Stepping in** This last step is one the bond company does not want to take. It means that the production is in trouble, and that its money is now at risk. So if it becomes apparent that particular production goals are not being met, the bond company will move from a review role to a participatory role. It will assign on-site representatives to monitor daily production activities. It will analyze and attempt to mitigate causes for cost overruns or production delays. If worse comes to worst, it will replace key personnel with those of its own choosing—in effect, taking over production from the producers.

The Practice of Insuring Success

It's sort of hip in Hollywood to bash bond companies. But the producers I've talked with who actually have had to deal with them see no reason for the bashing. Scott Rosenfelt, for one, has no problem acknowledging the important role such a company can play in helping an independent production get off the ground, and in helping stay on track once it's in motion. Naturally, no one can sell insurance to protect a movie's box office draw—that will forever rest in the hands of the movie gods. But to this end, completion binding comes in a close second. At a price of 3 percent of budget, it's a wise investment, one that provides objective insight, promotes professionalism, and actively protects quality.

Losing Sight of Process in IT

The studio production system is everything in Hollywood, where it's called the "yellow brick road." Following it will take you where you want to be. Corporate IT development could use its own yellow brick road. Many IT shops have identified such a path: They have successfully implemented project management methodologies and process improvement frameworks. These are used to guide production, ensuring at the least that certain crucial steps valuable to the organization are followed for each effort. Other shops have tried to get to that state but have been less successful. Their programs have yet to take hold across their development teams. And still others have not set a program in place, for various reasons (some demonstrably valid, most probably not). For all of these groups, however, an essential component of every successful management method or approach is the use of quality oversight—a way to periodically audit or monitor project teams to measure compliance with process. Achieving, continuing, or building for success isn't possible without it. In CMMI, this oversight component is called "Process and Product Quality Assurance." In ISO 9001, it's described under section 8, "Continuous Improvement." And in the PMBOK, it's covered under "Quality Assurance." When a shop establishes a project management method (no matter what its scope or maturity) that lacks this component, a number of problems can arise, as described next.

1. **Upper management loses operational insights.**   The line workers are the ones who typically engage most with the project management system. But it is still management that owns the system, and it remains management's responsibility to ensure that the system is meeting the needs of its project teams; that it's helping them meet their various missions. But without some degree of oversight, this understanding is hard to acquire, at least in an objective way. As a result, management will lose insight into certain levels of operational effectiveness. The consequence often is greater difficulty in trying to improve the environment.

2. **Projects may drift silently off course.**   Part of the purpose of quality oversight is to identify opportunities for improvement through observation. Another purpose that's just as important is to help projects stay on track, to follow their preordained paths. In the absence of such oversight, a project may find that it is drifting invisibly off course, that in navigating the specifics of project work, it has silently sailed into unknown waters. When this happens, a project team may find that it is on its own, that it must rely on its own resources and its own innovations to see it through. And that can lead to trouble. Worse, it can lead to trouble without upper management's knowing that the trouble exists. Many project failures can be traced back to this silent drift. The use of quality oversight may not be able to prevent the drift but it can call the attention of others to the problem, often early enough to make correction a simple matter.

3. **Quality and performance standards lose their meaning.**   When process compliance is not monitored or reported in a coordinated way, common concepts of quality and performance lose their meaning. They become open to local interpretation because global definitions are not being driven from the top. What success means for one team may be very different for another; likewise, with operational values; and so on. Quality oversight is needed to foster consistent expectations regarding quality and performance standards. Without it, teams are left on their own to decide what they should focus on.

4. **Organizational capabilities are diminished.**   The real strength of any project management system is that it establishes an "organizational capability" within a development shop. It institutionalizes processes and practices that better ensure organizational success. As an obvious and general example, look at companies like McDonald's and KFC: They have found very successful processes for making Big Macs and Original Recipe chicken, and they don't vary from that, not from cook to cook or from locale to locale or from nation to nation. It's their way of doing business, and all of their associates honor it. Quality oversight can help a development shop establish its own way of doing business. Designed properly, the system will impart a set of best practices to all team members. But without some form of supportive quality oversight, compliance may dissipate over time, unknown to management. The shop will then find itself reduced to reliance on individual capabilities—talent, energy, and initiative—to see its mission through. Its innate capability will no longer exist. The risk is obvious: Lose the individual, and very little may be left.

Hollywood Lesson

The companies that put up completion bonds in Hollywood have very little interest in *making* movies. They simply want the production process to go smoothly, under the assumption that a smooth, well-run process will lead to a professional product. That same thing can be said about IT management: They want the projects they invest in to deliver on the commitments that have been set for them. One way to help ensure this outcome is for project teams to follow the processes and practices that make up the organization's project management system. As with Hollywood's completion bond, compliance with the system won't automatically ensure a quality output, but it will go a long way to promoting the consistency, predictability, and repeatability needed to effectively control quality. With those objectives in mind, one of management's jobs, then, should be to periodically monitor project work to make sure that the various teams are indeed following process. This aspect of project management constitutes the next lesson of this book:

> **Lesson 12:** Support project management activities with a program of quality oversight, one that includes periodic audits, compliance reporting, and proactive coaching and mentoring.

Establishing Project Quality Assurance Oversight

Quality oversight has no official name as it moves into the world of IT. The most commonly used term, however, is probably *project quality assurance* (PQA), a broad term that sits as the support and auditing arm under quality assurance. (That's pretty much how it's treated under CMMI, ISO, and the PMBOK.) The role of PQA is actually fourfold: (1) to ensure that the system (the process program) is available to project teams; (2) to help project teams understand and prepare for program involvement; (3) to periodically audit project activity against the system; and (4) to report on compliance to the project team and executive management. This kind of PQA program can be implemented using five general steps:

- Design and document the approach;
- Perform the audits in accordance with the approach;
- Record results;
- Share those results with the organization; and
- Use the results as a basis for improvement.

Let's take a look at practical implementation of these steps.

1. **Commit to the system.**   A PQA program won't really do much good if the organization hasn't made a solid commitment to the use of its project management system. If compliance is only optional, measures of compliance will hold little value. Executive

commitment may be the single most important requirement for the success of any management program. A PQA program will need to spring from this commitment; it is the logical extension of this commitment. Therefore, shape the program's approach to reflect this commitment. If it's helpful, seek affirmation of the commitment from this layer of management.

2. **Audit for value.**   This is where the PQA program is shaped. The program may be large; it may be small. But chances are that management won't want to audit each and every component. Establish a manageable PQA program by being selective. Work with upper-level management to identify those artifacts and activities that add the most value to a project and start with those; the program can always be expanded later. Focusing on high-value points achieves two things: First, it makes sure that the audit result data acquired can be used as an indicator of general project performance. And second, it's a way to communicate to the project teams high-priority items relevant to the project management system.

3. **Plan the oversight, share the plan.**   PQA audits should never sneak up on a project. Rather, they should be an integral and anticipated part of project activity. A great way to do this is to create a PQA plan for the project. The plan describes what products and activities will be audited, when the audits will take place, the audit procedures that will be followed, and the criteria established for compliance, plus escalation and results reporting procedures. In short, everything a team needs to stay in compliance. By developing a plan early in the life cycle, the project team will understand what is expected of it and be prepared to meet those expectations.

4. **Teach, but don't test.**   PQA programs work best when they focus on the function of coach rather than cop. Moreover, such audits do not go over well when they are designed to test or trap people. Therefore, the program should be built to serve a support role for project teams. PQA is there to help them stay on process, and to help them get back if they move off it. To bolster this purpose, the organization should visibly reward compliance; the program can then be viewed as an avenue to help obtain an award. At the same time, noncompliance need not lead to heavy negative consequences, which would tend to turn people off process, rather than leading them to it. So management will need to strike this admittedly delicate balance according to the shape of the organization. But if the PQA program can begin from the view of a teacher and not a tester, that balance should be achieved easier and sooner.

5. **Share results.**   Some shops treat audit results as if they were secret reports. Others use them as personal leverage, as a soft threat. Both of those tacks are destructive to morale and counterproductive in the long run. Audit results should be treated as common property, open to all. The project team should receive them—and have the opportunity to comment on them before they are finalized. Management should receive them—and use them as a basis for evaluating their own contributions to operational effectiveness. And anyone else who has a stake in the performance of the system

should have access as well. A positive spirit of improvement requires this spirit of openness and cooperation; alignment toward common goals requires a common understanding of present positions. The proper appreciation and use of audit results can push both those agendas.

These are the general steps usually needed to set a quality oversight program in place. Big program or small program, the approach remains the same. Start with executive commitment; shape the program to reflect management values in the shop; openly plan the oversight so that everyone understands it; use audits as an opportunity to guide and support; and reward compliance. Project managers who adopt this approach will acquire the kind of insights into process performance and compliance that can be used as a foundation for future improvement and refinement activities. Figure 12-1 illustrates how a PQA program can be designed to serve the overall improvement needs in an organization.

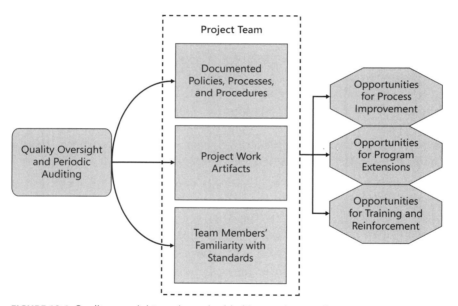

FIGURE 12-1 Quality oversight can be embedded in a project quality assurance program to drive improvements across multiple operational areas.

Benefits of Project Quality Assurance

Compliance is, of course, important for any system. This is particularly true when the system reflects and promotes an organization's mission and values. But compliance in and of itself should not be seen as an end goal. It's just a *means* to a end—the real goal being a desired blend of performance, quality, and economy. A PQA program can help management achieve this goal through the delivery of benefits that complement the strength of compliance. Here are three important ones.

- **Reinforces organizational values**   When the audits performed as part of the PQA program are designed to focus on high-value processes and practices, the kind of re-inforcements provided by the program will help those processes and practices become institutionalized over time. That is, they will become more and more ingrained into the culture of the organization. The PQA program will provide both front-end and back-end reinforcement. The front-end support will come from the PQA plan. This plan lets the teams know at the start of a project just what activities and artifacts will be ex-pected from them. The back-end support comes from the audits. Audit results are used to pinpoint coaching and mentoring needs and to promote future compliance. At the same time, they can be used to identify opportunities to improve the program itself, to better address organizational values. The ultimate benefit is enhanced ability to focus on what's really important in relation to project performance goals.

- **Provides visibility into system performance**   A well-practiced PQA program will pro-vide objective insight into project performance, with particular regard to the use of the management system as an aid to effective performance. The key word here is *objective*. Project management is in a position to provide similar insight. But that view may be clouded by close proximity to a myriad of project issues. Because PQA is more removed from the "heat" of a project, its observations may be freer from interpretation. In this way, the program can serve IT executive management as a great complement to the status reporting and progress assessments that come from line management. In fact, given this objective insight combined with its coaching and mentoring role, many peo-ple view PQA analysts as lieutenants at the service of organizational captains, including project managers.

- **Highlights coaching and mentoring opportunities**   The coaching and mentoring role just mentioned should not be underemphasized. It's a key benefit of PQA programs. Compliance should never be a tug-of-war between management and its team mem-bers. And audits should be neither traps nor tests. The goal is to see practice become habit, and for compliance to become invisible. PQA programs can help achieve this goal by identifying weaknesses and providing the guidance and ongoing support to strengthen performance over time. When this mission is stressed over one of mere compliance, members of the organization are able to see the program as the support tool that it is and become more willing and adept in its application.

As a producer working on 8th Street Films' carefully targeted independent productions, Scott Rosenfelt has experienced those same benefits from a very similar type of auditing program: the involvement of a completion bond company. The 3 percent or so of budget that Scott pays for the overage insurance provided by the bond company brings a degree of stability to his productions, a stability that extends into his investors' comfort zones. PQA, serving an oversight role for upper-level IT management, can up the confidence that project life cycles will follow paths and practices that have been preordained as important by the company.

Case in Point: Pitney Bowes

Based in Stamford, Connecticut, Pitney Bowes is the world's largest postage metering company. It's a global organization with an international client base, so it needs to maintain constant control of changing currency rates and varying postal rates. Much of that control comes from software embedded in its meters, and most of that software is developed by the company's Tech Central division. For the past couple of years, Tech Central has been rolling out a series of standardized processes that deal with the collection, management, and verification of postage and meter management requirements. The goal is to promote the completeness and accuracy of functionalities across the life cycle, so that the integrity of the meter firmware, when installed on the factory floor, is ensured. Early on, Pitney Bowes management understood the need to complement these new processes with oversight into their adoption and use. Accordingly, a process company called Olive was brought in to establish a product-and-process quality assurance program.

The program was designed to regularly audit project-specific activity once the teams had been introduced to the purpose and focus of the program and had undergone process training. Olive also designed the program to produce regular performance reports, which were issued to Pitney Bowes upper-level management. Pitney Bowes saw positive results from the program almost immediately. For starters, the company could quantitatively confirm that its requirements processes were indeed effective. The PQA reports allowed comparison of adoption rates with software defect rates. Sure enough, teams that tended to be higher in compliance tended to have lower defect rates. Moreover, management found that commitment to the process program seemed to grow with the introduction of the PQA program. Visible PQA activities seemed to communicate the importance of process to the organization at large; the ongoing visibility kept it in the forefront of managers' and team members' minds. Finally, the executive reporting provided by the program gave management a consolidated view on pockets of strength and pockets of weaknesses. The company was then better able to apply resources where they were needed to shore up the program.

Pitney Bowles used its PQA program in an optimal manner: not as a surveillance program but as a learning aid.

For a Deeper Look . . .

- David Hoyle, *Quality Management Essentials*, Butterworth-Heinemann, 2007

  Hoyle presents the concepts, principles, tools, and techniques used to establish quality management systems. The book takes a fairly high-level, executive view of the topic, but it's well organized and easy to read. A good look at quality assurance for project managers.

- Daniel Galin, *Software Quality Assurance: From Theory to Implementation*, Addison Wesley, 2003

  This book contains an overview of software quality assurance (SQA) forms, roles, and activities as they relate to software development within organizations. The stress is on SQA application, operation, organization, and control. Includes guidelines for developing the right mix of SQA procedures and work instructions.

- Michael West, *Real Process Improvement Using the CMMI*, Auerbach, 2005

  West focuses specifically on the Capability Maturity Model, but his observations on the concepts and techniques of process improvement, including quality audits and reporting, are general enough to be helpful to businesses operating outside the sphere of CMMI. Written in a plain, straightforward manner.

Chapter 13
Manage the Hot Costs

Six Sigma is a process improvement discipline that's been used by such companies as Motorola, GTE, and Ford Motors to streamline efficiencies and control costs. The program focuses on measuring performance and then using those measures as a basis for process refinement. Six Sigma calls this "data-driven decision making." The PMI's PMBOK, another improvement framework, places a similar emphasis on project management's use of performance and progress data as a way to shape future activity. These data-driven approaches to project management add an extra layer of rigor to the discipline, yet many shops forgo them. Instead, they rely on qualitative management to see them through, whereby experience, intuition, and judgment become the arbiters for decision making. Valuable as these attributes are, they tend to drive action based on perception rather than on fact. Because perception and fact often can lie quite some distance apart, the reliability of qualitative management is hard to bank on. Yet many IT projects are run this way, in accordance with the personal insights of project management and team members. Such "soft" decision making opens the risk for perceived value and performance levels to differ greatly from what's actually happening.

One of the reasons Hollywood projects tend to come in on time, on budget, and to spec is that production teams rarely rely on qualitative management techniques. When a movie's in production, every aspect of that production is regularly measured. Crew times are clocked; purchases are tallied; the number of script pages shot each day is recorded, as is the amount of film exposed. The detail even goes down to ordering a stapler. Every day these "hot costs" are summarized and presented to the producers. The producers compare them against budget and schedule figures to determine the current status of the shoot. The hot costs indicate if things are on track or off track; if the numbers show that they're off, it's a cue for the producers to confer with their colleagues and find a way to get back on track. That's good project management at work. This chapter looks a little further into the use of hot costs and how the same idea can be applied to technology projects as a way to control progress and enhance performance.

The Trailer Next to Sound Stage 4

Center Studios, located in downtown Los Angeles, is a sprawling complex of office towers and sound stages, facilities for independent movie and television production. Upstairs in the center tower is suite T-500, temporary headquarters for the production *He's Just Not That into You*, a romantic comedy starring Drew Barrymore, Jennifer Aniston, and Ben Affleck.

I arrive around 4 o'clock to meet with the executive producer, Michael Beugg. Michael shows me briefly around the offices, pointing out various members of his staff. As I walk and listen, I feel more like I'm in a typical corporate accounting department than in a movie production office. I'm introduced to the production accountant, the payroll manager, a couple of interns, and an administrative assistant. I'm kidding, of course, when I claim to be disappointed: "Pretty unglamorous," I point out. "I hope so," Michael replies. He's *not* kidding.

Michael's office is not in this suite. It's in a trailer outside, next to Sound Stage 4. That's where much of the movie's interior scenes are being shot. That's where the action is, and to manage it well, Michael needs to be close by. We take elevators down and move through long winding corridors until we're in the open air. Across from us are the stages—huge warehouse structures, one after another. A line of trailers are parked in front of each. The street is filled with activity. Crew members from multiple productions move in and out. A small group of extras costumed as Desert Storm troops drink Diet Cokes at a picnic table.

Michael shows me into his trailer. It's outfitted like a mini-office, with a small conference table, captain's chairs, a built-in sofa, cabinets and shelving, and a flat panel screen used for viewing dailies. Again, pretty unglamorous—and completely practical. It's this angle on practicality that I'm interested in. It's my second week in Hollywood and I've now spoken to maybe a dozen producers and studio executives. Only once was I in an office that you might call chic, that looked like the kind of producer's office you might see in, well, the movies. By and large, the views I've been getting are down to earth and business-like. I'm seeing more and more the business aspect of this industry, an aspect that is driven by the need—day to day—to manage, to control, but most of all, to know.

Michael has been pretty successful as a producer. His movies include *Little Miss Sunshine* and *Thank You for Smoking*. His background is a little different from that of the many producers who have worked their way up in the business through one of the trades. He has an MBA from Stanford. He laughs lightly when he says he doesn't spread that around. If people have to know that he went to grad school, he hopes they assume it was for theater.

Of course, I'm very interested in the business administration side of his job, particularly practices that deal with staying on budget. As mentioned earlier, Hollywood has an impressive record for bringing projects in on time and on budget. And the vast majority of these are not small projects. They involve hundreds of people over many months, moving easily through 40, 60, 80 million dollars. What's the trick?

A Cool View of the Hot Costs

"Trick" is the wrong word. Michael explains that there is no trick, no mystery to the method. Producing has its complex side, especially when it comes to motivating and directing large, disparate teams. For the budget, however, with its own large and disparate elements, the management techniques turn to simple and basic. First, he says, you need resources that specialize in budget management and are dedicated to this task for the life of the production. Michael's immediate team consists of production supervisors, production coordinators, and production accountants. They work to establish, monitor, report on, and—as necessary—adjust all spending activities.

If there is a trick, Michael concedes, it would be to manage the "hot costs." *Hot costs* are tallies of the daily expenses that go into production. Out of tracking these expenses come all of the controls needed to hit budget objectives. Michael's team uses these data as the basis for developing five regular reports to ensure that these objectives remain in everybody's sights. These five reports vary in content, source, and frequency.

- **Daily hot costs**   This is a listing and summary of all expenses incurred for that production day. It is line item–based and ties directly back to the budget. It is used to generate to-date totals and variances from expected positions. The report is highly detailed: It summarizes everything from labor times to food costs down to outlays for copier paper.

- **Daily production report**   This report comes in from the set. It summarizes the progress of the production crew. It lists what scenes and script pages were completed, how much film was exposed, how many takes were made, and how many takes printed. It contains a sound report from the sound crew. It also contains information on meal times and meal penalties, as well as summaries on the use of extras and associated costs.

- **Daily call sheet**   This is a planning tool. It details all activities for the upcoming day's work, and from this, the producer can calculate what that day should cost.

- **Weekly cost report**   This is a weekly summary from the daily hot costs. It presents spending totals of the week's work and contains to-date running totals that are then compared back with the budget. Weekly cost reports are sent by the producer to the studio, which uses these reports as a key tracking tool.

- **Weekly projection**   This is a projection of what expenses are most likely to be incurred in the coming week. Although the call sheets can serve as a basis for the projection, the strip board and the shooting schedule are also used.

The Clock Is Running but the Camera Ain't

That's a prototypical Hollywood producer observation. And it's always followed by a question: Why? If the clocks are running but the camera isn't, then nothing is getting made, in a very expensive way. We saw in Chapter 8 ("Budget to the Board") the emphasis Hollywood puts on budgeting. The script is important, the schedule is essential, the creative team is cherished—but the budget is king. It wraps around everything and constrains everything as needed. So production management pays particular and steady attention to anything that has potential impact on the budget. In fact, the studio production system itself would probably not have evolved as it did except for the fact that movie making is so expensive. The system is a money management machine as much as anything. And it's the job of the producer's unit—the production supervisors, managers, and accountants—to keep that budget focus in place, on top of the whole show. A producer's ability to make the budget work—or rather to work to the budget—can make or break a reputation. That focus is achieved by a systematic estimation process in preproduction, one that establishes a budget all key parties can agree to and work from. It is then maintained by constant tracking, reporting, and summarizing of expenditures, comparing estimates against actuals and adjusting work as necessary to remain in sync with original expectations.

Floating Over the Numbers

Separate, independent studies indicate that today the typical IT project still overruns its budget by about 43 percent.[1] Studies by four prominent research firms show that only around 20 percent of all IT projects ever finish within budget.[2] Another survey surmises that a third of IT projects carried out in the private sector run between 10 and 20 percent over the original budget.[3]

These numbers confirm that the IT world has a difficult time keeping its projects on budget. Why? There are many reasons, many of which are addressed in this book. Here's an obvious one: Project management in many IT shops just doesn't pay that much attention to the budget. Yes, project managers are frequently seen carrying their schedules around with them, or managing their resource lists, or updating their risk and issue logs. Nevertheless, within the sphere of project management, a deep level of benign neglect regarding the budget is common, in big and small shops alike. By contrast, the schedule is very often in the forefront because projects tend to be deadline driven. Resource listings are out in the light as well, because project managers often spend a lot of time juggling resources. Risks and issues get updated because they are aligned with the potential for crisis, which is a prime concern for project managers. But the budget—or, rather, the detail of the budget—is another matter. After the budget is approved, the document often is slipped into the back of a stack of other work and checked only from time to time. Project management doesn't realize the endeavor has gotten off track spending-wise until something prompts a reaction to the overage.

What's the source for this soft focus on budget management? Why do we who work in the IT business not place this issue dead center at the heart of project management considerations?

---

[1] Tim Wilson, "Affordable IT: Staying on Budget." *Network Computing*, June 3, 2005.

[2] Frank Schmidt, "What To Do When Your IT Project Is Late, Over Budget, and Looks Like It's Never Going to Work." Available at www.renovationproject.co.uk/article.cfm/id/12580 (accessed April 7, 2008).

[3] Bupesh Jain, "Survey: A third of IT projects exceed budget." Available at www.news.com/Survey-A-third-of-IT-projects-exceed-budget/2100-1022_3-6207696.html (accessed April 7, 2008).

Other businesses surely do. A lot of influences shape this condition, but four common, inter-related attitudes seem to silently promote this benign neglect:

"It's out of our control."   It is common in IT shops for project managers to not deal with dollar figures. These are accounted for at a higher or different level in the organization. But this arrangement does not mean that spending activities are thereby automatically withdrawn from project management's view. In fact, the opposite is true. Spending is still very much a part of that view, because the project's other parameters—schedules, resources, deliverables—directly drive costs. When the project manager can assess these parameters in light of the budget, even though its control is not local, the performance of the project can be better shaped to match what the budget will allow.

"No one takes it seriously."   In an IT consultant capacity, more than once I've had upper-level IT executives shrug off my concerns about a project's budget with a casual "Don't worry about it." The implication was that the work was going to have to get done anyway, no matter what the budget said it was going to cost. So the main thing was to concentrate on getting it out the door. In short, management was acquiescing to a budget being driven by the future—yet a budget's whole purpose is to drive the future. This response typically comes from organizations that see themselves as delivery-bound, as judged by due dates. In such organizations, budgeting activities accompany the other planning processes more out of habit than need. The resulting numbers are not taken seriously because from the outset, no one places much faith in the stability of the project's scope, or in the consistency of existing development processes, or in the company's ability to forecast accurately in the first place. And if project management has gotten away with it pretty cleanly in the past, why start worrying now?

"It's gonna change anyway."   Some IT people think that because a budget may be open to regular change, it's not worth managing. They have probably struggled in the past with budgets that weren't formally approved or baselined or version controlled. In such instances, budget management can become a nightmare. But the mere possibility of difficulty does not constitute a reason to forgo it. The way to avoid the nightmare of constant budget changes is to circumvent the confusion in the first place: through collaborative budget development, thorough stakeholder reviews, formal approvals, and tight change control.

"It's only funny money."   I recently worked with a major clothing retailer whose IT division does not charge back its services to corporate. Upper management views IT as a traditional part of administrative overhead, so IT activities simply represent a cost of doing business. As a result, project budgets mean very little to stakeholders. It really *is* funny—a set of spreadsheet numbers that merely pass from here to there. Surely many companies operate this way, however, so the solution is not to change this accounting practice but to remove it as an excuse not to pay close attention to the budget. As "funny" as it may be, it still retains, even in those environments, power as a barometer of effective performance.

These kinds of excuses do not fly in Hollywood, where it's all about the money. Accordingly, a slew of reporting avenues have been designed to monitor and control this money so that projects can meet their budget goals. This approach constitutes the 13th lesson of this book:

> **Lesson 13:** **Track and manage budget activity** through a prescribed series of regular status, progress, and cost reports.

Managing by the Numbers

As noted earlier, Six Sigma calls management by the numbers "data-driven decision making." This project management tool has at its core an array of mechanisms for gathering and categorizing data. Budget control in Hollywood is almost a paint-by-numbers activity. The tracking and reporting mechanisms are well set into place. Tools like Six Sigma use the same approach, and IT projects will be well served by use of a similar approach. The following six tips can be used by the project manager to move the IT shop toward a position in which a key ingredient to effective budget management becomes a matter of data collection and analysis.

1. **Leverage executive and stakeholder commitment.**   Budget management that is driven by a dependable flow of data into project management requires executive commitment. A good way to obtain this commitment is to leverage the budget approval process and upper management's acceptance of the baseline budget. Subsequent management can (and should) spring from that baseline. This is also the right time to expose management and key stakeholders to the budget reporting stream (see the next tip). In this way, a cross-management focus on the budget will be established early on in the project, typically at a time when it is most visible. Subsequent management activities will ensure that it remains visible—and familiar—across the life of the project.

2. **Establish consistent metrics.**   Here's the key to effective budget management: the consistent use of meaningful expense and cost data. The basic intent of budget management is to generate a set of reports that can be used regularly to track budget activities, with the goal being to stay within accepted budget parameters. Achieving this goal will require a close look at the organization and the kinds of projects it undertakes, followed by determination of the metrics that will deliver management control.

Here are some core cost report line items that usually warrant tracking:

- ❏ Key personnel work hours
- ❏ Ancillary personnel work hours
- ❏ Capital expenses
- ❏ Supplies
- ❏ Outside services
- ❏ Inside services
- ❏ Facility and overhead allocations
- ❏ License fees

These expenses typically are summarized in various kinds of reports:

- ❏ Weekly cost reports
- ❏ Milestone-based budget summaries
- ❏ Project closeout budget summaries

3. **Work from the budget.**   Manage the work as if the budget matters. In dealing with work authorizations, resource assignments, scheduling, and other project tasks, begin with an assessment of the budget. In the planning path described in this book, establishing the scope comes first; analysis of that scope reveals a logical work breakdown, leading to schedule and resource allocations—from this final step, the budget is born. Now manage back from that point. Assess with a view to adjusting cost only when other views concerning schedules and scope prove impractical. Making the budget the first consideration in dealing with such change will allow better control of the budget, as well as protection of other key project parameters.

4. **Distribute the data stream.**   Budget management should be seen as a team activity, the same way it is in Hollywood. Key project roles should come predefined with the reporting obligations that each role is responsible for. The project manager should not be alone in this. Think of roles like senior architect, programming lead, test lead, and technical writer—they all manage large sections of project work, so they all have a hand in budget distributions. It's a good idea, then, for key resources to regularly report to project management with data concerning their activities. When teams are set up this way, with everyone contributing to budget status right from the start, big jobs are made more manageable, and the numbers received from across the teams give a finer picture of budget status and movement.

5. **Live with the budget.**   Pull out the schedule, the resource matrix, and the risk and issues log. Now lay the budget on top of all of these documents. It's possible to drive the effective use of all of those other tools by making budget control and assessment a cornerstone management activity. If the first consideration with a specific effort is what it might do to the budget, then project management can address the schedule and resources, and any risks attached, to keep the budget intact, or can reshape it as appropriate. That's why it's important to live with the budget as a key project artifact. Refer to it regularly in the following contexts:

- ❏ Planning reviews
- ❏ Status meetings
- ❏ Milestone meetings
- ❏ Re-planning meetings
- ❏ Progress reports
- ❏ Performance reports
- ❏ Strategy meetings
- ❏ Lessons learned sessions

   Handle it always in the forefront and with the attitude that it will change and will need to be adjusted, but with an appreciation that that reshaping will need to cleanly reflect the evolution and status of the project at large. Project managers who achieve that aim have accomplished most of what people expect of them in that role.

6. **Tout your performance.**   Make your project's budget results a key part of project closeout reporting and lessons-learned activities. Raise its visibility as high as you can—even if the results are not what you would have liked to see. This will help the organization at large pay more attention to the budget and thus to the budgeting process and budget management activities. Although this path may point out a few embarrassments, appreciate that it's meant to. Take it instead as a means to making budget management one part of your project management system that is continually being improved. Figure 13-1 below depicts how these steps might be formed into a basic process flow.

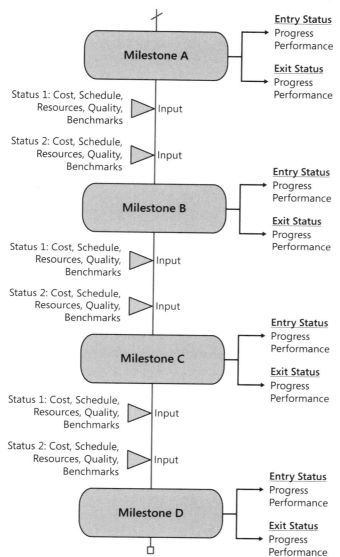

FIGURE 13-1 Adopting a numbers analysis view of budget management leads to greater stakeholder buy-in and more accurate status and forecast reporting.

Benefits of Managing Through Measures

Simply put, the best way to control a budget is to pay attention to it. And the best way to pay attention to it is by careful analysis of the numbers that go into it and spring out of it. Reports that summarize such activity will be useful to many stakeholders across the life of the project. But through this concentrated focus on budget management, project management and upper organizational management should realize a set of specific benefits, ones that not only target their capacity to control spending in the present but help to more accurately forecast spending commitment in the future. Here are four of these benefits:

- **Meaningful status reporting**   A red, orange, or green status indicator on a status report may be a convenient visual cue but doesn't really communicate much about status. And descriptors such as "all's good" or "right on target" or "things look to be slipping" reveal little cause and less actuality. Back these forms with data, however, and they begin to mean something—convenience combined with depth, summaries projected from detail. Meaningful status reporting is crucial to reliable status reporting, and that's what managing by the numbers can provide. And it makes concrete analyses (such as earned value analysis) possible.

- **Data-based forecasting**   Status reporting is important because it tells where the project is at the moment. But the job of project management is to do more, to forecast where the project ought to go. Without data to drive forecasting, projections can't help but fall to subjective limitations. Success is possible with use of techniques like judgment and intuition alone, but outcomes in such instances invariably involve a certain degree of luck, which can't be counted on. A better path is to manage by the numbers as a way to bolster judgment and intuition, to give them added dimension. The use of data delivers the ability to predict in a much more rational manner, one with a decision path guided by logical and empirical objectivity.

- **Better decision analysis**   A business adage states: "It's better to know you know than to think you know." Knowing makes it easier to answer questions like "How did we get here?" and "Why did we do that?" Managing budgets by regular analysis won't solve all budget problems, but it will provide a firm basis for making certain decisions, and it will clarify why other decisions were made along certain lines. That kind of tangible rationale can be a great learning tool. It's a way to make decision analysis in the present both objective and concrete while establishing a potential decision analysis repository that can be used to support similar points of decision making in the future.

- **Better future forecasting**   Hollywood is superb at budgeting because it has a long history of paying attention to budgeting. As more technology projects are managed with a focus on budget control, so too will IT professionals see a growing ability to establish and control future budgets. The use and institutionalization of meaningful cost reports will set into place a foundation on which effective budgeting practices can be built and improved.

All of these benefits are at work in the Hollywood system. When I observed Michael Beugg studying hot cost reports, call sheets, and weekly production reports, I was seeing the core of production management at work. None of the bustling business of movie making could have been in progress on Sound Stage 4 had not this activity been quietly under way out in the trailer. It wasn't glamorous. There was nothing glitzy about it. But it provided support for both the glamour and the glitz. That should be a good cue for technology projects to consider adopting a closer approach to budget management, perhaps making it a much more core-based project management practice. For managers who begin to pin their decisions more on the life of the budget as the impetus to schedule and scope, the ability to bring in projects on budget—and also on time and in scope—will be significantly improved.

Case in Point: Micronetix

In the late 1990s, Micronetix was a software company specializing in client tracking systems for county and state agencies. The company had development contracts with various human resources divisions in Georgia, Rhode Island, and Washington when it landed its largest account, a health records management system for the state of Texas. The development phase was slated to run 14 months, with a series of periodic payouts set across that schedule. The two owners of the company were pretty astute when it came to designing automation solutions, and they had a crack team of technicians working for them. But they were project management novices. Faced with this really big project, they moved from their development lead roles into management oversight and set about learning just what project management was all about. After a few months of work, they began to get something of a handle on it. They were parceling out work in manageable chunks. They were communicating well with their teams and with their Texas clients. And they were keeping a keen eye on the quality of the output. Things looked as if they were going smoothly. Work was heavy but uneventful, and best of all, the client was happy. But a key element was spinning unchecked: the actual cost of running the project. The two managers were conscious of the investment needed to run a job from four states away (Georgia to Texas) but were not overly concerned. The contract, after all, was worth just over $1 million, and the payments were coming in on schedule. In the end, it was the hot costs that got these managers. They simply did not track cash in versus cash out; they didn't count incrementally or assess incrementally. By the client's standard, the project was a success. It came in after a year, on schedule and on budget, and the system worked well. But when the two managers finally looked at what was left at the end of this impressive project, they found that there was practically no money to show for it. They had not realized it moving from month to month, but the project's hard costs just about equaled the budget. What should have resulted in at least a modest windfall for Micronetix turned out to offer little more than a moment of pride. When their accountant tallied it all up, the number in the profit column was not much to look at. What could they do? Just one thing. They wrote out two checks, splitting $404 between them. I know this all quite well—one of those checks was made out to me.

For a Deeper Look . . .

■ Lawrence Putnam and Ware Meyers, *Measures for Excellence: Reliable Software on Time, Within Budget*, Prentice Hall PTR, 1991

The authors target the management of small- to medium-sized software projects, with an emphasis on progress control through the use of regular measurement. The book includes practical techniques for performing software estimates, productivity measurements, and quality forecasts and then describes how to track these as they unfold across the life of the project.

■ E. M. Bennatan, *On Time Within Budget: Software Project Management Practices and Techniques*, Third Edition, John Wiley & Sons, 2000

The focus of the book is presenting tips, techniques, and best practices that have proved useful for completing software projects on time and within budget. Includes lots of real-world case studies and examples.

■ Donald J. Reifer, *Software Management*, Seventh Edition, Wiley-IEEE, 2006

Now in its 7th edition, *Software Management* provides pointers and approaches to deal with the issues, challenges, and experiences that shape overall project management performance. The book provides insight into specific management tools and techniques that work to align schedule, resource, and budget expectations. It also addresses the skills, knowledge, and abilities that project managers should possess to operate effectively in this domain.

Chapter 14
Cut as You Go

When IT projects get into trouble, the contributing factor that's most readily identified is defects. Having to fix defects is the major reason why schedules and budgets get extended. Rework almost always necessitates new cycles of definition, development, and verification. Most IT shops rely on testing activities to uncover defects. At the same time, most IT shops treat testing as an end-of-cycle activity—that is, one that occurs near the end of production processes. The trouble with this approach is that defects aren't discovered until late in the game, when there may not be adequate time or resources left to address them all. Furthermore, when discovery happens late in the process, the true depth of the problem may be only partially uncovered. The visible failure may hide a deeper-level defect yet to be found. This problem is particularly common when "waterfall" life cycles are used, but they can appear in any life cycle in which testing is treated as a separate responsibility, distinct from development. This risk is easy to see in movie production, in which testing means editing. If the editing isn't begun until the shooting is over and the cast and production crew have disbanded, the post-production team has to live with whatever it's got, good or bad. And if the footage hasn't been carefully screened to that point, it might not be enough in terms of both content and quality. That's why editing begins early on in the production process. Editors begin cutting scenes together as they are shot, ensuring that the various shots fit together into scenes, the scenes into sequences, sequences into acts, and the acts into a full movie. The philosophy at work here can be directly applied to IT projects in the form of early test planning and iterative test execution. That's what we'll look at now in this chapter.

Way Down East

Most people associate film editing with post-production. This is a pretty valid association because most of the editing that gives a picture its final look, shape, and feel happens then. During this phase, the editor and the director are at last able to work together, generally un-distracted, to make their vision real. But the job of editing begins long before post-production. The editor is a key hire who gets involved early on in the project, usually in preproduction planning. Editors need to have the same understanding of the scope, mood, and design of a film that the director of photography has, or the production designer, or the stylist—perhaps more so, because of the specific impact of how a movie is cut on the audience's percep-tion. Recognition of the importance of on-the-go editing is not a recent development. When D.W. Griffith made the silent screen classic *Way Down East* in 1920, he had to shoot a climactic chase across a frozen river broken by ice floes. He knew he'd have to match action from shot to shot; otherwise, the chase would lose its dramatic punch. So he brought his editors—James and Rose Smith—out on location with his company, and in a shack in the dead of Connecticut winter he had them develop and rough cut footage as it was shot. It's the same in Hollywood today, except that now the shacks are insulated and have wheels. Editing is a vital part of production, not just post-production, for very practical reasons.

Cutting to Ensure Increase

Take Gus Van Sant's 1998 remake of Alfred Hitchcock's *Psycho*, for example. That was an *exact* remake of *Psycho*, shot for shot, angle for angle. Van Sant needed his editor on set practically the whole time, working right next to him. They had to keep confirming and re-confirming that what they were getting through the lens was a mirror of what Hitchcock had gotten 38 years earlier.

I hear this anecdote from Jim Behnke, a producer who's just worked on another very exact remake: *Omen 666*, a redo of the 1976 horror classic *The Omen*. He uses *Psycho* and *The Omen* as examples because they cleanly highlight the important link between production and editing. This link aids in the realization of dramatic vision and establishing narrative drive, but its primary purpose is a business practicality: Integrating cutting with shooting increases overall production efficiencies. In the foregoing examples, there was a pressing need to edit on the go in order to match what had been done already. But two additional drivers are more compelling: The first is hard costs. A production team will be very hesitant to strike a set and move on to a new stage or a new location if they are not comfortable that they've gotten all the coverage they need to bring that part of the story together. Having to go back for "pickups" can be very expensive. The second driver is a simple one: schedule affinity. It simply takes less time to make a movie when the editing begins while the picture is still being shot. To take a pure "waterfall" approach to the production life cycle and not begin cutting until everything has been shot would extend the studio's schedule and leave a heavy bulk of work for late in the game—adding both cost and risk to the project. So editors begin their work of editing early, not late, and always with a view toward the focus they'll apply in post-production, but with a clear charter to assemble as much as possible during production into as polished a form as possible.

Cut, Print, Shape

The technology disciplines conduct testing on a rising continuum, starting with unit testing and moving on through integration, system, and user acceptance testing (with perhaps a dose of regression thrown in for good measure). This same continuum of verification is found on a movie set. To ensure that what's being filmed and put together will do the job of telling the story, the director and the editor (and others) rely on three ongoing forms of review: on-set playback, working with dailies, and shaping the answer print.

On-Set Playback

Jerry Lewis invented video assist in 1960 when he was making *The Bellboy*: He strapped a video camera to a Panaflex movie camera for instant playback, and history was made. Today all professional cameras support video assist. Directors, editors, and performers alike have come to rely on it. They can watch each take of a shot and judge its merits. They usually won't move on to a new setup or locale until they're comfortable that what has just been filmed will work in the finished product. The video playback lets them, in effect, begin to cut the picture in their heads, giving them confidence that they are getting the right amount of coverage.

IT folks can liken video playback to unit testing. It's testing the smallest unit of a movie—the shot—to ensure that it's been properly constructed.

Working with Dailies

For key production personnel, work does not stop at the end of the shooting day. There is still more to do. The film that was just exposed is taken to a processing lab, developed, and then copied to DVD. These DVDs are then screened by the director, the editor, the producers, the performers, and others. This happens daily—hence the term "dailies." They are all looking for the obvious, of course: Is the image in focus? Is the block right? Did a microphone drop down into the frame? But the director and the editor are looking for more. They want to see the potential for continuity and rhythm from shot to shot. When shooting resumes the next day, the editor goes to work shaping this material into a rough cut of certain script sequences.

This level of checking is very similar to integration testing in the field of technology development. The editor takes stable units and glues them together (literally), repeating this process to set major portions of a system into place.

Shaping the Answer Print

As a movie nears the end of its production phase, the editors are now very close to having what's called an "answer print," a complete—if still rough—version of the assembled shots, scenes, and sequences—that is, the movie. This phase of movie production has an approximate parallel in the software and systems worlds: system testing, in which individual components are linked into a cohesive system to ensure that they all work together. It is at this point that the editors and the director of the picture embark on a focused and collaborative effort to apply the fine spit-and-polish: pace, rhythm, unity, dramatic drive, subtle nuances. Elements like sound and visual effects and music also are added in. Here at the final stage of editing, the goal is to shape the picture in its best form for its penultimate purpose: to be screened for the studio. IT people call this presentation *user acceptance testing*. (For more on user acceptance testing, see Chapter 16, "Study the Test Cards.")

Hollywood sees editing as an iterative process. Right from the planning stages, the producers account for editing requirements beginning in production. The use of video assist and video playback, the screening of dailies, assembling rough cuts, and working toward answer prints are activities that are staffed, scheduled, and budgeted, and also discussed with key stakeholders to ensure adequacy. As noted, editing translates to testing in the field of IT—unfortunately, in most cases, not with the same level of attention to staffing, scheduling, and budgeting. Let's take a look at some of the consequences.

Waterfall Ahead

Way Down East ends with the heroine stuck on an ice floe, about to go over a waterfall. In the nick of time the hero arrives, jumps from floe to floe, grabs her up, and whisks her away to safety. They live happily ever after. Over the years, waterfalls have played the role of villain in more than one movie. When it comes to testing for IT projects, the waterfall can be just as dangerous—specifically, in the context of the waterfall development life cycle. In its classic form, the waterfall breaks a development project up into separate and distinct phases—for example, analysis, design, coding, testing, and release. The idea is to finish one work phase before beginning the next, with one team passing on its work to the next. This approach is seen in construction a lot: The foundation guys come in first, then the framers and roofers, then the electricians and plumbers, and so on. That's a sequential workflow, not an iterative one, and it's been known to promote problems when it's applied to technology development.

Separating Us from Them and Then from Now

The waterfall life cycle has been around for years in the world of IT. It's gotten a lot of criticism for its perceived rigidity, and many shops that use it tend to modify it somewhat to their cultural needs. But it's still probably the most popular way to structure and manage a development project. The problem with the waterfall method, particularly from a project management viewpoint, is a separation of job roles. People don't see duties as being linked. They tend to pass work "over the wall" to the next team. Consequently, teams tend to be shaped as us-them alliances, with work that will happen "now" considered "ours" and work from "then" considered "theirs." This division has special impact on testing because testing in the waterfall method tends to be a down-line activity—and when things get crunched, they tend to get crunched at that end of things. Other life cycle models try to take a more integrative approach to project management. Development approaches like RAD, XP, Agile, and Spiral all try to shorten work cycles so that each phase of a project gets to cycle through numerous times. This approach tends to strengthen the testing process. But most shops still wrestle with problems that, if they aren't introduced during testing, inevitably show up there.

The End-of-the-Line Crunch

Waterfall method or not, testing can be a big headache for project managers, especially in an organization that doesn't emphasize test strategies or one that relies, no matter what its method, on late-stage testing. The big risk (the one that tends to turn into the big problem) is "crunch time." With a deadline date that's set in stone and a project that's slipping its schedule, the outcome is inevitable: The project manager has no choice but to squeeze timelines for those end-of-line phases—including testing. The result: poor defect identification and removal and thus rework. When test activities are planned and managed in this way, crunches of various types can be expected.

- **The time crunch** Late-stage testing has a hard time being effective due to an inherent time limitation. By this phase in a project, the schedule is typically running out. It's very common, in fact, that the test time has been condensed in response to extended design or development needs. With only so much time, test teams can look thoroughly at only so much work. A tough choice then arises: Skim thinly over most of the work, or look deeply into a small portion of the work. Either way invites both compromise and risk. (And it most assuredly guarantees rework.)

- **The load crunch** Let's say instead that late-stage testing can indeed be effective. Given the right number of resources with the right experience, the test activities may be able to uncover most of the defects within a software release. But that leads to another problem, one of bulk. So much discovery happening all at once makes it difficult for a development team, which at this point may have been considerably reduced, to address everything that's thrown back to it. Instead, the team is forced to pick and choose among fixes, and management must accept that production defects may very well remain.

- **The people crunch** Even if it's somehow possible to avoid the time and load crunches, a third type is likely to remain: the people crunch. This kind of crunch can arise because testing is not an end-of-line activity—it's a feedback mechanism. The testers feed defect data back to the programmers, who then make corrections as necessary. The problem with late-stage testing is that the programmers—or at least a significant number of them, perhaps the most senior of them—may have been moved on to other work. The architects, designers, and other specialists may have likewise been reassigned. Reassembling them to address defects may be problematic at best. As a result, the team that is available is back to the choice of what to fix, having to accept that not everything can be.

- **Customer confusion** All of these problems lead to customer confusion. In these kinds of situations, the customer has probably not been privy to the specific details of test activities. What the customer experiences instead is a relative instability in the product. Often, customers don't have the experience or exposure to separate the instability into minor and major problems. So, the system will just look broken, and attempts to explain what happened to get things the way they are can be a sore point of confusion. Here's a surefire benchmark: A project that has reached this stage with its customer can be safely categorized as in serious trouble.

Hollywood can't afford these kinds of crunches: time crunches, load crunches, or people crunches. Too much is at stake to allow any of those windows of risk to open. And any significant customer confusion—the customer here being the studio executives—can get an entire movie shut down on the spot. That's why the production system enforces an early and ongoing focus on editing: While filming is still in progress, the editing team is cutting the evolving material, making sure it stands well on its own and confirming that it will integrate successfully later on into the whole. This approach, which aligns cleanly with the importance of testing on an IT project, constitutes the next lesson of this book.

> **Lesson 14:** Ensure ongoing product integrity by the early integration of iterative test activities across the project life cycle.

Integrating an Iterative Test Approach

Chapter 5, "Time Box the Projects," looked at the benefits of managing scope through the use of fixed-development time frames. This strategy promotes an iterative-type approach to construction. It's effective because it allows development teams to deal with manageable bundles of work, instead of a whole barrel load dumped on them at once. Likewise, when testing is set up as a last-phase activity, test teams are again at risk for an overwhelming work load. Unfortunately, this happens so often on technology projects that it's almost the expected norm. But such an approach does not work well. A better tack is to bring the philosophy of iterative development into the realm of testing. Testing iteratively not only helps manage test loads more efficiently but supports more focused and thorough testing, which leads to better quality. Of course, adopting this approach is likely to require some degree of organizational change and, with that, executive commitment. But if it probably will add value to the project management tool kit, here are six tips to consider when setting an iterative approach in place.

- **Establish an iterative strategy.**   To develop a plan of appropriate scope, begin with simple principles and expand as required by the needs of the shop: Build and test. Prioritize functionality. (See Chapter 5.) For my own management projects, I develop test plans for functional tests (driven by use cases), user interface tests (because these are often not defined in use cases), performance tests (load-, stress-, and performance-related), data integrity tests, and security tests. Although developing a test plan of this nature can feel like a lot of work, the payoff is the knowledge that the application is being tested from a variety of perspectives.

- **Plan while planning.**   This means to make test planning an integral part of project planning, one that has a similar degree of the visibility you would give to the budget and the schedule. By default, this will bring testing into the forefront of project considerations. Not all of the detail needed at this point to define test cases and scenarios may be available yet, but it should be possible to articulate the test approach—with its iterative evolutions—as well as what is expected to be tested, who will likely do the testing, when it will probably begin, and so on. The point is not to get the detail complete. The point is to involve stakeholders in the planning process. When project management, IT management, the technical team, and business partners are allowed to understand and shape the test approach, the activities that stem from that approach are likely to proceed much more smoothly.

- **Appoint a testing manager.**   It's surprising how often this step is omitted. Someone within the project team needs to coordinate test activities independent of the project manager. And this is true whether testing will use a big-bang approach or an iterative one. It's critical that someone hold explicit responsibility for managing which tests are complete, which are under way, and which are to come. Just as important is the need to coordinate the flow of defect data and defect resolutions back out to the development teams. In lieu of a recognized test manager, these needs can only be addressed through personal initiative. Admirable as those who rise to the challenge may be, that's a test strategy destined to deliver headaches.

- **Test between builds.**   The whole key to iterative testing is testing between builds. This will require the early involvement of test teams; they will need to know the content and schedules of upcoming builds so they can prepare for them (cases, scenarios, environments, data, and so on). The purpose, however, is not to test to deliver but to test to build. These iterative test cycles will be used to progressively remove defects and confirm functionality, with one cycle building on the foundation of the other. And because the size of the iterations will be smaller compared with a one-time dump, the test activities should move with more focus and depth, resulting in cleaner code (Figure 14-1). Moreover, this can all happen in parallel with development, helping to bring down the wall that can seem to exist between the two teams. The result will be a closer partnership and a better integrated, more reliable end product.

- **Test in layers.**   Testing in layers simply means testing using different audiences. The diversity of audiences brought to the testing table at this point in the project life cycle will depend on the layout of the organization and the specific nature of the project. But the more feedback acquired in moving through the iterative cycles, the closer the product is likely to align with customer needs. Test audiences may include programmers, interface experts, human factors specialists, message and servicing experts, and, of course, customer representatives. For more on this topic, see Chapter 15, "Edit to the Investment," and Chapter 16.[1]

- **Re-plan from test results.**   This is a great project management technique because it can be used to ensure that expectations remain synchronized across stakeholder

---

[1] A good extended discussion about some of these points can be found in Bryan Campbell and Glenn Ray's *Iterative Development Testing Approaches: Managing Iterative Testing in an Agile Development Project*. Available at www.bryancampbell.com/Articles/Test_strategy_long.htm (accessed April 7, 2008).

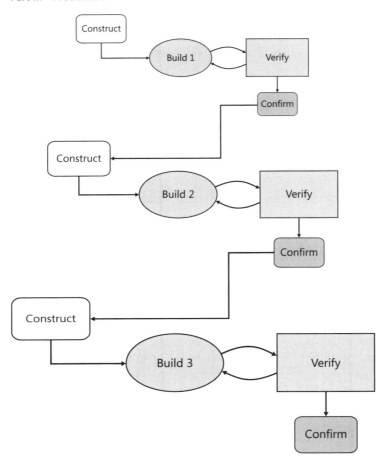

FIGURE 14-1 A strategic iterative cycle of construction, verification, and confirmation can lead to more effective test management and better test results.

groups, who have now become invested in a large part of core production. The idea is to review test results not simply to assess quality but as a basis for shaping the direction of future project activity. For some reason, this step of re-planning is very often skipped during test phases, yet it is not only very useful but wholly appropriate. Even with a fixed deadline date, the re-planning can establish new priorities regarding functionality, new alignments with respect to resources, or other adjustments that may be needed. Including stakeholders in this re-planning process—assessing status, analyzing options, making decisions—will harness agreements and energies to move in the same direction, even in situations in which testing has been crunched past comfort levels.

Those six general points can be expanded to form the foundation of an iterative test approach for a particular IT shop. Each of the steps is driving toward one of three management objectives:

1. Early introduction of the test strategy as a key part of the overall project management strategy;

2. Early introduction of test activities as a way to ensure on-going product integrity; and

3. Apportioning of test packages into manageable, workable bundles.

The evolutionary track this approach supports is illustrated in Figure 14-1.

Benefits of Iterative Testing

Mark Twain once said, "Everybody talks about the weather but nobody does anything about it." To paraphrase Mr. Twain, everybody talks about testing but nobody seems to do anything about it. Fact is, it's not that difficult to address some of the shortcomings found in current test strategies. Because most of those shortcomings are not technical in nature (they have little to do with a team's ability to test) but are introduced through weak project management structures, addressing them is not so complicated. With adoption of some of the recommendations described previously, these shortcomings will begin to dissipate. In their place will be the following benefits, reflecting both heightened performance and (always a relief) increased confidence.

- **Harmony with test performance obligations**   Testing tends to go smoother when it has been coordinated across key stakeholder groups. With adoption of recommendations like the ones described previously, test considerations are introduced early in the project life cycle. This is done mainly through the creation, review, and approval of test plans. Involving stakeholders in these planning activities will establish common expectations of what kinds of testing will be used, and what kind of support each of those test types will require. Reaching agreements about the obligations regarding that support will go a long way to clarifying the subsequent depth and reach of test activities and to harmonizing expectations about test performance.

- **Better defect identification and removal**   Integration of iterative test cycles into construction-build cycles reduces the work load and feature scope of test activities. As a result, testers can focus on smaller units of work, which should increase their ability to spot defects and to facilitate the clean removal of such defects by the development team. Furthermore, the ensuing cycles will give the test team and the development team opportunities to revisit previous work, to confirm that it remains functionally intact, as well as verifying that it remains intact through subsequent integrations.

- **Reduced rework**   If a project manager who is otherwise a raving lunatic reduces the amount of rework by, say, 30 percent, people will shout out: "Hero!" Excessive rework is the main culprit in all projects gone bad. Ironically, thorough testing is often the source of rework; that's how the need for rework is discovered. But needed rework typically is problematic only when discovery happens late. With use of the tactics just described, selectively or en masse, the early detection of issues will prevent larger problems from conglomerating. Problems tend not to become buried or compounded. As a result, the need for major rework when the product is finally being integrated is significantly diminished.

- **Smoother deployments**   There's nothing more embarrassing than bringing something to a customer, plugging it in, and watching it blow up. To one degree or another, this probably has happened to all IT project managers. A solid testing program will help avoid such moments. Through a regular, modulated focus on integration and conformity across the production life cycle, it becomes possible to better ensure that defects and anomalies are identified well before they are passed on to the customer. A cleaner product emerging from production will mean fewer issues when it comes to deployment. Implementations will thus be smoother. Improved operational productivities will more quickly follow.

- **Improved quality**   This is the ultimate goal of any well-managed test program. With use of a well-designed, conscientiously applied program, the product that emerges from the process will inevitably be of higher quality—better integrated, more reliable, and closer aligned to its originating business mission. More important, the customer should find the same improvement. In one sense, the role of project management can be summarized as follows: "Visualize the value." A solid testing program can go a long way toward that visualization. Seeing the mission realized will lead only to increased customer satisfaction.

Taken together, these benefits will contribute to the highest level of the project management mission: quality and reliability delivered on time and within budget.

Case in Point: Public Health Software Systems

Public Health Software Systems (PHSS) was the company that in the 1990s developed immunization tracking systems for state and federal health care agencies, mainly public health departments. At the time, a renewed national focus on immunization rates for preschoolers had pumped millions of dollars in federal funding into various state initiatives, with automation being one of the hottest objectives. PHSS not only had the slickest software for this niche market but had developed it around a core-configurable engine that made customizations and extensions much easier to accommodate. State after state signed contracts for the PHSS system. Even the Centers for Disease Control and Prevention (CDC) showed keen interest. But a testing-related problem was evolving. The three testers the company employed knew quite a bit about recording and managing health records but were technically weak, so they tended to focus on surface testing only. What's more, the development habits in PHSS led to mass throws over the wall onto the testing team, usually full releases at one time. This work pattern further pushed the need to surface test; there just wasn't time to go deeper, even if the testers had been inclined to do so. What happened as a result was that a crucial flaw in the core engine got by unnoticed. It had to do with how data entry screens were indexed in a reference table (the engine managed all screen components as database records). With the indexing off, immunization histories would get jumbled after a table accumulated about a thousand records. Naturally the testers, dealing with simple data sets, never encountered the issue. To them, things looked like they worked fine. The programmers were the ones who could have spotted the problem. Had there been a bridge between coders and testers and had test activities been forged as an ongoing partnership between the two, the issue would have popped up almost immediately: Even a casual glance at the screen tables would have revealed the cross population. But the problem got by and out into the marketplace, and soon systems everywhere began to behave in mysterious ways. The company was quick to respond, and the fix was a relatively easy one. The perception of unpredictability, however, was harder to erase. States lost trust in the system. Competitors' products were being looked at with more enthusiasm. The CDC set up a board to look into the "PHSS situation." There was some negative press. The company got through it, but its reputation took a hit—all because of a basic issue with testing. This case serves to underline the importance of testing as an ongoing and shared activity within a development shop, one that is not allocated as a downstream exercise but rather is integrated as an extension of development itself.

For a Deeper Look . . .

- Rob Cimperman, *UAT Defined: A Guide to Practical User Acceptance Testing*, Addison Wesley Professional, 2007

  Cimperman's text offers an informal explanation of the relationships among testing, software development, and project management. The focus is on helping project managers and test teams better integrate work flows and project objectives. Practical without an overwhelming amount of detail.

- Elfriede Dustin, *Effective Software Testing: 50 Specific Ways to Improve Your Testing*, Addison Wesley Professional, 2002

  This book presents 50 best practices, pitfalls, and solutions centered on effective test management. Chapters look at test planning, test design, documentation, test execution, and test team management.

■ James Shore and Shane Warden, *The Art of Agile Development,* O'Reilly Media, 2007

Shore and Warden mostly focus on the use of Agile and how shops can effectively deploy Agile methods, but they also provide a lot of good information on the need to establish early and active customer relationships during product development. Their book describes how to achieve increased customer satisfaction through ongoing customer involvement.

Part IV
Post-Production

Here we look at topics that center on the end of a project's life cycle, specifically on how project components are assembled, tested, and validated.

Chapter 15
Edit to the Investment

When a motion picture is being cut together during post-production, the editor and the director work as a team. Their job is to physically glue shots, scenes, and sequences together to establish the rhythm, pace, and dramatic tone of the movie suggested in the original script. Those qualities were, after all, what the studio and its executives responded to in the first place; they were the "sell points" that kicked the project into gear. Because that's what the executives paid everybody for, that's what they're naturally going to want to see on the screen. And so the editor and the director work, in this last phase of production, to craft a final product that meets those expectations—optimally, to bring the script to life. As an aid to this task, they create what's called a "cutting continuity" or a "continuity script." The continuity script *is a record of every shot in the film, in the order it's been spliced together. With allowance for some degree of artistic variation, the continuity script is expected to closely mirror the shooting script. In other words, the continuity script serves as a record that can be used to trace the shape of the final product back to the original script requirements.*

IT projects have not just a similar need but the exact same need. Before a technology solution is placed before a business group for user acceptance testing, project management should be able to demonstrate that the components of the solution trace cleanly back to the project's system and business requirements. When this is the case—when such traceability exists—both the project team and the business groups can move forward with confidence that the integrity of the business mission is intact. In the IT world, this domain is called verification—*chiefly achieved through peer reviews. And it includes a set of activities that work to objectively verify affinity with the business mission. This chapter looks at tips and techniques that support the use of peer reviews in the same way that a continuity script is used to support the final mixing of a motion picture.*

The Butcher's Wife

The job of first assistant director is to keep a production moving along according to schedule. The role is very much like that of a stage manager for a play. You can easily spot the first assistant on any picture set. Just look for the camera. There you'll see a team of four or five people: the director, the director of photography, the focus puller, the camera assistant—and the first assistant. The first assistant director is the one wearing the communication headgear, which allows communicating via radio to all of the department heads, providing whispered instructions during shots, and coordinating setups between shots. Whereas the director deals with relatively few on the set (the camera crew, the sound crew, the actors), the first assistant deals with everybody. And in reality, first assistant directors are not assistants to the director at all. Directors are part of the creative team, but first assistants are part of management. The first assistant does help the director in making sure that things are ready on the set, but the real role for this position is in assisting the producer to ensure that everything goes as planned. To do this requires keeping a constant eye on a multitude of production factors. One such factor is the script. Throughout a production day, the first assistant regularly confers with the script supervisors (another management role) to make sure that shooting schedules are being adhered to and that the production is getting the coverage it needs. If that view gets lost—if what's being shot doesn't line up with what's in the script—things can get messy in post-production. And by then, if it's not impossible to fix, it's going to be terribly expensive.

Carey Dietrich is a first assistant director who has worked on such films as *Walk Hard: The Dewey Cox Story*, *Zero Effect*, and *American Beauty*. I meet her in Culver City, at a coffee shop just down the street from CBS Television Studios. I explain that I'm working on the link between post-production editing—how the post team ensures that what's being cut reflects what's called for in the script—and how technology teams can better ensure that their end products reflect the demands of the requirements. She's not exactly sure what I mean about the technology part of that link, so I briefly explain the development-test cycle and how it supports delivery of the kind of solution the customer originally signed up for. That part she gets, so she describes the process the production team follows to confirm that each day's work will add up, all in all, to the movie that's contained in the script. A key part of this, naturally, is tracking the shooting schedule, shot by shot, every day, by the first assistant director and the script supervisor. But other practices come into play. The production team uses on-the-set video playbacks to check performances as they go. They screen dailies each night to check the footage that's been shot. And they edit rough cuts of scenes and sequences while production is still in progress. (For more on this, see Chapter 14, "Cut as You Go.") Combine all these together and by the time production wraps what the post team is left with to put into final form should be ample for the needs of the project. Of course, there can always be a hitch, and to illustrate this possibility, Carey tells me about *The Butcher's Wife*.

The Butcher's Wife was a movie about the benignly clairvoyant wife of a local butcher who subtly influences the lives of everyone in her Greenwich Village neighborhood. The original plot interwove a series of light romantic stories, each with equal weight, each spinning into and out of each other. Carey was the production's first assistant director. Preproduction on the project had gone well. And by the time principal photography began, the design was comfortably in place. Now the hitch: The movie's central character, the butcher's wife, was being played by Demi Moore. Moore had just come off the megahit *Ghost* and was now recognized as a star with major box office draw. She arrived with her own thoughts about how the story should be played out, and because the draw was in her favor, the producers did not stand firm with the original design. Right away, things went into flux. The director, Terry Hughes, continually had to realign his prepared approach to that of Ms. Moore's. That sent department heads scrambling on the set, revamping their own directions. As a result, the video playbacks and the dailies and the rough cuts weren't referencing any baseline, so the department heads did not feel comfortable commenting on them. The collaborative view that is so essential to efficient production dissolved. The result in the end was not so much a mess as it was a conglomeration of work that had to be sifted through and sorted out. "How did the movie do at the box office?" I asked. "It actually did pretty well," Carey said. But getting there had been tough going. Her point was not an assessment of the creative process; it centered on a much more practical observation: All the preview techniques at hand will add only so much value if the key stakeholders are not actively involved in the review process. That was the link I was looking for; in the business of technology development, it's called *peer review*.

Divergence and Discontinuity

A common characteristic of troublesome projects is poor quality. When a team develops something that proves on delivery to be less than suitable for its intended use, the fallout can ripple in many directions: The team may be confused about what went wrong. Resources may have to be reallocated to address the situation. Subsequent planned activities may have to be readjusted. Customer confidence may erode. Poor quality can come from many sources. The most direct one is incompetence, the basic inability to do the work. But in technology development, that's also the rarest. Most people in IT tend to be competent. A more likely source of poor quality is less direct but imminently more common: weak communication. Weak communication has long been recognized as an issue in any organizational design or culture, and many attempts have been made to identify potential solutions. This chapter takes a narrower focus. The focus on communication as it relates to quality actually centers on the issue of formal product inspections. It's a clean assumption: Inspecting a product before releasing it will identify defects to be corrected, leading to a product of higher quality. Coordinating inspections with a team—in effect, applying more eyes to the view—also will cause quality levels to rise. Such "coordinated inspections," then, can be thought of as procedure-based communications, as a type of directed formal communications—often called peer reviews. With peer reviews, a group of related stakeholders follows a defined procedure to inspect a product's attributes, and the group's judgment regarding suitability-to-purpose of those attributes will control whether the product moves forward in the production process.

Numerous product problems are possible with reliance on only incomplete or, at best, informal communications. In the absence of a consensus viewpoint, the accuracy of a product is tough to determine. (Does it truly represent all its requirements?) The workability of a product is hard to establish. (Is its present form appropriate for the next production stage?) The integrity of a product may not be easy to confirm. (Will it integrate well? Is it maintainable?) A well-designed peer review process can address all of these problems and actually prevent their adverse impacts.

Hollywood's use of a continuity script serves as a way to trace the requirements of the original script right through to the finished film. And it provides a running checklist that promotes inspection from external parties. These parties can rely on the cutting continuity to confirm, step by step, that the end product is coming together in the anticipated final form. It drives effective communication near the end of the production process. In the field of IT, such a practice can be used to drive communication and inspections not just close to the end of a project but across its full life cycle, as summarized in the next lesson of this book.

> **Lesson 15: Adopt peer reviews** as a technique for promoting the continuity of quality as project deliverables are developed.

The following section explores how this lesson can be put to productive use.

Continuity of Quality

Peer review is a great technique for providing continuity of quality across the life of a project. Look at any project's work flow. From phase to phase, new components emerge. Just about all stem from previous ones. Most build on each one. If defects or nonconformities slip in at any phase (as they are likely to do) but go unchecked, the quality of the resulting products will inevitably suffer. On the other hand, if work is inspected at discrete intervals, the opportunity to discover quality problems arises. Through such inspections, components can be cleaned before further work or subsequent integration. The first path leads to the usual project problems: iffy quality, rework, vexed expectations. The latter leads to the opposite: verified quality, production efficiencies, and stable expectations. This latter path can be set into place by adopting certain peer review practices and formalizing them into a process. So let's look next at how to structure a workable peer review process in a typical IT shop. The first consideration is the question of what to peer review.

Helpful Reviews

Peer review can be applied to *anything* over the course of a project. But not *everything* has to be peer reviewed. There are no rules regarding what's in and what's out. But some commonsense guidelines are in order here. For example, reviewing too much can weigh down the project team and may make reviews less effective; reviewing too little may cause problems down the line. To decide which products to review, look to those that tend to have the most impact on project success. These are typically products that deal with project parameters (schedules, budgets) and promote product quality (verified functionality). Select review-worthy work products accordingly. By way of example, here's a list of products that mature organizations include under their peer review programs.

- **Plans** Plans establish the commitments and expectations for a project. That's why it's essential that they be inspected through peer reviews. A project may have many plans: the budget, the schedule, a communication plan, test plans, quality plans, and so on. Each describes activities that will drive the use of resources as well as the production process. Before these plans are executed, provide any key stakeholders with the opportunity to review them, reshape as needed, and then share common agreement that they are suitable to the demands of the work.

- **Requirements** Here's another critical piece of work to submit to peer reviews. The requirements are essential to shaping the scope and reach of a project. They document customer objectives and business needs and also capture the systemic and technical functionalities the solution must address. Without firm agreement on the requirements, it becomes difficult for project teams to move synchronously. Peer reviews can be used to establish this synchronicity early on and to maintain it over the life of the project.

- **Designs** Designs have an extremely high impact on the technical success of a system or software solution, so they almost always benefit from the scrutiny of a peer review. The review can be used to verify that the designs are adequate to the needs of the requirements, that they are executable in light of development platforms and standards, and that, when realized, they can be adequately supported in operations.

- **Code reviews** This is admittedly a technical form of peer review but still one that can prove very useful. Code reviews involve examination of system and software code by technical team members to gauge its conformance with development standards, its overall integratability, and its performance with respect to the originating requirements.

- **Test results** Test results reveal the underlying quality of work products. Before work is passed on for further refinement or integration, and certainly before it's moved into a customer's domain, ensuring that it meets an acceptance quality standard will be essential. Peer reviews can be a very effective way to confirm that these quality standards have been met.

Once this assessment has revealed what should be placed under peer review activities, it's time to begin shaping a peer review process.

Shaping a Peer Review Process

Support the organization's need for peer reviews by developing for it a peer review process. The intent of the process is to provide a framework that can be followed when work—and understandings of that work—need to be shared across teams. A good peer review process will support collaboration and coordination. A basic peer review process can work just as well as a detailed one. A basic process will move through eight general steps. Let's take a quick look at each.

1. **Select.**   First, make a strategic decision about two things. For this project, what work products will be put through the formal peer review process? (For more on this, see the previous section.) Then, for each of those products, who will do the reviewing? Selecting the right review groups is essential to holding productive reviews. Such groups typically fall into one of two categories: upstream stakeholders and downstream stakeholders.

   Upstream stakeholders may be people who . . .

   ❏ Provided content for the material;

   ❏ Are affected by a commitment contained in the material;

   ❏ Oversaw production of the material.

   Downstream recipients may be people who...

   ❏ Work with the received material;

   ❏ Will need to approve resulting work products;

   ❏ Will be accountable for the suitability of the resulting work product.

   Look at the makeup of the project's stakeholder groups. Comparison with the attributes in the foregoing lists will identify the best reviewers for the project.

2. **Plan.**   The peer review process should be instituted as part of the project management methodology. The steps in the process should be planned, and the plan executed and monitored (the definition of project management). The plan for any particular project need not be complex or overly detailed, but it should contain what every good plan contains: the who, what, and when of the work. For peer review plans, here's a core set of data to consider for inclusion.

   ❏ The work products that will be reviewed;

   ❏ The stakeholders who will review each product;

   ❏ The expected dates for individual review periods and review meetings;

   ❏ A brief description of the process, procedures, and tools available; and

   ❏ Identification of the process manager and meeting facilitators.

3. **Distribute.**   With the work product completed and the reviewers informed, send out the material to them. This can be achieved by "pushing" it out, as through an e-mail. Or the relevant documents can be "pulled" down from a preset Web site. Whichever path is chosen, it's important to make sure that the material is easily accessible.

4. **Review.**   Once the work product has been distributed to the right stakeholder groups, give them time to inspect it on their own. Here are three tips to make this review period productive.

❏ Allow people plenty of time to review the work. Don't spring it on them.

❏ Provide guidelines for how to critique the work. In other words, let the reviewers know what elements of the work they should be scrutinizing. (These guidelines will naturally be contingent on the type of work product under review.)

❏ Provide tools to aid the review. Most often this is a blank inspection report, a form the reviewers can use to record their notes and comments and rate issues as they appear.

This kind of preparation should ensure that the selected reviewers are ready to contribute productively to the upcoming peer review meeting.

5. **Convene and comment.**   Here's the visible act of the peer review: the review meeting. (Actually, most of the work should come before and after this middle step.) Here everybody comes together to discuss the work according to their review notes. This is an opportunity to ask questions, clarify understandings, raise issues, and generally discuss the quality and suitability of the product. Treat this review as a formal meeting. Ensure that it's properly facilitated, that a note taker or recorder has been appointed, and that attendees have been properly prepped to contribute accordingly.

6. **Revise.**   The wisdom of peer reviewers will help make a project's work products better. Through the act of reviewing, convening, and commenting, the review team will provide a set of changes—some perhaps small, others perhaps large—that can be applied to the work to make it acceptable to all parties. Take this input now and revise the work accordingly. Depending on the extent of the revision, another peer review round or only a quick informal review may be required. Either way, a point close to general consensus and approval has now been reached.

7. **Baseline.**   A baseline is an essential ingredient for coordinated work. It represents the official version of a document. The main intent of the peer review process is to get a team satisfied enough with the state of a work product that it can be baselined. Once it's baselined, the project team can work from it with confidence; by default, it represents the official version of the information at hand. Without recognized baselines, teams may end up working with outdated or unapproved materials, or with current data sets mixed among current versions—typically resulting in backtracking, rework, and efforts at reorganization. With a baseline, people can more readily work in agreement and in the same direction.

8. **Change control.**   This is really the final destination of any peer review process: control of the approved baseline. The process itself provided the steps needed to get certain material in front of a particular set of eyes; from there it was scrutinized and refined for value; and from there its final form was approved. A common consensus regarding this material now exists. Here's where change control comes in. From this point on, any changes to the material should go through a formal procedure that is itself a type of mini peer review: Requests for changes are documented, assessed, and decided on

by duly recognized members of the project team. With adherence to this coordinated sequence, change does not get out of hand and products do not drift out of shape. Through change control, the integrity of baselined work products remains intact. This is illustrated in Figure 15-1.

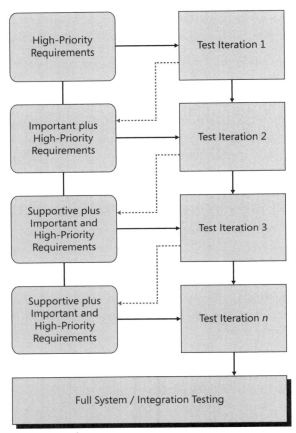

FIGURE 15-1 Peer reviews can be used to ensure that critical requirements are accounted for as project work products evolve.

Benefits of Peer Reviews

Peer review practices are not complex, nor are they difficult to implement. Most IT shops, large or small, should be able to create some form of process that supports periodic inspections. Such a process can deliver distinct benefits to the effectiveness of development activities. Here are three benefits every IT shop can realize by instituting peer reviews.

- **Reliable defect identification and prevention**   This is the driving purpose behind peer reviews. Inspecting work products before they are embedded into or integrated with other work will uncover defects much more effectively. With application of this process over time, the resulting end product should be likewise that much cleaner. Additionally, peer reviews help in detecting potential nonconformities more readily. These are not defects per se as much as they are "disjoints," mismatches that, when paired with other components, may result in operational or interface defects. Resolving these nonconformities early, when they are isolated, will prevent such introduction and likewise lead to cleaner end products.

- **Shared vision**   Here is a great byproduct that comes from conducting peer reviews. Not only does the team have the opportunity to remove defects and nonconformities, but the very act of reviewing the work materials with a collection of appointed reviewers helps establish a shared vision of what the work should be across the team. This goes a long way to aligning scope, progress, and quality expectations. Such alignment is crucial to a project's ability to measure and monitor success. If those understandings are skewed in different directions, there may well be little agreement regarding what success really means, or how it might evidence itself. When they are aligned, the recognition of success becomes much easier to achieve.

- **Work product integrity**   The expected endpoint for each peer review is an acceptable baseline of a work product. That work product's integrity can be assumed because the very action of the peer review is to confirm that integrity is present. A well-designed peer review process will help protect this integrity through formal change control. In other words, baselines cannot be altered without requests for changes being formally documented and (peer) reviewed by an appointed change control body. In this way, the practice of inspections is carried on even as a product continues its developmental evolution.

In Hollywood, the cutting continuity is used by editors to document, in effect, the cuts they are making as they assemble strips of film into a finished movie. The continuity traces back to the script and can be viewed by upper-level production personnel to ensure that the finished work really does adhere to the script. That's a facilitated form of quality inspection. IT shops can facilitate a similar process through the use of a peer review process, one designed to define, coordinate, and manage the inspection of work in progress by qualified and relevant reviewers.

Case in Point: MCI Worldcom

"We'll fix it in production." That's what the development manager of the Local Number Portability (LNP) project said to me in late 1998. Thing was, the development team wasn't even close to deployment. We were still gathering requirements. But the manager, Rudy, wanted to go forward with some preliminary design work, hoping to get a jump on an already aggressive schedule. This was in Atlanta at the Business Division headquarters of MCI Worldcom. Shortly thereafter, the company would file for bankruptcy in a financial scandal that rocked Wall Street. On this occasion, however, the deviation from best practices was of a much more localized nature. The LNP project had been initiated to help customers transfer phone service while keeping their old phone number. We were building the central database that would keep track of all those numbers. Rudy knew the fundamentals of how this database should be shaped; he didn't want investigations into detail to hinder progress that could be made now. By "fixing it in production," he meant that if the design proved inefficient, his teams would revamp the data through production updates. I was a temporary consultant at MCI. Rudy had been there 10 years. I followed his lead, which was pretty much in line with the entrepreneurial sales culture that made up most of the company at the time.

It's possible to run-and-gun on some kinds of projects, but LNP was a different matter. It was a *big* system that needed to interact with similar kinds of systems from other phone companies. Interaction and interfacing: that was the essence of LNP. This kind of scope required a lot of coordinated documentation—which is where the real trouble started. The LNP group was not big on peer reviews. The requirements team would hastily compile one set of functionalities and throw it over the wall to designers, who would interpret it according to their own architectural views; this would then be tossed to developers and testers; and on and on. Meanwhile, the cycle went on, and with more discovery came more refinement, often of work facets that had been already shaped into something of a final form.

This onrushing stream of thin communications combined with a narrow work focus across teams to generate work that was off the mark. Needed capabilities were not represented. Interfaces did not work well. Components did not integrate effectively. Finally, management recognized that maybe this work was beyond the reach of its internal resources. It brought in an outside systems contractor, a specialty company from Canada that had provided similar portability solutions for other phone companies. This company was able to quickly leverage its experience and methodology (they were ISO 9000 registered) to reshape the work for market readiness. I was not privy to the costs this alternate track required, but I did see the frustrations from the schedule delays, and the embarrassment of having to communicate Worldcom's weak status to outside members of the telecommunications community. This unfortunate experience perfectly highlighted the importance of a sound peer review process, one that encourages communications and critical questioning. I made a note to share this insight with Rudy once deployment had run its course. By the time that happened, however, the Securities and Exchange Commission had initiated a peer review of a much different nature.

For a Deeper Look . . .

- Steven R. Rakitin, *Software Verification and Validation for Practitioners and Managers*, Second Edition, Artech House Publishers, 2001

  Rakitin offers a concise and practical introduction to the basic principles of effective software verification and validation. Chapters discuss formal inspection processes, proper configuration management, effective testing techniques, and the use of quality measurements as a mechanism to drive future improvements.

- Rex Black, *Managing the Testing Process: Practical Tools and Techniques for Managing Hardware and Software Testing*, Wiley, 2002

  The focus of Black's book is on the tools and resources typically needed to manage both large and small test initiatives. Emphasis is placed on fitting the testing process into the overall development and maintenance processes.

- William Gibson and Keith Powell-Evans, *Validation Fundamentals: How to, What to, When to Validate*, Informa, 1998

  Validation Fundamentals explores the relationship of validation with quality assurance and how the two can be bonded to build high-quality products. The book covers such topics as testing protocols, certification, validation reporting, and sign-offs. The focus is not on technology development, but the advice is sound enough and general enough for application there.

Chapter 16
Study the Test Cards

In a general sense, user acceptance testing *may properly be seen as the ultimate goal of every technology project: It's the culmination of the technical team's work. Yet for many IT projects, it is a dreaded exercise, carried out in a perfunctory manner and sometimes with reluctant cooperation. That's usually because the project has experienced problems along the life cycle, some of them perhaps introduced by the users. By the time of acceptance testing, then, the project team may have only a tenuous grasp on the integrity of the product and is wary of presenting it as a finished form. Thus far in this book, we've looked at a lot of the potential kinds of problems that may affect IT projects. Scope, resource, schedule, and budget issues all can cloud a team's ability to focus on the job at hand and turn out high-quality, integrated work. But whatever the nature of the problem, the work will always fall into question. In such situations, the results of acceptance testing are almost always the same: Users readily discover defects unnoticed by the team, and when this discovery continues as a pattern, they will quickly assume, no matter what the severity of defects may be, that the product is unworthy and that the team has failed in its mission.*

Hollywood faces a comparable situation: It also works to present a product to its end users, its intended viewing audiences. And it runs the same risk of having its products snubbed if the early audiences don't respond to it. But Hollywood's studios have a way of addressing this, and it's a method they use for every production they undertake. It's called test screening, *but it's more than that name implies: It's actually a process of test design, test preparation, and, finally, testing by screening. And it's an effective way to ensure that a movie is indeed ready for mass audience presentation. That's the subject of this chapter, and we'll see how it can be linked to the practice of user acceptance testing in IT shops. Applying some Hollywood practices to this phase of the project will allow the shop to enter into testing activities if not with full confidence then at least with a solid spirit of partnership among the players.*

Changing the End

Even after a movie has been completed by its production team and accepted by the studio, more work needs to be done before it's released to the public. The studio wants to know that's it got a marketable product. If it believes it's holding a hit, it will be anxious to confirm that. If it thinks it might have a stinker, it will want to know how bad. These are important insights to acquire because marketing a motion picture can be almost as expensive as—and on occasion more expensive than—making it. If things look promising, there'll be no hesitation making the additional investment. But if they look shaky, it may be time to hedge some bets. That's where test screenings come in.

The first step is to recruit the audience. The marketing folks do this with a very specific demographic in mind: the movie's intended audience. Is the picture aimed at young males? Does it target older females? Not a lot of guesswork is involved here. This audience has been known pretty much since the days of preproduction; in fact, the entire movie was shaped to speak to this audience. The marketing folks will venture out to a selection of towns that can deliver that audience. (Las Vegas is one of the most popular because of its constant rush of visitors from all over.) There they'll entice viewers with food and giveaways and prizes as they work to fill the theater. They'll also work to squeeze in some off-target audience members, wanting to get a feel for how other demographics may respond to the movie.

Next, they'll explain what's happening to the audience. The audience members need to know that they'll be part of a test screening so that they'll watch with an appropriately critical eye. Often the audience will be reminded that the film being shown is a rough cut, and that things may change before the final release. The audience, then, will have the chance to supply those changes.

Then the marketing folks will distribute the chief research instrument of the test screening: the comment cards. Just after the screening, the audience will be asked to fill out the comment cards, which are really carefully designed questionnaires. They are prompted to relate how they liked the storyline, how they liked each of the main stars, which minor characters they liked best, and what they liked best and worst about the movie overall. These cards are then carefully collected and thoroughly analyzed, and the results tabulated. Next, the researchers may ask a portion of the audience to stay after for a free-form focus session. This session is a facilitated group discussion in which perceptions and attitudes can be explored more freely. All of the collected data is then used by the studio executives to decide what course of action to take next.

It's not at all uncommon for the results of a test screening to drive a studio to change a movie. Most of the time, the changes are relatively small: adjustments to how certain scenes were edited, varying the screen time for certain minor players, modifying the music. But sometimes they can lead to major changes. *Fatal Attraction*, *Titanic*, and *Mary Poppins* are all movies that were revamped because of response from their test screenings.

That's Hollywood doing the thing it may just do best: listening to its audience.

Working with the User

In the world of IT, the equivalent of the test screening audience consists of the sponsors who commission the shop's development efforts and the users who will put them to work. Typically, however, the role of this IT "audience" is viewed differently. In Hollywood, the audience is always on everyone's minds. By contrast, in IT, the audience is kept at a distance; no one really wants to engage the users until the production process has just about finished. Although this practice is intuitively counterproductive, it's nevertheless popular, in part because of its practicality and convenience and in part stemming from the preference of many users. A typical development shop will usually engage with its users at two points in a project. The first is during requirements definition, when the business and technical specifications are being detailed—at the very *start* of a project. The next point of engagement is when it's time for the users to come in and test the product that's been built—at the very *end* of the project. What's gone on in between those two points may be a mystery to the users. What the users have been up to in that same time may be a mystery to the project team. But to many development teams, this is a practical separation of worlds. IT shops that avoid dealing with customers during the bulk of production do so for a number of reasons. The technical people are often worried that heavy interaction will result in too much change, that user discussions will trigger more ideas to be added into the mix. Or they think that the users will want to meddle in how the technical solution is being shaped. Or they object to the users' observing the team as they work because then it's more likely that they'll get in the way. Such "practicalities" don't hold up well when examined closely but have been traditional aspects of the customer-vendor relationship. Moreover, sometimes the customers like it that way—they may well prefer to go away while the techie-type work gets done and then come back to pick it up when it's finished.

Nevertheless, aside from convenience, "practicality," and preference, what emerges from this approach is a perfect recipe for a classic project management problem: users who are dissatisfied with the product they receive. When the production process is characterized by separation of parties as described, expectations are sure to diverge to some degree. The system that results may look fine to the team that built it; it may even work without a problem. But it might not be what the user had in mind, and if it doesn't match expectations, the discrepancy is likely to be viewed as a fault. More commonly seen, however, is the following scenario: The system that's ready to be tried out is not completely clean; the technical team may even be aware of weak areas that need to be explored. They're hoping that the users, with their business knowledge, can help with the exploring. But the users are likely to see a much different situation: a system so full of bugs (real or not) that it seems virtually useless. How could the tech team have failed so miserably? That's usually when the finger pointing starts—along with the scrambling and the late hours and, with all that, a further separation of parties. That's the classic project management problem, and one that every project manager wants to avoid. Yet it's a pit that IT shops fall into time and time again. That's the subject of this chapter, with a specific focus on the practice of user acceptance testing, that point in the project life cycle in which the users get a chance to take the system for a test drive. It's very much the same as assembling a test audience to preview a new movie. It's an opportunity to see how people like what's been made, and to discover any problems with it that need to be addressed.

Users come into the acceptance testing process primed to see their expectations realized. They are looking to confirm a few basic desires. First and foremost, they want to feel confident that the solution is fully functional—that it addresses all of the features and capabilities they need. They also want to confirm that the system is usable, that it is easy to maneuver and work in. Users will also want to verify that the system, as is, is sustainable—that it will operate efficiently in their real-world, real-time business environment. And finally, they'll want to feel comfortable that the system is solid—that it's been built so that the customer can rely on it and trust it with their business. Meeting these customer wants indicates a good acceptance test. From there, it's pretty certain that the project will be deemed successful. But falter in just any one spot, and the whole perception of the work may change.

Hollywood's practice of considering audience needs early on in production, and then eagerly listening to it before a picture's broad distribution, constitutes the essence of the next lesson of this book:

> **Lesson 16: Establish an approach for acceptance testing** that calls for early planning, regular communication, and cooperative collaboration between users and project team members.

Fortunately, this practice is not difficult to implement. It simply calls for a shop to shape a process around acceptance testing that promotes it not as a well-ordered, final activity but as an open-ended, ongoing early one. Let's take a look.

Listening to the User

It's an age-old business maxim: Make the customer happy and you'll be happy. The nice part about applying it here is that most customers encountered by IT people are pretty reasonable folks. They know that systems may have bugs, or may need to be tweaked, or may need some additional fine tuning. So they don't necessarily mind when such things crop up. But what they do mind are surprises. It's the unexpected that throws them (just like everybody else). And the unexpected is almost always the result of failure of one party to listen to the other. User acceptance testing is a key point in any project's evolutionary progress. My own professional experience bears this out. In mature shops, in which project teams and sponsors are primed to listen to each other, user acceptance testing normally goes smoothly (even when it's not completely successful). In less mature shops, in which similar processes are not in place, user acceptance testing is usually a dreaded activity—and its outcome is a roll of the dice.

A basic process for user acceptance testing is presented next. This process steps through six basic activities that can be used to ensure a more coordinated test event, but it also includes, within the activities, specific actions that will promote collaborative listening—if not for everything about the project, then at least for those activities essential to customer acceptance.

1. **Involve key users early.**   User acceptance testing is all about verification—verifying that the requirements were realized, that the system flows like the business flows, and so on. It's also about coordination, making sure that the test event is ready to go and that everyone knows the jobs he or she needs to do. That's the purpose of this first activity. Make acceptance testing planning an activity that occurs early in the project life cycle and one that is shaped through the direct involvement of key users. These users may be part of the sponsor team; they may be the operators of the system; they may even be champions of the project. Whoever they are for the project, identify them and engage them. Ideally, this should happen in line with approving the requirements. Establishing relationships and beginning test planning at this time will position the project team to effectively tie the testing strategy to the requirements. With the help and input of the shop's users, it's also possible to establish acceptance criteria, which will serve as guide for interpreting test results later. This is a key listening point in this process. It establishes a commonality of understanding that should be supported throughout the acceptance testing process.

2. **Use facilitator sessions to create test plans.**   One reason user acceptance testing can turn into a nightmare is because teams don't adequately define what will be tested and how. Avoid that by developing test cases in partnership with the users. Bring them together with test teams, and, in a formally facilitated session, work out the details for how acceptance testing will be conducted. The goal here is to end up with a plan that is also a contract, one that users will expect the testing team to abide by and vice versa. This is a second listening point; that's why it works best when it's conducted as a cooperative workshop.

   Here are some planning points to keep in mind:

   ❏ Plan to keep test cases and scenarios as close to real life as possible. This will ensure familiarity when the users are finally in front of the new system.

   ❏ Plan to put together solid test data. The test data should reflect data in the users' world, and there should be enough of it to stress the system in a real way.

   ❏ Plan for the right number of testers from both sides of the house. It's important to include enough users to give the system a true operational load, with the right mix of technical members and business users to provide for the right balance of insight.

   ❏ Plan for the right environment. This is important. As close as is practicable, plan to mimic a production-like environment for the testing process. If getting at least close isn't possible, consider releasing hidden problems into the real environment.

❏ Plan to test usability. User input here is particularly important. The intuitive maneuverability of a system will go a long way to user satisfaction with the product.

❏ Finally, plan for how test cases results will be recorded and scored. This will give all testers a consistent and predictable way to eventually interpret test results.[1]

3. **Base test cases on the requirements.**   Although planning for user acceptance testing must come early in the project, creating the test cases can come closer to test time if preferred. Be sure, however, that the cases built for this purpose trace to specific requirements. Make sure, too, that they trace to user-approved requirements. Then shape this traceability into acceptance criteria both parties will use to evaluate test results. This third activity will support the most visible portion of user acceptance testing: executing the test cases. If test execution can clearly demonstrate fulfillment of the requirements, the product by default should be viewed as acceptable.

4. **Provide pretest training.**   Here is another listening point. Don't begin acceptance testing by placing users in front of a strange workstation. This will only cloud their ability to effectively move through test cases, evaluate performance, and appreciate the work that's been done. Instead, prep them for the testing process by giving them pretest system training. The training need not be extensive. It should, however, seek to establish a comfort level the users will need to move through their work efficiently. The listening point here also has to do with comfort. Here, project teams and users have the opportunity to reaffirm the test plan and move in unison toward the acceptance goal.

5. **Support test execution.**   A surprising finding is that many development shops turn over acceptance testing to their users, carte blanche, while the technical people pace hallways somewhere, waiting. Naturally, that's not the way to do it. As this process we've been walking through implies, acceptance testing should be considered a major part of the shop's project activities. All of the foregoing activities will ensure that the project team and the users are ready for testing. Now the testing process needs to be facilitated. Part of the project team will help execute it. But it also needs to be managed. That's a key project management duty. As with any other phase in the life cycle, make sure this one is adequately resourced and properly scoped, and that key activities are addressed.

6. **Examine and use the results.**   This last activity seems obvious, but it bears special emphasis. By this time, test execution will have run many test cases through the new system, generating many sets of test results. On the basis of the criteria established earlier in the test plan, the testers will have scored these results. Now it's time to make a data-driven decision: Does the quality of the system warrant acceptance? These

---

[1] For more on this, I recommend Jonathan Kupersmith's *Putting the User Back in User Acceptance Testing*, B&T Training, 2007.

results are important; they constitute empirical evidence of acceptability. Accordingly, project management will need to rely on this evidence. Review it with the users; discuss it; evaluate it. Use it as the basis for an objective judgment. If the project teams have moved through the five previous activities, a reasonable assumption is that project and user teams are now in sync regarding the completed project.

These six steps constitute a simple process for making user acceptance testing a proactive, anticipated activity, rather than an unfocused, ambiguous one. The results derived from this collaborative activity are just like the test cards audiences turn in to market researchers after a preview of a new movie. Studios pay close attention to the numbers and comments on these cards, by which the voice of the audience comes through clean and clear. The studios listen to that voice to make adjustments to their pictures as needed. User acceptance testing results should serve the same purpose. The voice of the customer is in those results. Project management can prepare for and see through successful user testing by listening to that voice throughout the project.

Benefits of User Acceptance Testing Together

The interactive togetherness provided by the user acceptance testing process just described can foster a smoother user experience. The main benefit it can provide, of course, is a harmonious interpretation of the test results. But there are ancillary benefits as well, benefits that lead up to this main one but also support other areas of project management and project performance. As discussed next, three such benefits are collaborative involvement, cooperative evaluation, and insight into production.

- **Collaborative involvement**   The user acceptance testing process delineated in this chapter promotes the early involvement of the system's users. This involvement is used to establish the approach and strategy for acceptance testing. But it also is used to bring the users in sync with the technical team. The collaborative activities within it serve as a way to harmonize understandings and expectations regarding the test effort. Set up front and reinforced over the project life cycle, they foster a smoother approach to acceptance testing.

- **Cooperative evaluation**   User acceptance testing events can run into trouble when the user side and the project team side can't agree on the outcome of the tests. If the results are unclear or inconsistently interpreted, follow-up actions can be hard to determine. But with a more cooperative and proactive approach to testing, guidelines for noting and scoring results can be established. Use of these guidelines will lead to consistent interpretation of the results. User teams and project teams will then have a foundation on which they can base decisions for future action.

- **Insight into production**   When users are involved early on and regularly in the acceptance testing planning and execution process, they achieve a degree of understanding of the development process they may have formerly lacked. From this understanding may come an appreciation for the complexities of system development, and from this appreciation a more flexible attitude in discovering and evaluating defects. Likewise, the exchanges with users should give the technical team members better insight into the users' business domains and the demands those domains may present.

User acceptance testing signals that a project is nearing completion. A large part of that project's success will then rest on the quality of the product that's being delivered. But another part rests more in the perception of project performance. If the users (sponsors and operators alike) have been involved with the project team in establishing quality benchmarks early on and in shaping how those benchmarks will be verified, they may recognize the project as being successful even if certain aspects of the product require revision.

Case in Point: Agilys

Agilys is a value-added reseller (VAR) for midrange IBM computers used in the hospitality industries. The company pairs a home-grown property management system with these boxes and sells them to hotels, resorts, and office complexes. In 2002, Agilys was engaged in a major upgrading of its mainline property management system, moving it to a thin-client, SOA-based architecture. Although it was a significant effort in terms of manpower, the company considered this to be a relatively simple technical exercise—after all, it just involved rewriting an already existing system. That was one of the reasons for management's decision to go light on testing, and to forgo completely acceptance testing with select members of its user community. The project manager conferred with senior management and concluded that the job could be handled by some of the business analysts and some of the developers.

About seven months later, the new version was announced with fanfare in the press and slated for demos at tradeshows. (It was probably at that point that Agilys managers became converts to the idea of user acceptance testing.) The folks who had done the testing had performed essentially "skim testing." Lacking detailed knowledge of business process flows, they just skimmed over the surface of the interface. When the company got to the first trade show, however, it was a different story. The attendees were industry experts and knew how to move around in such a system. As soon as anyone initiated anything close to a complex transaction, the system crashed. This went on all day, until Agilys pulled the plug. It was an embarrassing show, with old customers disappointed and potential new customers lost. The press that followed was almost as bad as the embarrassment itself. That put the new release absolutely off the map. The company issued new press releases, sought to pacify its client base, restaffed a design-development-test team, and settled in for three months' worth of rework. This time around, management contracted out test duties to a local service firm.

For a Deeper Look . . .

- Rob Cimperman, *UAT Defined: A Guide to Practical User Acceptance Testing*, Addison-Wesley Professional, 2007

   UAT Defined offers an informal explanation of the relationships among testing, software development, and project management. The focus is on helping project managers and test teams better integrate work flows and project objectives. It is practical without an overwhelming amount of detail.

- Elfriede Dustin, *Effective Software Testing: 50 Specific Ways to Improve Your Testing*, Addison-Wesley Professional, 2002

   Dustin presents 50 best practices, pitfalls, and solutions centered on effective test management. Chapters look at test planning, test design, documentation, test execution, and test team management.

- James Shore and Shane Warden, *The Art of Agile Development*, O'Reilly, 2007

   This book focuses on the use of Agile and how shops can effectively deploy Agile methods. It also contains a lot of good information on the need to establish early and active customer relationships during product development. It describes how to achieve increased customer satisfaction through ongoing customer involvement.

Chapter 17
Count the Box Office

Previous chapters have taken us through the full extent of the Hollywood production system, from initial development all the way to test screenings of the hoped-for final cut of the movie. Now we move to a last step, one that's actually out of the control of the system but is nevertheless a reflection of the performance of the system: counting the box office. After a studio accepts a movie in finished form, it creates release prints from the negative. These prints are then shipped to theaters for domestic showing. The studios count on advertising and word of mouth to bolster the popularity of the film so that it maintains a long theater life—the more weeks, the better. The more popular it is domestically, the more successful it is likely to be on DVD and on the international market, and on the Internet, and so forth. The surest measure of this early success, of course, is ticket sales. Box office receipts come back to the studios daily, and they keep careful track of how each new release is performing. This is where the hits are separated from the duds. The hits are praised (by everyone who made them) as innovative entertainments. The duds are analyzed by unsentimental suits who compare costs against income and trace the line of decision making to determine what went wrong, how wrong it went, and which name plates to remove from which office doors. The hits are actually analyzed in much the same way, in order to determine a success pattern that can be leveraged again. In either case, it's an issue of lessons learned. The production system is not just about making movies efficiently; it's about maximizing its own efficiency. It does so by self-analysis. That's the subject of this chapter, which also relates it back to IT shops and demonstrates how IT shops can use lessons learned to make their own project management systems stronger.

The Bucket List

Hollywood studios used to make practically all of their own movies. Studios had their own sound stages—row after row of them; their own cabal of directors, writers, and stars; their own costume departments, their own camera departments, and so on. In short, they were self-contained production factories. But not anymore. Today's studios are not so much in the business of movie making as they are in the business of deal making: making deals to commission new pictures and, more important, making deals to distribute new pictures. It's the distribution end that really interests them, putting product into the channel. That's where the money comes from. Studio executives see it as something of an inconvenience that they have to commission a movie in order to sell one. But that's the way it goes. Each year a major studio may sponsor 30 or so productions, signing up some to produce, signing others after they've been made. The amount of money tied up in these deals is naturally quite significant. In a distribution deal, the studios typically get about 30 percent of gross revenues in return for covering production costs, advertising, and release prints. Filmmakers rail at that percentage, but it doesn't leave much room for mediocre performance. Those margins are such that if a movie manages only to cover its production and marketing costs, it's considered a failure. The studios count it as a bad investment, an opportunity lost. So to Hollywood, the box office is everything.

In earlier chapters we saw the detail and energy that producers put into developing new projects and planning green-lighted ones. And we saw how the studio production system carefully controls the process of getting a project in the can. A logical assumption might be that once this has been accomplished, the only thing to do is kick back, relax, and hope for the best. But that's not what happens. When a picture goes into release, the real job of the studio, as a financial entity, has just begun: to count the box office. In the movie business, studios buy (or commission) a film; they then license that film (or a package of films) to theater chains, striking the best deal they can and aiming to average revenues out across the slate; the chains ship the films to local theaters; concurrently, advertising runs; people line up to buy their tickets. Then the process moves in reverse. Each week (and often daily), the theaters send ticket receipts up to the chains; the chains send them up to the studios. Tallies are totaled; profits are split. While all this is happening, the studio's financial analysts are examining the incoming numbers. Table 17-1 shows an example of the kinds of analysis they undertake. These numbers are for the top five theatrical releases for a week in January 2008.

TABLE 17-1 Sales Analysis for Top Five Releases for Week of January 18, 2008

Rank	Title	Gross (Mil)	Weekly Change	Days in Release	Theaters	Average (Thou)	Total (Mil)	Worldwide
#1	Cloverfield	$41	No change	3	3,411	$12.02	$41	NA
#2	27 Dresses	$22.42	No change	3	3,057	$7.33	$22.42	NA
#3	The Bucket List	$15.15	-22%	27	2,915	$5.19	$42.70	NA
#4	Juno	$10.25	-25%	47	2,534	$4.05	$85.37	NA
#5	National Treasure	$8.14	-28%	31	2,963	$2.75	$198.03	NA

Look at *The Bucket List*. The analysts know that that picture has been in theaters for 27 days now—a good run as movies go. They know that for the week of January 18 it made about $15 million, and—being shown in almost 3,000 theaters—it averaged about $5,190 per. They also know that that week's total is down 22 percent from last week—evidence that the movie's attraction is wearing off. And they know that so far, the picture has grossed about

$43 million. That's a little disconcerting for the movie's studio, Warner Bros. *The Bucket List* cost $45 million to make and half again that to promote. Already now the lessons are beginning to arrive. What did the movie open against? *27 Dresses, Blind Date, Cassandra's Dream, Day Zero, The Great Buck, Howard, The Guitar, Mad Money, Still Life, Summer Place, Teeth, The Witness, Kicking It, What Just Happened?,* and *The Mysteries of Pittsburgh.* Nothing overwhelming. What was the weather like? What was happening in the news? What new deals are Jack Nicholson and Morgan Freeman signing up for, and how's their current clout? And on it goes. The studio executives are going to want to know everything and anything about what might have affected the picture's performance.

The Bucket List had a happy ending. By the time its distribution channel had run its course, it had generated upwards of $150 million. But the point of note here is that the end total was not a surprise to the studio. Warner had tracked that revenue stream from day one; the analysts compared it with what their original projections had indicated, and they examined every element of the product itself and its release environment to understand why the market performance was the way it was. No doubt here's one lesson that came out of that: Put two ill-matched buddies together, send them off on a sentimental quest, and represent them with two stars who can play crusty, and what have you got? In the parlance of Hollywood, you've got bank. A good question is what Warner Bros. is going to do with that lesson. A fair guess is that right now, someone, somewhere, is trying to figure out how to make a sequel about two terminally ill, irascible codgers who for some reason need to get together to do something bittersweet. Plenty of films have been built on less.

Hollywood has a brain. And it approaches both success and failure head on. IT people may see a different situation in their own world. IT has brains, sure. But many times project teams take both success and failure lying down, glad to be finished with them, glad for it all to be over. The thing the organization tends not to do, at least not very seriously, is to look for lessons learned. Success and failure generally are not assessed in order to determine why things turned out the way they did. Most IT professionals, however, would readily agree that such assessment could be of the utmost value. Without that kind of knowledge, project teams often encounter the same project management problems over and over again.

The Unconscious Organization

From years spent moving into and out of corporate IT shops, on both long- and short-term engagements, I would probably have to characterize most shops as largely unconscious. I mean "unconscious" the way a paramecium or an earthworm is unconscious. The paramecium and the worm are no doubt alive, but they're not very self-aware. They're built to respond appropriately to things like environmental changes and hunger and reproduction, but they don't do much strategic planning about any of that. They act on one biological imperative when they need to and then move on to another.

Lots of IT shops operate the same way. They move mainly through reaction. They focus on the day-to-day job of development—creating, enhancing, maintaining, supporting systems, services, or whatever for whichever clients happen to be in the immediate vicinity. The driving impetus in these shops is to get the work done—just get it done. More often than not, that means overtime, rework, backtracking, and missteps. But because success here is simply a measure of output, those conditions are not recognized as problematic in and of themselves, nor are they seen as contrary to a larger business mission. In fact, many shops see them as *essential* to the business mission, part of the cost of doing business. If a certain situation at hand needs attention, the shop reacts this way or that until the threat or problem seems no longer imminent. Little thought is given to thinking about past experience and how it might apply in present performance. Less thought is given to expending energy to avoid the potential for similar problems to appear in the future. The unconscious shop is uncomfortable expending energy on potentialities; it needs all its energy to deal with present realities.

These kinds of shops are often labeled "ad hoc" or "chaos-driven." That's not a style of management—it's a *lack* of style, a problem of *no* style. And it's not a technical problem, even when present in a technology shop. It's a management problem. And it's just as prevalent in most business domains. Management that seems forever caught in the "now" is stuck there by one or more of the following conditions:

1. Management is measured by short-term results and pressured to focus on the here and now.

2. Management may be technically astute but lacks training or experience in strategic planning or organizational design.

3. Management is averse to the challenge of change.

4. Management is not empowered to provide leadership to its customers or its internal teams; rather, its main charge is to sustain the status quo.

Running a shop this way will have a tangible impact on project management's ability to operate in a consistent and predictable way. Most project management activities depend on understanding past performance as a way to control present conditions. Resource staffing, cost estimations, risk identification, and scope definition, for example, all need to be shaped as accurate reflections of similar elements from past experience. In the absence of that experience, how accurate can those reflections be? A shop that hedges this concern by relying on the experience and judgment of individual team members is not making much progress toward addressing the real issue. It's the *organization* that needs the experience and the knowledge. So it's the organization that must provide the ways and means for its individual workers to come together and collect that knowledge.

What's needed for the organization to become conscious is to recognize itself as a self-contained entity whose past experiences and present actions can shape its future state. An important step in this direction is to use tactics like lessons learned sessions and project closeout meetings as avenues to assemble key stakeholders and discuss specific issues of performance with regard to specific project activities, whether current ones or those from the past. Uncovering these lessons will provide the organization with a base of knowledge that can be leveraged to improve future performance. The value of this knowledge base is hard to overstate. The topic of lessons learned is often viewed as a minor project activity, yet eminently qualifies as a major one.

Organizations that embrace this practice with the rigor it deserves position themselves to be more effective and more responsive. They can anticipate with more accuracy because they "remember" more. They can react with more exactitude because they can "access" more. They can move more quickly to a desired destination because they "know" more. In other words, they are smarter. Of course, this rigor takes energy and commitment, and adopting it will entail a certain amount of change. But without this evolutionary motion, an organization will have a difficult time growing; the limitations it operates from will stymie growth. It may even have a hard time sustaining its current level of performance as its limitations drag it down. Companies that tend to operate in chaos also tend to have a fairly brief life course.

The Hollywood practice of not just counting but analyzing the box office can illuminate the value to be had from self-analysis. The studios are continually examining market performance in light of present plans in an attempt to maximize future success. They are committed to a lessons learned process that involves every key player in the studio, from the executives on down. They rely on the validity of the analyses that come out of this process, and they incorporate those lessons into new planning strategies. Surely corporate development shops could benefit from a similar lessons learned approach. That brings us to lesson 17 of this book:

Lesson 17: Use the lessons learned review as a way to establish a learning organization capable of leveraging knowledge management toward continuous improvement.

Leveraging Knowledge Management

Establishing lessons learned as a formal project management tool supports two goals within an organization: knowledge management and continuous improvement. *Knowledge management* can be thought of as informed decision making; it's the technique of making decisions, in part, through an assessment of past experience. Lessons learned can provide a documented wellspring of insights from past experience. *Continuous improvement* is the practice of regularly (and consciously) assessing organization performance to look for opportunities to make that performance more efficient or effective. A lessons learned process can help by documenting previous performance outcomes for later comparison and analysis.

Ultimately, the purpose of a lessons learned process is to promote the recurrence of successful outcomes while precluding the recurrence of unsuccessful outcomes.[1] Such a process is not difficult to initiate, nor does it need to be complex in nature. In general, moving in this direction will require two actions: first, to define, organize, and shape an approach to eliciting lessons learned; and second, to provide mechanisms to access, search for, and use those lessons. Let's take a look.

Define, Organize, Shape

The goal here is to define the shape and focus of the lessons learned process. As described next, six basic steps will lead to this goal: define, establish, collect, organize, store, and distribute.

Define   Think about the kind of process most appropriate to the shop's mission and then put it on paper. The process should answer the whens, whos, and hows of planning for and conducting lessons learned sessions.

- **When**   How often will sessions be conducted? A review of lessons learned can be done with each project phase, or with certain deliverables or milestones, or simply at the end of each project. Decide on the timing, and then mark that in the process.

- **Who**   Who will attend the lessons learned sessions? As a rule, it's a good idea to involve as many different viewpoints as possible. So attendees may include technical team members, customers, project managers, quality auditors, shop managers, certain reporting parties, and any other appropriate ancillary parties.

- **How**   Define how the sessions will be planned and facilitated, and then define how results will be distributed. For more on this topic, see the following sections.

Establish   Lessons learned sessions should not be treated as ad hoc chat fests. They need to be focused. And a good way to focus them is to standardize a set agenda of discussion points. These are the subject areas that should be addressed when project management meets with stakeholders to elicit the lessons. These discussion points should be centered on those management practices that are particularly valued in the shop. Is resource management of particular interest? Is quality of utmost importance? Work with upper-level management to decide what areas to investigate with special emphasis. Meanwhile, here's a list of typical discussion topics:

Schedule affinity	How well did we schedule the project timeline?
	Was the work breakdown representative of the actual tasks?
	How did the actual timeline play out?
	What factors had the biggest impact on schedule affinity?

---

[1] For more on this, see David Fair, *Concepts and Practices in Finding and Applying Lessons Learned*, U.S. Army ARDEC, 2005.

Budget	How well and accurately did we budget for the project?
	Did our original expense categories account for actual expenses?
	How did we do at staying on budget?
	What factors had the biggest impact on budget affinity?
Resources	How well and accurately did we plan our human and other resources for the project?
	Did our initial expectations of team size and for skill sets prove to be well founded?
	How stable were our resource needs across each phase of the project?
	What factors had the biggest impact on resource use and availabilities?
Product quality	How well did the main project artifacts turn out?
	Were integrity, reliability, and performance targets met?
	What kinds of quality issues did we encounter?
	What factors had the biggest impacts on our ability to deliver on our quality commitments?
Team makeup	Did we have the right people on the project?
	Did we have the right blend of business, technical, and managerial expertise?
	Did we have enough people? Too many? What were our utilization rates?
Teamwork	How well did the team work together on the project?
	Were there any inter-team or intra-team cooperation issues?
	How well was the team able to communicate across each phase of the project?
	Were we able to coordinate and collaborate successfully?
	What factors influenced the level of teamwork we achieved?
Customer management	How well did we manage our customer?
	Were communications smooth and open?
	Did we have access to the right business stakeholders?
	How can we work better with our customers in the future?
Scope control	Were our original definitions of scope accurate for this project?
	How well did change control work? Did we experience unexpected or un-authorized shifts in scope?
	Were we able to baseline scope-related artifacts effectively and then man-age change to them as it occured?
	How can we identify and manage scope better in the future?

Once the kinds of topics to be addressed at a lessons learned session have been defined, it's time to bring the meeting together.

Collect   Make the lessons learned session a part of the project's official (and approved) work flow; include it as an activity in the WBS. One possibility is to conduct a series of sessions at certain steps in the life cycle, or a single session can be presented at project end. However it's planned, treat the sessions as formal meetings. Establish an agenda, target and invite the right set of stakeholders, appoint a qualified facilitator, and arrange for comfortable facilities.

Then conduct the meeting and document the lessons. Someone (or some team) will need to be designated as the official recorder. Make sure the lessons are being collected accurately; periodically review them with the meeting members; and double check them all at the end of the session.

Organize   Once the lessons have been documented, they need to be organized. Eventually, they should be stored in some kind of repository (see next section); to do that effectively will require a system for organizing them. Organization can be accomplished according to select-ed themes, project name, project type, performance impact, frequency, or any other number of attributes. This organization will go a long way to shaping how the shop's people will then access and move through the lessons.

Store   Storing the lessons learned sounds simple and obvious, and it is. But it's also key: Collecting lessons learned is an important task, but an even more important task is using them. For the company to use them effectively, access to the information is essential. And that access must be both easy and productive. So it's important to plan how to set up the lessons learned repository. There are many ways to do this, but any approach should account for how the organization's folks will get into and move through the repositories. The follow-ing are some points to consider:

- How lessons will be displayed;

- How lessons will be sorted (by theme, project, date, and so on);

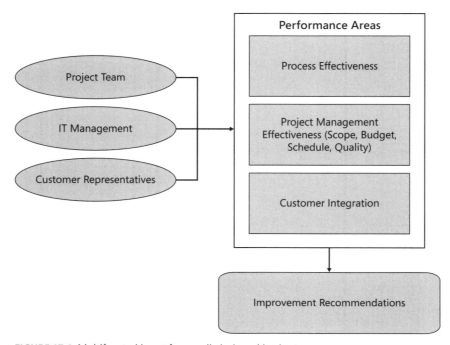

FIGURE 17-1 Multifaceted input for a well-designed budget.

- How user can search for and find lessons;

- How users will read, print, and export lessons;

- How lessons can be shared; and

- How users can update and add to the repository.

Distribute   With the lessons in place, it is now up to the organization to distribute this knowledge out to its people. See the following section for more on this process.[2]

Figure 17-1 illustrates how a lessons learned process can be configured to facilitate viewpoints and observations from both project stakeholders and customers.

Present, Access, Rely

The real value of lessons learned comes from using the information derived from this kind of review. Many shops make something of an attempt to capture this information, although that attempt may be only half-hearted. But few really embrace its use. To remedy this failing, the organization should establish mechanisms to present the lessons to its people, give people access to this presentation, and then encourage them to rely on the lessons as a source of valuable project management information. The presentation can be accommodated by storing the lessons in some form of repository (say, a SharePoint site, an intranet location, or even a shared corporate folder). Access can be ensured by making sure that the repository is well organized, easy to use, and readily located. Reliance can be achieved through the example of upper-level managers. Their use of the repository will show others its importance to the shop at large. This can be further supported by communicating the major uses of the repository. Three ways in which IT shops can (and should) use lessons learned include input into decision making, input into planning, and input into risk preparation and mitigation, as described next.

- **Input into decision making**   Lessons learned should be made available to all levels of the organization, including executive and upper-level management. The prime intent of these lessons is to help avoid repeating past mistakes. Problematic projects often come into an organization as problematic to begin with. Reviewing lessons learned can be a way to assess what kinds of projects tend to do well in the shop and which ones tend to be challenges. When upper-level management uses the lessons as a type of sounding board, bouncing new proposals and opportunities off them, they can better position the organization to take in projects primed for success.

- **Input into planning**   Project managers should be encouraged to access lessons learned as part of the project planning (and replanning) process. A learning organization is one that is focused on continuous improvement. One area that can benefit

---

[2] For more on this, see Thomas Crowles, *Criteria for Lessons Learned*, Abstract #1169, Raytheon, 2004.

from this focus is planning. Planning by its very nature is a collection of estimates, and estimates are at best simply approximations. Studying lessons learned can be a way to make planning more effective by making it more accurate. A good topic for any lessons learned session is budget and schedule affinity. How did actual compare with original estimates? What factors tended to influence this outcome? How could we have estimated more effectively? How could we have managed actuals more efficiently? Lessons learned can contribute answers to these questions. They foster better techniques and practices for all planning activities.

- **Input into risk preparation and mitigation** Project managers should be given access to lessons learned as a tool to manage risk. Many mature organizations maintain a risk mitigation repository as an aid to project management. The repository holds a history of prior project risks and documentation of how each was handled. Project managers have access to this repository and may reference it when they encounter what may be a recurrence of a previous risk. Complementing this database, lessons learned can be a great source for adding to this repository. Risks that turned into problems usually crop up as lessons. Discussions of why a particular risk was not avoided and how the problem emerged, as well as ideas concerning how such a situation might have been circumvented, can contribute value to risk preparation and mitigation for current projects.

These three practices make the use of lessons learned valuable to any development shop. The lessons can be an aid to decision making. They provide good reference material for planning purposes. And they can be used to avoid or mitigate current risks. Realizing these activities simply requires a conscious act on the part of the organization: to make collection and documentation of lessons learned an institutionalized practice, one that is given a visible and prominent place in the project management methodology.

Benefits of Leveraging Lessons Learned

A look at the major project management frameworks will reveal a common attitude toward lessons learned. For each of its 22 process areas, for example, CMMI recommends periodic involvement by upper-level management to understand and review how things are going. The PMBOK supports the practice of postmortems, lessons learned sessions held by the team at the end of a project to assess performance and quality. ISO 9001:2000 requires procedures to support continuous improvement, including examinations of past performance weighed against objectives and targets. Whether a shop chooses one of these three frameworks or designs its own lessons learned approach, the resultant benefits are likely to be the same. It's not how the approach is shaped so much as that it is put into place to begin with. Two such strong approaches, described next, are within reach of any shop.

- **The conscious organization** As noted earlier in this chapter, a consistently effective IT shop needs to be a "conscious" IT shop. A conscious shop understands where it currently stands, remembers what paths it took to get there, and uses both to assess directions available for further movement. Lessons learned can help an organization achieve such consciousness—to become aware of its actions and the consequences (profitable or not so) of those actions. By using lessons learned, the shop can then begin to shape not only its work but its identity as an enterprise in order to perform better.

■ **The learning organization**   Once an organization has made an official and organized commitment to examining its performance, it becomes not only conscious but a learning organization as well. This is the key to long-term successful project management and to successful process improvement—and to general business success as well. After all, effective production processes and efficient operating practices are not bestowed on any team automatically. The team—the unit, the shop, the organization—has to work to acquire the knowledge and insights that can lead to predictable effectiveness and repeatable efficiencies. Lessons learned can play a big part in unveiling that knowledge and insight.

Box office performance is the surest sign of movie success. A generous take means smiles all around for everyone. A slim take, and folks aren't as pleased. But in either case, the box office draw leads to detailed analyses. What vein did we hit or miss? What decisions probably led to this outcome? Can we repeat them next time around? Can we avoid them? The analyses all drive toward better production choices, better production efficiencies, and better end product quality. IT shops can benefit in a similar way, by adopting a lessons learned approach that emphasizes examining project performance against expectations and using the subsequent insights to manage projects more effectively in the future.

Case in Point: Advantage Computers Inc.

Advantage Computers Inc. is a company that was built on lessons learned. The company started off small with a simple service: Its people captured digital stills of a homeowner's property, artifacts, and assets and then cataloged them for potential insurance purposes. They started with a simple camera and simple shots; the service was not complex. But the principals had a natural interest in customer service and in making the most of whatever potential the company had. So they made a point of talking with all of their clients, as often as they could, asking what else they might be able to help out with. From a few clients who were art collectors, they learned of the need to capture very-high-definition images of paintings and sculptures as an aid to both detecting and avoiding forgeries. Accordingly, they upgraded their equipment and began offering very-high-resolution images taken from multiple angles, with some images from as close as ¼ inch from the object. This capability led to an expansion of their business, not only to other collectors but to art galleries and museums as well. They continued to confer among themselves and with their customers, during and after engagements. After a while, they learned that the value of expensive objects can come not just from their fixed shape but from their proficiency moving. So the company expanded its service offerings further to include digitized high-definition video recordings of objects in motion (curios, antique cars, and so on). Such video communicated a quality-of-condition that a still image could not. This application further expanded the company's business to luxury goods dealers in the automobile, yachting, and aircraft industries. Following that path, Advantage Computers today has moved from offering a simple insurance-supporting property catalog service to a multiproduct-line company offering a wide array of multimedia services to a broad client base. The company attributes its success to its focus on customer service, to its genuine interest in what its customers have to say, and to the lessons that have come from that.

For a Deeper Look . . .

■ Kimberly Wiefling, *Scrappy Project Management: The 12 Predictable and Avoidable Pitfalls Every Project Faces*, Second Edition, Happy About, 2007

The theme of Wiefling's book is taking advantage of lessons learned. She documents common project pitfalls that most every development project can expect to encounter in one form or another. She then presents ways to address each, mitigating their adverse impacts on project performance.

■ Thomas Crowles, *Criteria for Lessons Learned*, Abstract #1169, Raytheon, 2004

This is not a book but a slide presentation available from Raytheon. In its compact form, it presents a very good introduction to the structure and use of a lessons learned program. It provides guidance on how to design the program for broad application, how to collect and organize lessons, and how to then use a lesson repository to strengthen the management of current projects.

■ David Fair, *Concepts and Practices in Finding and Applying Lessons Learned*, U.S. Army ARDEC, 2005

This is like the document above—not a book but a slide presentation. It features good definitions of what makes a lesson valid and applicable, provides clear descriptions of how to organize and categorize a lessons repository, and presents a flowchart that depicts a generic lessons learned collection and distribution process.

Part V
Wrap-Up

This section summarizes the themes of the book by revisiting the general needs of project management within corporate America.

Chapter 18
Honor the System

This chapter presents the final component of the project management approach, described throughout the book and designed to address typical performance considerations and quality concerns of the IT shop. As emphasized beginning in Chapter 1, "Follow the System," and highlighted throughout the others, an essential attribute of any management system is a commitment to adhere to the methodology: In order for the system to prove its usefulness, it must be used. Stories abound in the IT world about organizations that have gone to great lengths to create management systems—project methodologies, improvement programs, and other such process ventures—only to have them dissipate in an atmosphere of failed returns. A close look at most of these initiatives probably would show that some were poorly engineered—too heavy, too off-base, too radical. But most of the time the fault lies elsewhere, in the implementation effort. Weak and unfocused implementations have probably derailed more new management systems than any other single factor. In my experience, IT organizations on the whole tend to minimize roll-outs over development. This preference may simply be a cultural bias. After all, it's more exciting to build a software system than it is to package one. But when a shop is seeking to make change, the conscious dissemination of that change becomes the key driver to successful absorption of the change into the culture. This absorption is not an automatic thing. Yet many IT managers take that approach when they seek to roll out components of a project management system.

Hollywood probably has an edge over IT in this respect. The studio production system is not project-specific or even company-specific (at least at the macro level). It's an industry standard, and people typically learn it by working in it year after year. But the point remains the same: The system is followed; it is honored through use. And it has become as refined and as effective as it stands today because of this continuous use. That's a point that could benefit IT management; the key to a successful project management program is to help the organization use it and commit to its use over time. Let's begin, as usual, with a look at how this is accomplished in Beverly Hills.

The System Is the Solution

It's the last day of my last trip to Hollywood. There's a November wind blowing down Los Angeles' Beverly Boulevard, but it feels more like spring than fall. I've just turned off Ventura Boulevard, past Rodeo Drive, and I'm looking for a specific landmark: a street corner with a Bentley dealership on the left and a Mercedes-Benz/Audi lot on the right. Two blocks up I spot it, and just across from the lined-up Mercedes I find the offices of Intermedia. Intermedia—actually, International Media—is an independent production house focusing on its own high-end properties (like *Terminator 3*) and it also partners as coproducer on films for the majors. Intermedia Film develops, produces, and distributes genre movies, primarily action films with midrange budgets, usually between $15 million and $30 million.

I'm at Intermedia this morning to see Patty Long. Patty is a staff producer for the company (most producers are freelance), and she has an impressive record as production manager for both theatrical films (like *King of California*) as well as a host of TV movies (like *Thief of Time* and *Skinwalkers*). It's this TV expertise I'm particularly interested in. Most of the industry professionals I have spoken with have focused on theatrical productions, movies shown in theaters, produced specifically for the big screen. But they all mentioned at least briefly the fine rhythm of TV production, especially that first cousin to the movie, the one-hour drama. Shows like Fox Broadcasting's *House* or CBS's *Miami: CSI* have exactly 11 days to shoot, 12-hour days that they are—but no more. If the crew can't get the shot in that time, there's no replanning or redesign. They simply go with what they've got, or drop the shot altogether. This requires hypervigilant planning and production efficiencies. Patty's particular exposure to this level of production made her a great source for information on this last topic: the value IT shops can find in staying on process, in following their project management system, in finding the project management solution through the system.

The Machine Rolls On (or Over)

Patty's office is on the second floor of the Intermedia building. A big picture window overlooks the Mercedes and Audis parked below. I'm offered chilled bottled water (just like at every other studio meeting I took) and motioned to a blue teak chair. Patty sits behind a busy desk crowded with what look to be scripts, budgets, plans, and other production material. A rainbow sea of numbers flows continuously across a flat panel pushed now politely over to one side (but not so far as to fall out of range of her peripheral vision). I start by asking her about the production process in general, and she explains the high-level steps in the same informed and consistent manner used by Bill Fay, Jack Crowley, Alan Blomquist, Marty Ewing, and all of my other interviewees. But Patty's experience as a producer and production manager in both movie and TV work seems to slant her discussion toward an emphasis on the control provided by the system, not just its reliability or its familiarity.

She explains the value of this control along three paths. First, it delivers an overall framework for constructing the movie product, a product that can vary widely from production to production. It sets into place predetermined work phases of fixed duration, each with a documented allocation of resources. Second, it provides a very well-delineated definition (and separation) of job roles. Through the system, everyone on the production team—and this can be a hundred or more people in the same place at the same time—understands just what their responsibilities are and what their contributions should be. This promotes smooth work flows and orderly communications. And third, she explained how the system's design pushes progress toward goals. A suite of built-in assessment tools—daily status accounting, hot costs, production reports, call sheets—combine to create an ongoing, always reshaping picture of schedule, budget, and scope affinities. With these three layers of control in place, Patty says, you're going to go off track only if (for whatever reason) you're not doing your job well.

To illustrate this point, and Hollywood's overall reliance on the system, she recounted the story of a young TV commercial director who'd been given the chance to make a major movie. This was a guy whose early success had given him an inflated image of his own abilities, so he came to the set as a maverick with a "my way–highway" attitude. As a result, he moved at his own pace and in his own way, interacting with cast and crew in ways that probably set him apart as unique but came across to people used to a different rhythm as disjointed. That disjointedness began to evidence itself in the work immediately. Setups took longer than needed, and some of the scripted work was not being completed. The director quickly became frazzled with the pace the production staff was working and at one point had to call for a break to collect his wits. The line producer was watching all this with a look of dismay on his face. Finally, he quietly approached the first assistant director and asked what might be done. "I'm not too worried about it," the first assistant said. "Either he'll catch up to the machine or the machine will produce the work without him."

From what I saw on the sets of *Yes Man*, *Liberty*, and *He's Just Not that into You*, that first assistant director was exactly right. The smoothness evidenced by these teams was at the same time obvious and invisible. With the rhythm of the system in place and up and running, it was easy to imagine the work getting done even if the director didn't show up—pretty unlikely, of course, but Patty's story does underscore the value of the system. Sure, creative results can be obtained through innovation and improvisation, but with so much on the line, studios must limit how much ambiguity they can accept into the risk mix.

The Surety of Familiarity

Wes Anderson is an up-and-coming director known for his dry wit and deadpan look at life in such movies as *Rushmore* and *The Royal Tenenbaums*. He's at Century Center now in downtown L.A. on an apartment set for *The Darjeeling Limited*, a comedy about the coming together of three distant brothers. The day is almost spent, and the script supervisor is worried. Anderson's shooting a lot of coverage, and that's slowing the schedule up—and burning a lot of film. The first assistant director is looking at tomorrow's call sheet, wondering if it's still any good. The supervisor and the assistant take advantage of a break to visit the producer's trailer parked behind Studio 2. They share their concerns and then ask, "Should we say anything?" The production manager thinks a moment. What he thinks is, *The Royal Tenenbaums* cost $12 million to make and netted $71 million. "Let's see how it goes," he says. "We'll look to make it up later."

Cut clear across the country now to New York, to a side alley off West 54th Street that's been dressed to look like a dead end to nowhere. Sidney Lumet is getting ready to shoot a scene for *Before the Devil Knows You're Dead*, a gritty crime drama. Lumet's been in the business since 1948, when he started directing for TV's "Studio One," a live weekly omnibus. In the alley, with the weather turning cold, it's nearly 60 years later, and at 83, Lumet is on his 45th feature. The shot requires a complicated Steadicam move, so the director is carefully pacing it out with his cameraman, the director of photography, the soundman, and the subject of the shot, actor Ethan Hawke. The first assistant director notices his watch and walks over for a quick decision: It's twenty to twelve. Do the guys think they can get the business mapped out relatively easily? If so, we can push out lunch (for which service and times are itemized in everyone's contract) with little or no problem. If it's complicated, maybe we can break now and come back to the shot afterwards. Lumet and team confer. The shot's important. It should be done right. Let's break now and pick it up fresh after lunch.

Now jump back in time three quarters of a century. It's 1931 and we're on a Universal back lot with Todd Browning, Carl Laemmle, and Bela Lugosi shooting *Dracula*, a movie being styled in the new "mystery" genre. It is late afternoon, and the three are next to a plywood castle façade going over the day's work. Coming in and out of the discussion are the director of photography, the editor, the art director, the script supervisor, and the effects supervisor. The production manager is the last one over and comes with the day's production report. They compare the scenes they shot against what they had planned to cover. They look at the amount of film exposed, the clock-in and clock-out times of the crew, the amount of unexpected carpentry that had to be set into place. Finally the production manager goes over the next day's call sheet; the group disbands and everybody goes their own way, ready to return tomorrow, prepared for another day's work.

Three different movies by three very different directors separated over 75 years in time—yet they all share a common vocabulary, a common frame of reference, and a common approach to organization and assessment. The three productions could easily have been partners on the same project. That unifying quality comes as yet another benefit from the studio production system. But the element that remains dominant—at least in Patty Long's view—is the control: budget control, schedule control, scope control, quality control. This quality constitutes a kind of virtue that extends far out from Hollywood. It reaches into any collection of activities set out to create a product, whether that product be movies, coat hangers, or software systems. It's the range of control all project managers strive for.

Hesitation in IT Shops

Less mature IT shops frequently are hesitant to move from an ad hoc, personality-driven state to one governed by defined project management policies and practices. The six most common reasons cited for this reluctance to make a change are discussed next.

"Everything's fine."   If everything's fine in an IT shop, then a project management system is probably not necessary. Better yet, such a system probably is already in place—whether it's readily visible or not. If the shop enjoys adequate control over schedules, budgets, resources, and quality, then nothing need be changed. Ignore the lessons in this book.

Unfortunately, when a lot of IT managers, faced with a proposal for change, announce that everything's fine, what they're really saying is "Don't bother me with that right now." They may feel that they already have their hands full—how could they possible undertake another directive? Or they may have grown used to the staccato rhythm of reactive management, thinking (as mentioned back in the Introduction) that shift and loss are natural to the mix of IT development. Maybe they've seen such a system fail elsewhere and have been left with little faith in a methodological approach. Then again, maybe they just don't know a lot about project management as a formal discipline and wish to avoid unfamiliar waters.

The point is that very rarely is everything fine in the domain of IT project management. Even if it's fine now, that could change in a minute. The umbrella constraints of shifting business needs, complex environments, diverse stakeholders, stretched resources, and integrated technologies can't help but challenge project management's ability to guide individual projects. Even with the aid of a system, these challenges will remain. As noted in the Introduction, the reality of these constraints begs the need for a system of some kind. Management that is not able to appreciate the value in using a project management system or understand how it might tangibly contribute to organizational success is electing to not manage. One of the chief jobs of upper-level and executive IT managers is to establish an organizational model of conducting business and then provide the awareness, tools, and support needed for its associates to operate successfully under that model. Project management techniques fit naturally under that responsibility.

"We've got other fish to fry."   Things in an IT shop may not be fine, but technology folks may cite yet another reason for resistance to a project management solution: "We've got other fish to fry." (Let's hope those other fish are bigger fish.) What this means is that the organization has problems in other areas that are more pressing, that demand more immediate attention. And that can very well be true. If customer ranks are thinning out and profits are drying up, it's reasonable to assume that management is going to congregate around those issues, pushing others aside. If new market technologies are displacing the company's core set, that may become a major distraction. The shop may have leadership problems or restructuring issues. If the building is on fire, management will probably not be well disposed to hearing about the promising potentials of a project management system.

The angle to explore here is the source of those "bigger" problems. Weak project management can lead to a shrinking customer base and falling revenues. It can forestall strategic movement, introduce conflicting expectations, and help set an organization out of joint. A perceptive manager will recognize a possible link, with the need for some root cause analysis on the part of a few people in the shop.

The insight that's needed here is the ability to fit the role of project management into the context of overall organizational success. When this can be accomplished, the success chain becomes clearer, leading up from specific project management activities to the higher mission, and from the higher mission down to certain others. If management can view the organization itself as a system—and what organization is not a system?—then it is better able to see a project management system as an important and necessary contributor to organizational success.

"We're too different."   Most IT professionals have probably either heard or claimed some version of the following: "Sure, that's probably a great idea for most shops, but what we do is too different for those kinds of blanket answers." This response is particularly common from organizations encouraged to try one of the popular established management frameworks, like the PMBOK, CMMI, or ISO 9001. In actuality, most IT shops are indeed "different." They have different customers, they deal with different technologies, they shape different environments, they address different business needs. But *different* does not mean *unique*. In fact, a cross section of IT shops—no matter what the industry or domain focus—probably will demonstrate more that links them in common than sets them apart. They each have to understand customer needs. They have to approximate a technological solution. They have to order a sequence of production activities. They have to realize the solution, validate its suitability for use, and package it for the customer. And each has to do these things through the commitment of time, money, and resources.

The managers who emphasize their uniqueness to counter movement toward standards often think of methodologies and process programs as fixed paths with rigid requirements. But that's rarely true. The PMBOK, CMMI, and ISO 9001 are actually based on the premise of interpretation, taking a set of recommendations and integrating them into a culture-based program. So a project management system should never be "someone else's solution." It can be, and indeed should be, a customized method that springs from the foundation of a specific shop and takes advantages of current organizational strengths and best practices. In fact, it can be argued that the more unique a shop perceives itself to be, the more important it is to document that uniqueness in an external, communicable form.

"A program will weigh us down."   This is a common complaint. Sometimes it's born out of a false perception, sometimes out of concrete observation. It's easy to think that project management methods are by nature heavy things that add lots of overhead to development activities. Many books (like this one) that seek to explain such approaches to method are hundreds of pages long. If that much space is needed to explain the thing, so the thinking goes, then it must be heavy. On the other hand, it's easy to find existing programs that are bloated and lead-based, that address too much detail down to too fine a level. These kinds of programs can and do weigh down organizations. It's very easy to overengineer a project management system. Creating policies, procedures, forms, and templates is pretty easy work. The key is to start with a strategy to right-size the system, to position its purpose as one that will seek to reduce work rather than compound it. Efficiency almost always comes by paring down, not by adding to.

To create a light, flexible, and effective project management program, it's important to keep four things in mind. First, don't try to solve every issue at once. Instead, focus on a manageable set of productivity targets. Next, start light. Create basic procedures and guides that ensure high-level motion in the right direction. Then, set these in the hands of team members to use, but don't expect perfection. Give time for gradual absorption over time, supported through available training, coaching, and mentoring. Finally, plan to grow the program over time. As more and more people become accustomed to it, begin to enhance the program to help manage an extended set of activities. This approach will help avoid creating a heavy program. Instead, the result will be one that's able to stick in the culture and become the basis for further refinement and development.

"We've already tried that."   Sometimes a shop will try to implement a project management system and the effort will fail. Lack of initial success can have some long-standing repercussions. The people involved can easily lose faith in the whole idea of standardized project management. They never want to hear about it again. When they say, "We tried that and it didn't work," it's safe to assume that they mean it. Something no doubt went wrong somewhere. And that something going wrong was probably accompanied by a lot of lost time, money, and patience. How can an organization be brought back on track after that? To be honest, sometimes it's impossible. Sometimes that battle brings the war to a close. In other instances—usually softened with the passage of time—there can be a refocus back to the original intention. For these occasions, it's helpful to look at the initial effort and pinpoint why it did not fulfill its intent. Was the program poorly designed? Was training inadequate? Did it lack management support? When people take the time to think it through, the reason usually becomes obvious. Sometimes it's not hidden at all—no thinking is needed; everyone knows why it didn't work.

Regaining the faith needed to try again can be a tough hurdle to get over. It helps to begin if possible with some evidence of benefit, some indicators of a positive ROI. In line with that, part of the intent of this book is to offer evidence that certain project management practices really do work. They tangibly help in managing a project and in driving it to its desired goals. The evidence comes from the Hollywood production teams that use these practices: There are things we can do to change our environments for the better.

"Our customers won't support it."   Management may think that developing a defined project management system means adding layers of new work that will pass on additional costs to the customers, costs they think the customers will have no interest in paying for. That's a common view—but it's backwards. The better view is to see the system as a way to control or even reduce costs. Moreover, institution of such a system should not be looked at as something that's done for the customer, although it should realize positive outcomes for the customer. Its purpose is to help the organization better realize its mission, and that mission more often than not happens to include profitability. When customers deal with well-run IT shops, they may sense that there's a machine in place but the details of that machine needn't concern them. They are content with receiving timely and solid work products.

As a counterpoint to this line of thought, sometimes management cites a lack of customer support as a way to avoid having to say, "We don't want to pay for it." That's the stickier issue of the two. In order to create a project management system—big or small, light or heavy— the organization is going to have to make an investment. And this investment is not a clean purchase. It's not like cutting a check and then pulling something out of a box. The shop must build it itself, and what it comes up with may be a reflection of its own commitment to a solution. That may be enough in and of itself to make management back off.

The project performance statistics that dog the IT industry will probably continue along the same trend line so long as the foregoing views are embraced by upper-level and executive IT management. On the plus side, these views are only rarely cited as "excuses"; only a small percentage of management uses them as superficial substitutes for the truth. Most simply don't have exposure or experience to see past them. Perhaps as the appreciation for the discipline of project management grows, and with it a realization of its benefits, greater adoption and better shop performance will result.

Project Management as an Operational Asset

C-level management—CEO, CIO, CFO—loves stability. It's usually an indicator that everything's going as planned, and in the sense that "going" means up, not down. Employees like stability, too. Studies have shown that retention rates are higher in stable companies than they are in companies going through periods of dynamic challenge or change. Catharsis can be fun, but not every day. Employees prefer to wake up to work days that promise as little chaos as possible. And there's another party that loves stability: Wall Street. Financial analysts and investment professionals evaluate companies in part on the basis of their operational stability. To them, stability signals that management has a firm handle on the ins and outs of its particular business domains.

A well-designed project management program can help contribute to operational stability. Appreciation of the full reach of technology across the business enterprise serves to highlight the influence a program management program can have on a company. Technology project management doesn't just happen within the IT shop; it's a way for IT to reach out into the organization. A well-run project management program can help the company at large achieve smooth, predictable operations. This is in line with recent financial analysis developments: Wall Street is beginning to pay more and more attention to companies adopting quality and process programs like Six Sigma, ISO 9001:2000, CMMI, and ITIL. These programs are counted as contributors to operational stability, and operational stability is regarded as a market asset.

As a mediator of stability, then, a project management program can deliver distinct operational benefits to the organization. Four big ones are discussed next: the triad of predictability, consistency, and repeatability; synchronous customer relations; effective strategic and tactical planning; and enhanced performance.

Predictability, Consistency, Repeatability

The triad of quality performance attributes consists of predictability, consistency, and repeatability. From those attributes comes control. And when control is combined with appropriate design, the result is a high-quality product. The people in an IT shop are there to deliver intelligent and appropriate designs. The project management system is in place to deliver the control. In shops in which control is largely absent, the operational scenario typically includes frustration and inefficiency: People spend a good portion of their time and effort figuring out what to do, not doing it. They improvise communications and work flow solutions anew, solutions that may well have been addressed previously by others. They find that because of false starts or misdirection, they have to revisit the same decision or the same work over and over again. Even worse, it's not that they aren't following a system; it's that by necessity they invent a new one each time out.

Look to the project management approach, then, as a way to align missions, people, and activities. As an applied standard, it will serve to establish work patterns and work rhythms in the shop. These patterns and rhythms will foster better communication and coordination within projects, between projects, and across projects. In working to a common standard, the members of the IT shop will soon find that they also are moving toward the same shared vision. By happy coincidence, this benefit—a harmonizing, solidifying force within the shop—leads directly to improved relations with the customer.

Synchronous Customer Relations

IT shops that implement a project management program can realize a benefit that is surprisingly very often overlooked or underappreciated. And yet it is both very real and very influential. Operating from a run-and-gun approach, IT shops often unwittingly train their customers and business partners in bad habits, perpetuating inefficiencies and fulfilling prophecies of poor performance. But when the shop implements a coordinated program, it begins to train customers and partners in the proper ways of technology development. That makes life better for both parties. From the perspective of the IT team, the customers begin to support their collection, analysis, design, and deployment activities. The predictable rhythm of the system and its standardized set of work product and artifacts together help to serve as a road map for planning interactions and charting progress. From the perspective of the customer, the IT people seem to have their act together. When the technology teams work with the business teams, they seem to do so in a consistent way, asking for the same kinds of materials, sharing the same kinds of documents. Over time, this consistency breeds a level of comfort that leads to confidence. And when this new, predictable way begins to demonstrate its effectiveness through better quality, the confidence compounds, and with it, willingness to participate fully in the process. At its peak, this benefit promotes the kind of transformation that can ultimately move to bridge the gap that exists between IT and other business units in corporate America.

Effective Strategic and Tactical Planning

A healthy organization uses planning for two overarching purposes: (1) to point itself in a particular direction and then (2) to set itself in motion toward that direction. Good planning— sound, realistic, practical, and informed—is like a reliable map in the hands of a skilled navigator. The chances of getting to a desired location are pretty good. On the other hand, poor planning usually means landing in some suboptimal location, perhaps only partway to the goal, maybe way off course from it. The cliché is that organizations that fail to plan, plan to fail. Like a lot of clichés, this one carries a lot of truth. Planning emerges, then, as an important organization activity. Organizations need to consider planning along two lines: strategic and tactical. *Strategic* planning is typically used for the original pointing. *Tactical* planning is used more often for the kicking into motion. Both are essential for success.

A project management program can serve as a valuable aid to support organizational planning activities. For strategic planning, it serves as a repository of project management values, establishing the thresholds, milestones, and benchmarks used to define success. These organic elements—subject to refinement and adjustment over time—need to be reflected in the organization's strategic position. For tactical planning, a point of interest is that the project program can itself often be considered the plan. The program, after all, is essentially a series of established steps and activities that are followed when projects are taken on. That in and of itself is a pretty good definition of a plan.

Enhanced Performance

Here's the bottom-line benefit: enhanced performance, by an organization better at its core mission and better able to manage the business framework of that mission. How does an organization operate at this level? With project scopes that are well managed. Schedules that are seen as reliable and deliverable. Budgets that can be taken to the bank. And well-developed products that perform in line with expectations and needs. These attributes are routinely evidenced in high-performing IT shops. They are hallmarks of maturity, discipline, and captured experience. They represent a shop that is driven by an embedded organizational capability, whereas less mature, less effective shops tend to be driven by individual capabilities.

Of note, project management methodology, on its own, probably can't take an IT shop to this level. But it should be seen as a powerful contributor to that goal, with the potential to significantly shape a shop toward that end. And in the end, that should be the goal of any technology organization. Effective project management is a shared partner in achieving that goal and is undeniably one of the most important components of successful operations.

The Lean Machine at Work

To see firsthand the advantages of working through a system, a look around should suffice—the evidence is everywhere. A Hollywood movie set is a great place to see it in action, although it's pretty difficult to get access when a shoot is in progress. Many of the "names" behind a movie—famous actors, famous directors, famous producers—will require "no guest" sets as a way to protect their limited privacy. (I probably managed to get onto so many sets simply because I told the executives that I had no specific interest in rubbing shoulders with Jim Carrey, Drew Barrymore, Jennifer Anniston, Shia LaBeouf, or Ben Affleck, fine people though I'm sure they were.) But those who are permitted access will see a large, coordinated crew executing a series of very diverse tasks, all in anticipation of a singular outcome. The activities taking place here represent a highly specialized collection of skill sets, some technical, some artistic, some literal, some interpretive. Each requires its own space, its own toolkit, and its own moments of precise attention and focus. The system accommodates all that. To illustrate, one aspect of smooth production that struck me right at the start was how *quiet* it all was. For example, on the set of *He's Just Not That into You*, I was surrounded by dozens and dozens—maybe a hundred—people: stylists and makeup artists, camera and sound crews, gaffers and grips, supervisors, prop masters, set decorators, seamstresses, assistants, and interns (interns everywhere). With a crowd of that size, bustling and in near-constant motion, generation of a loud cacophony seems almost unavoidable—but it was just the opposite. Not silence, of course, but there was very little in the way of extraneous conversation, superfluous talk, or pitched volume. Communication did not have to be loud or overt to be effective. I could see this stemming from the system. Its emphasis on procedures and role definitions provides distinct avenues for executing work activities. People don't get in each other's way. They focus each on their part of this huge, collaborative machine—hence, that quiet professionalism.

This same degree of finesse can be observed from the bleachers of a football stadium. A great team is a similar kind of machine operating from a tried-and-true system. In 2007, the New England Patriots had a perfect regular season record—16 wins and 0 losses. Could that have come about in the absence of a system?

Not a football fan? Visit a concert hall and listen to (and watch) the performance of a classical symphony. The 80-piece orchestra on the stage is bringing off an incredibly complex integration of timing, notation, syncopation, rhythm, and mood. And, to boot, it's doing it in real time. That's a system of high order at work. In fact, we are surrounded by proven systems, some as mundane as the set of highways and traffic lights (or public transportation) we maneuver en route to work every day, others more obviously complex or inherently more interesting. But we depend on them because they have developed into efficient benchmarks of order. We follow them because they work.

Here now is the last lesson of this book:

> **Lesson 18: Honor your project management system.** Use it to plan, manage, and monitor projects. Commit to this use over time. And work to continually refine and improve the system.

Let's consider, in brief, some ways to put this lesson in practice.

The Secret to Project Management Success

The 18 lessons presented in this book point out a series of activities and practices that can be used as the basis for an IT shop's project management system. These lessons come from the motion picture production industry, where they have proved effective after decades of use. Of interest, most of these practices are already familiar to the IT industry. The difference is that the IT industry has not been able to integrate them into the habit of development to the same degree. But why has Hollywood been able to establish a system that addresses complex project management, while the IT industry, whose projects are clearly just as complex, lags behind? Perhaps the answer is simply time and the relative maturity it brings. Hollywood has been in the business of film production for 100 years. Maybe that time span has given it the maturity needed to understand how to produce its kind of product in the most expeditious manner. The technology industry has been at its job, as we know it today, for perhaps 25 years—a big difference.

But there's a second aspect of the secret to Hollywood's consistent success with its system, which is not something that resides in the mystery of the practices. Rather, it's how the system is put into place. Because the success of any system cannot be realized until the system is honored, implementation is key. Six effective practices in this area, seen at work in Hollywood as well as in the hallways of corporate America, can be used to help "institutionalize" best practices in an IT shop—to integrate them into the culture so they become habit. These six practices are:

1. Executive commitment to the system

2. A system sized to the needs of the organization

3. Involvement in its development from the people who will use it

4. Ongoing governance and insight

5. Accessible training and coaching

6. Recognition of performance

Let's quickly look at each.

Executive commitment   Executive commitment to the system may be the single largest contributor to project management success in any organization. It may also be the dominant reason why many project management programs fall short. An effective project manage-ment approach requires sustained action over time, and sustained action requires executive commitment. If an IT shop is one that recognizes the need to change some of its project management practices, such change will be realized only through some sort of investment. Energy, time, and money, to a variable degree, will have to be allocated. It's the executive branch of the company that usually controls the expenditure of energy and money over time, so without this support little lasting change will occur. The commitment from management must be twofold. First, it must ante up the investment needed to design and establish the program. For some organizations, this may represent a significant investment; for others, it won't be so large. As a point of interest, this is the area in which executive commitment is not especially difficult to achieve. Management—enlightened management, that is—is rarely averse to acting when it knows it should, and if it knows its approach to project management needs adjusting, it will usually act. "Investing" in a "solution" makes simple business sense. That's the easy part. The tougher aspect of commitment comes next, after the solution has been introduced. This is when commitment can wane. If results are soft at first or are slow to materialize, the impression can arise that the new approach isn't so effective after all. In a business landscape often judged on quarterly performance, long-term commitments often lose momentum. But the long-term view is essential to the success of a project management program. The program needs time to be used, to be exercised across its scope, for people to grow accustomed to it, and for its strengths and weaknesses to become fully understood. Only with the time for this to become known can the program really be used to push the overall mission of the organization. In beginning to seek sponsorship for the program, seek out management and emphasize the importance of this trait.

Right-sizing   As mentioned elsewhere in this chapter, it's relatively easy to create a project management program. Policies, guidelines, templates, and checklists can all be generated without too much difficulty. For this reason, it's also easy to overengineer a system, to make it too big or too complex, to want it to address every project management issue right out of the gate. It's wise to resist that temptation. Especially early on, a light program sticks bet-ter than a heavy one. Instead, look to "right-size" the solution; create a project management methodology that suits the needs of the organization, one that's sized to fit its culture. A good starting point toward this goal is to identify the major project management issues the shop needs to address and then prioritize them. Maybe there's a need to manage scope bet-ter. Maybe the shop's approach to estimation is too casual. Perhaps it's not seeking firm com-mitments and approvals from stakeholders. Take a look at the shop, speak with the folks who can be expected to move into and out of the system during the course of an average project, identify needs that should be addressed. Then share these needs with associates and, with their input, stake out which ones to work on first. With an approach engineered from this perspective, the solution that emerges will be readily implemented, one that is designed for tangible results, and one that can be enhanced, extended, and improved over time.

Involvement of associates   It's not particularly difficult to define a project management methodology. There are lots of references to draw on, lots of sources of expertise. But a mistake many people make when they set out to create such a program is that they rely almost exclusively on external expertise: organizations, books, standards, consultants. They forget to involve the members of the organization in the design and development of the approach. When this happens, the organization complicates its path to success three ways. First, it sets the program up to be viewed as something from the outside, as if the folks within the organization were not up to tackling the problem themselves. This may put a distance between the tools and techniques of the approach and people's willingness to engage them. Failing to involve the line workers may result in longer roll-outs due to extended learning curves. Because the elements of the program are foreign to the associates, they will need time to become familiar with them. Finally, a program built in isolation or imported from the outside may be subjected to extra scrutiny, more so than if it had been developed in house. If the program has faults or needs adjustments, people may be less willing to give it the benefit of the doubt and work to improve it.

The better path is to involve the shop's associates right from the start. Leverage their experience. Seek their insights into best practices. Incorporate their expertise into the solution. Then they will feel that the program reflects their concerns and focuses on their needs. Accordingly, they will be more likely to embrace it. And because it begins with a degree of familiarity built into it, they will be more likely to use it over time.

Governance   Governance links program use with the strategic mission of the company. Hollywood uses industry tools like completion bonds and production reports to ensure that a project stays on plan and on process. For corporate IT, governance includes periodic project auditing, usually (but not necessarily) by an objective third party. The audits seek to provide insight along three lines: They can be used to document organizational awareness and compliance with the system. They are also effective at identifying problems or sticking points in the system. And they can be used to collect performance measures for trending program effectiveness over time. Governance also is important for the broader message that it communicates: It represents an executive commitment to the program and thus serves as a reminder of the system's importance to the organization. Acting as the eyes and ears of upper-level management, governance helps to keep program use as a front-line tool within and across project teams. Without governance, teams may feel that they are required to go it alone, or they may make the assumption that the program is not really crucial to mission success. With it, the program can better stand as an integral part of organizational culture, so much so that after a while, its use becomes invisible.

Training and coaching   Training and coaching probably are just as important as executive commitment. As borne out by my own experience, most people most of the time have no objection to following a program or a system as long as they know how to do so. It's when something new is presented to them, without the tools to understand or take advantage of it, that the new program is pushed to the side. Comfort and familiarity are preferred paths to take. If the organization will invest in the effort to make its associates comfortable and familiar with its project management approach, then chances are that it will be used more widely and more often. This familiarizing process is usually accomplished in two ways: through initial training and then with ongoing coaching and mentoring. *Training* orients associates to the scope, reach, purpose, and use of the program. It serves as a coordinated introduction to the facets of the materials and prepares the associates to view the program with practical application in mind. *Coaching and mentoring* takes a further step in the realm of applicability. Coaches and mentors provide ongoing, real-time help with use of the program, even to the point of participation in various program activities. Guiding associates through initial use reduces anticipation over the unknown. A continued presence in the environment helps promote compliance for the same reason. After a few cycles through the process, people begin to acquire confidence in it and feel comfortable working with it and then become able to see the benefits the program can deliver.

Recognition   The final tip is to reward people who work in the system—and to make this reward visible. The idea behind this is simple: The project management used by the organization is owned by upper-level management. It is management's way, in part, of running the company, project management being a key business activity. Accordingly, the program will reflect the values and priorities that drive the business. People who work outside the system may be misaligned with these values and priorities. Those who work within the system are much more likely to support them. Of course, with introduction of any new program or approach into an organization, a ramp-up period, when people move at different speeds deeper and deeper into the program, is to be expected. This motion toward adoption can be promoted (and accelerated) by recognizing those who move first and move well. Recognition can take many forms. Simple acts like handing out certificates or posting notices in newsletters can go a long way toward giving people deserved attention for accomplishments. Little gestures like presenting anniversary cakes or awarding gift certificates can do the same thing. In many mature shops, compliance is tied to performance reviews, and people can receive financial rewards and promotions by demonstrating commitment to the system. No matter what path is taken here, the idea is to demonstrate the importance of compliance and to provide visible evidence of this importance to the organization's associates.

Patty Long, production executive at Intermedia Films, has gotten her share of that kind of recognition. Her expertise working with Hollywood's production system has been well recognized. In an industry in which 90 percent of producers and production managers are freelancers, she sits as an executive within a profitable international production company. For her, as for all successful Hollywood producers, honoring the system really is the best way to do business.

Case in Point: Thoughtmill

Thoughtmill was an Atlanta-area software services company founded in the 1990s. It took on many types of work, but it specialized in Web-based e-commerce applications. The late 1990s were a great time for companies like Thoughtmill; business was going gangbusters. That soured quickly, though, with the dot-com crash of 2001. The company shrank down to a small set of employees and was then acquired by a large systems integration company, American Systems Corporation (ASC). ASC wanted Thoughtmill as an independent division, one it could leverage for its software expertise. ASC dealt heavily in federal defense contracts and sought, with Thoughtmill in its stable, to bid on lucrative U.S. Department of Defense contracts. However, one step remained: In order to submit bids, the company had to be recognized as operating at CMMI Level 2, an industry-recognized maturity rating that centers on project management. Thoughtmill had some superb technicians on staff, but its project management office was not so advanced. It practiced project management by fiat—that is, it redressed problems with resources: more people, more money, more meetings, longer work hours. ASC knew that large government contracts demanded a better approach. That's where I made my entrance.

Thoughtmill hired me in 2004 to design and implement an internal project management program that, once deployed, could be rated at CMMI Maturity Level 2. ASC funded the initiative. I recruited a team and we worked on the program for seven months. When it was ready to go, we deployed it out across the project teams, and when enough work had been run through the system, Thoughtmill was appraised and rated at Level 2. ASC gave kudos to Thoughtmill's management. And then everything went downhill.

With the appraisal accomplished, Thoughtmill and ASC thought the work was all over. They had the gold star on the door, so they turned their attention to other things. As a result, the project management office, which had gone along with the program only reluctantly, quietly began to ignore it. At the same time, executive management decided to no longer fund the governance roles that provided the program's coaching and auditing services. Thoughtmill's executive director wanted me to go into sales. He thought there was a lot of money to be made in selling project management consulting services.

The rest is history. With the executive push gone and the emphasis on governance removed, the program dissipated. Thoughtmill slipped back into its old habit of project management by fiat. The lucrative contracts did not appear. At the same, the general software development market softened, so the other kinds of contracts slipped away, too. ASC watched all this from afar for a while; then, seeing little value in Thoughtmill's independence, it absorbed the company into its own brand.

Market conditions aside, Thoughtmill made the classic mistake surrounding its project management system: It invested in building the system but not in its use. It saw the program as a one-off and not as an operational commitment requiring time. More telling, the company had little to no faith in the initiative's core premise: that project management works best when worked through a framework. Thoughtmill built the program only because it was told to. The result: wasted work, wasted money, cultural misdirection, and disappointed expectations. When a company has a system in place but doesn't honor it, that's the fallout that can be expected.

Today, Thoughtmill's former offices sit empty. As Shakespeare wrote when he wanted everyone off the stage: *Exeunt*.

Chapter 19
The Lessons Reviewed

For the upcoming movie Yes Man, *a helicopter was chartered every morning to pick up the film's star, Jim Carrey, from the helipad on the rooftop of his hotel and set him down at the particular location where he'd be shooting. One such location happened to be the Blue Moon Café in West Los Angeles. The only place nearby the helicopter could land was the local Little League baseball field. But the sheriff's department said no to a permit—it looked too much like preferential treatment. The producers (no doubt bringing out the checkbook) asked: What can we do? The sheriff's department liaison thought it over: Well, if you paid the permit fee to shoot* the movie on the baseball field, then okay, we could probably do that. Now, nothing in the movie took place on a baseball field (or involved a helicopter, for that matter), but the producers readily paid the fee, and for as long as they were at the Blue Moon Café location, they paid a second unit video crew to shoot Jim Carrey's helicopter landing in the morning and taking off in the afternoon.*

The point here is not that star power means getting anything the star wants. In fact, the helicopter wasn't even Jim Carrey's idea. (He didn't give a hoot if he got to the set by helicopter or car or monorail.) It was the producers' idea. And here's why: The studio was paying Jim Carrey the equivalent of $30,000 an hour, clocked from the time he left his hotel to when he arrived back at the end of the day. If this star were to end up stuck in a car somewhere, for who knows how long, in Los Angeles traffic—well, that could blow the budget.

The real *point: Treat your business like a business.*

Treat Your Business Like a Business

This story may very well offer a subtheme for this book: A business that's run like a business probably will do okay. That's Hollywood's view of it. Through the rigors of its production system, it takes a firm business approach to every aspect of movie making, from development to preproduction to production itself, and on to post-production and distribution. The studios treat it like a business because it *is* a business—*big* business, over 9 billion dollars' worth for 2007 alone.

In general, do IT shops tend to operate like a business, with the same attention paid to plans, expectations, costs, and commitments? No doubt some or even many IT shops are managed that way—but in the industry as a whole, something is lacking. As a result, the technology disciplines have a problem when it comes to reliably and consistently bringing in projects on time, on budget, and to spec. Perhaps Hollywood has something to teach us in this realm.

The preceding chapters looked at 18 project management lessons, delineating specific routine practices of motion picture production teams, that can have direct bearing on how technology development projects are planned, run, and managed. Let's take a quick, final look at each lesson.

Lesson 1: Establish a Project Management System

Motion picture production is a complex, time-consuming, and expensive undertaking. Yet most movie projects come in on time and on schedule, with the full script in evidence on the screen. The secret to this success is Hollywood's commitment to a proven production system, one developed over its 100-plus–year history. The system guides every step in the process, from project development to measures of box office success. In the IT world, this can be applied as **Lesson 1: Establish a project management system.**

IT shops should support their project management efforts by establishing a project management system that provides the policies, procedures, and tools necessary to plan, manage, and monitor project activities. The benefits:

- Promotes consistent, predictable project work flows
- Adds visibility into product development activities
- Institutionalizes organizational values and priorities
- Serves as a foundation for continuous improvement

Lesson 2: Manage Your Applications Portfolio

The major studios focus much of their energy on finding, developing, and producing properties that will show a long shelf life. Ancillary rights, sequels, spin-offs, and merchandising rights all leverage the value of an existing product. Moreover, the studios carefully balance their production mixes to establish the right blend of current projects so that the potential for strong box office returns is maximized for each. This leads to **Lesson 2: Manage your applications portfolio.**

IT shops should provide their project management teams with access to an accurate applications and systems portfolio. Such access will give project managers the ability early on to define scope and to identify key stakeholders. The benefits:

- Establishes a current architecture of operational capabilities
- Underscores interactions and interdependencies among systems and projects
- Supports the assessment and approval of new project work

Lesson 3: Establish Project Assessment and Approval Guidelines

Hollywood thrives on creative faith and enthusiasm, but these attributes are not what it uses as its business drivers. To get the green light to move into production, a project must show strong potential for success in the marketplace. In order to assess this potential, the studios undertake sophisticated and thorough analyses of a particular project's facets, from genre popularity to audience appeal. The goal is to reduce risk by demonstrating market need, and for IT shops this can be interpreted as **Lesson 3: Establish project assessment and approval guidelines.**

Project management success is a factor that an IT shop can influence early on, by ensuring that only viable, relevant projects are moved into initiation. This can be accomplished by establishing a set of project assessment and approval criteria that governs how projects move from concept into implementation. The benefits:

- Provides common guidelines for evaluating and assessing new project requests
- Promotes examination of potential or pending projects against business missions and goals
- Helps establish a balance between work loads and resource levels

Lesson 4: Devote Time for the Development of Requirements

Nothing gets produced in Hollywood without a script—not a script outline or a "promising" first draft, but a solid, workable script with identified peaks and draws. From this script, everything else springs: the cast, the schedule, the budget. Studios invest heavily in script development and provide writers and creative producers ample time to get this foundational product in shape. IT shops can borrow from this practice through **Lesson 4: Devote time for the development of requirements.**

The production of poor requirements is a major cause of project problems. An IT organization can circumvent many of these problems by providing its teams with sufficient time and resources to develop customer and system requirements. The benefits:

- Fosters closer business-IT partnerships
- Establishes a solid understanding of project scope and functionalities
- Promotes better project estimation and planning
- Facilitates smooth change control across the project life cycle

Lesson 5: Employ Incremental Development Windows

Most scripts come in at about 80 to 100 pages. Most production schedules run about 50 to 60 days. And most movies run at about 2 hours. Hollywood is a time box machine. It understands the amount of work that can be done in a typical time frame, so it shapes its products around those time frames. This time boxing provides a framework for controlling the scope, schedule, and cost of a picture. From this can be derived the next lesson: **Lesson 5: Employ incremental development windows.**

IT projects can suffer when they try to cram too much work into too little time, or when they try to conquer more than the resources can reasonably attack. This imbalance between scope and resources (people, money, time) can cause major shifts in budgets, schedules—and morale. By managing efforts within preset time boxes, organizations can better fit scope to resources. The benefits:

- Promotes achievable results within sustainable time frames

- Allows for the manageable segmentation of work

- Supports the review, approval, and confirmation of incremental results

Lesson 6: Use WBSs as a Basis for Estimation and Planning

Hollywood devotes extensive preproduction time to planning. The script serves as the foundation for this planning. Production managers and assistant directors analyze the script and break it down into ordered segments. From this comes the "strip board," which is used to identify various production needs, such as number of locations, number of night scenes, need for special equipment or effects, types of costumes, numbers of extras, and so on. It's an approach that breaks the script down into workable and plannable elements. That leads to **Lesson 6: Use WBSs as a basis for estimation and planning.**

WBSs are great tools for organizing work activities, accounting for required work phases, and leveraging planning data. By providing a standardized WBS to its project management teams, IT shops can foster consistency, repeatability, and predictability across project work flows. The benefits:

- Breaks down project work activities into manageable increments

- Establishes a structure for estimating budgets, schedules, and resources

- Creates a delineated picture of scope

- Can be used to define organizational standards for project work phases

Lesson 7: Identify Needed Knowledge and Skill Sets

Different creative talents tend to express themselves better in certain genres. Some are better at comedy; others are better at drama. Some do well with "big" pictures; others excel at intimate pictures. Such differences are well appreciated in Hollywood, and production crews are staffed accordingly. The studios look to bring on people who have demonstrated an affinity to the type of project at hand and show a record of performance with that type. Project managers can follow a similar path for their projects through **Lesson 7: Identify needed knowledge and skill sets.**

Appropriate staffing is essential to the success of any IT project. IT shops with fixed staffs may be somewhat constrained in determining team assignments, but this limitation can be mitigated in part in the planning process, by having project managers identify needed knowledge and skills drawn directly from the specifics of the project's domains. The benefits:

- Promotes the appropriate assignment of qualified technical and support staff
- Ensures consideration of a project's technical scope and focus

Lesson 8: Establish Budgets and Schedules That Tie Directly to the WBS

Motion picture production plans are detailed documents that can easily run 100 pages or more. The bulk of the plan contains the schedule and the budget. The scopes of both the schedule and the budget are derived from the strip board, or script breakdown. Schedule, budget, and strip board then become intricately linked. Guesstimates are kept to a minimum; rather, line by line, time and expense items can be directly traced to pages in the script. That level of detail can be transferred into the world of IT through **Lesson 8: Establish budgets and schedules that tie directly to the WBS.**

A standardized WBS can serve as a foundation for project planning, especially in terms of budget and schedule development. The benefits:

- Ties estimates directly to defined work activities
- Provides a basis for budget and schedule fidelity across the life of the project
- Serves as a basis for project monitoring and control
- Serves as a basis for progress and performance reporting

Lesson 9: Obtain Commitments from Key Stakeholders

A motion picture is produced through the collaboration of a dozen or so specialized departments. From the camera crew to the art department, each has its own contribution to make. So each department needs to work not only to its own goals but to the goals of others as well. That's where the contracts come in. Every key player of a production crew signs a contract when joining the team, and this contract cements the understandings that surround contributions, collaboration, and coordination. From this we can take **Lesson 9: Obtain commitments from key stakeholders.**

IT shops should establish procedures whereby key project artifacts are reviewed and approved by relevant stakeholders throughout a project's life cycle. The purpose of this approval process is to give stakeholders an opportunity to understand work products as they are being produced, and then to commit to working from them further down line. The benefits:

- Establishes commonality of agreement across key stakeholder groups
- Defines boundaries for contributions and commitments
- Sets an entry point for coordinated change control
- Promotes a shared definition of success

Lesson 10: Focus on the Delivery of Required Functionality

By the time production has begun on a movie, most of the inspiration has already transpired. The team is now engaged in the process of executing the script. Some new ideas may emerge, but by and large, the script guides the production. The producers and the studio executives are continually on watch to make sure that what they bargained for in the script is showing up in the dailies. This can be adapted for technology projects as **Lesson 10: Focus on the delivery of required functionality.**

One critical area of focus for project management is the delivery of required functionality. IT shops can promote this responsibility by providing mechanisms to prioritize requirements early on in the life cycle and tools to trace requirements across subsequent development phases. The benefits:

- Highlights essential and critical functionality
- Establishes a baseline for traceability
- Establishes a baseline for verification

Lesson 11: Manage Through Incremental Progress Targets

Call sheets describe what the movie crew is going to work on for each particular day: the scenes to shoot, the actors needed, the props, and so forth. The production manager issues call sheets at the end of the day to be applied to the next day. This way all members of the crew understand what will be accomplished next, and what role they'll play in making that happen. Taken into an IT shop, this practice could be read as **Lesson 11: Manage through incremental progress targets.**

In methods like Agile and Scrum, projects teams hold stand-up meetings every day to discuss immediate work. IT shops don't have to use Agile or Scrum, but they could benefit by assigning work in incremental pieces, planned to fit a whole, and then monitoring team progress based on delivery of these pieces. The PMI PMBOK calls these assignments "work authorizations." IT shops can use this tactic in various ways, to good effect. The benefits:

- Aligns work activities with project requirements
- Organizes work teams toward tangible outcomes and throughput
- Provides mechanisms for incremental monitoring and control

Lesson 12: Welcome the Quality Auditors

When production companies embark on a movie project, the investors often ask them to put up a completion bond, a form of insurance that guarantees the picture will be completed even in the advent of budget overruns. That guarantee provides risk reduction to the production team, but it comes with a caveat: If the crew can't demonstrate that it can come in on time and on budget, the bond company has the right to replace those people with its own, and to finish the film in its own way. IT projects can take from this **Lesson 12: Welcome the quality auditors.**

Setting a project management program into place in an IT shop is an important step. But it needs to be accompanied by the support of governance. IT shops should provide periodic project auditing to ensure that project teams are staying on process, that they are following the program. The benefits:

- Promotes affinity to organizational standards and practices
- Provides measures for compliance and improvement
- Adds visibility into process performance and effectiveness
- Ensures avenues for coaching and mentoring

Lesson 13: Track Scope, Schedule, Budget, and Quality on a Regular Basis

Production managers receive and prepare a variety of production reports. One is called the "daily hot costs" report. This report details, from the biggest down to the smallest element, the monies that have been expensed from the previous day—whether a big cost like film shot or the purchase order issued to buy a stapler. Keeping track of these hot costs on a daily basis helps ensure that significant cost overruns will not occur, and that if overruns do result, they will not arise unexpectedly. This leads to **Lesson 13: Track scope, schedule, budget, and quality on a regular basis.**

The regular reporting of project progress is a proven way to keep a project on track within its bounds. To promote this kind of control, IT shops should provide project managers with standardized reporting mechanisms. Such mechanisms regulate the reporting of scope, schedule, budget, and quality data. The benefits:

- Provides guidelines for regular monitoring and control
- Facilitates insight into project progress at manageable intervals
- Allows for proactive adjustments and refinements of plans and resources as needed

Lesson 14: Test Early, Build Often

As soon as a picture starts shooting, the editors start editing. They're cutting for two reasons: first, to make sure that what's been shot fits together before the current sets are struck, and second, to make sure that the director is getting the right kinds of coverage and performances needed to tell the story in the best way possible. From this can be derived **Lesson 14: Test early, build often.**

When testing is viewed as an end-of-the-line activity, a project can find that it's due for a lot of unexpected surprises. Instead, IT shops should promote early test planning and early testing as incremental work becomes available. The benefits:

- Promotes early control of functional delivery
- Facilitates traceability of requirements
- Strengthens down-line quality and integrity
- Integrates development activities with quality control activities

Lesson 15: Test to Verify Requirements

The editor cuts the film into shape with the director. Although some latitude is possible in expression here (pacing, timing, rhythm), these professionals rarely deviate from the script. They are in fact cutting to the script, accounting for it scene after scene. They understand that this is what the producers signed up to see, so they have the obligation to ensure that the finished product reflects the original intentions embedded in the script. This can be effectively applied in IT shops as **Lesson 15: Test to verify requirements.**

By establishing mechanisms for requirements traceability and tying test cases directly to business needs, an IT shop can establish a path for demonstrating a product's allegiance to requested functionality, thereby affirming the business mission of the project. This aligns technical teams and business teams along synchronous paths of understanding and expectations. The benefits:

- Provides guidelines for requirements traceability
- Promotes verification of functionality before deployment
- Establishes benchmarks for quality and performance

Lesson 16: Focus on User Acceptance Testing

When the director's cut of the picture has been delivered, the door to production is still left open. Now the picture is screened for test audiences, to gauge their initial response to it. On the basis of this response, the studio may order some refinements, some changes, maybe even some reshoots. The thrust here is to rely on the audience as the ultimate arbiter of quality. Strong test screenings usually point to strong market performance; poor test screenings usually indicate that something somewhere has to be reworked. We can borrow this in similar form, expressed as **Lesson 16: Focus on user acceptance testing.**

When IT shops focus on end user satisfaction, project success is more often realized. Accordingly, it's important to factor in the importance of user acceptance testing—not as a *de rigueur* exercise but as an essential part of product evolution that forges a partnership with end users. The benefits:

- Promotes product validation and operational integrity
- Provides avenues for product acceptance from appropriate user groups
- Fosters coordination of turnover and implementation activities

Lesson 17: Conduct Project Retrospectives Across Stakeholder Groups

The surest mark of success for a movie is its box office receipts. Studios pay close attention to these numbers. If the numbers are strong, they assess what it is they have done right that led to such performance. If the numbers are weak, they analyze the project to see what might have been improved. Both approaches are geared to lead to the same thing: succeeding the next time around. We can adapt this as **Lesson 17: Conduct project retrospectives across stakeholder groups.**

Assessing project performance—whether the outcome be positive or negative—can provide a basis for future success. A good avenue for this assessment is to conduct lessons learned sessions with both project team members and business stakeholders, to identify what worked well for the effort and what may need further attention. The benefits:

- Provides a basis for improvement

- Provides a mechanism for future risk identification and avoidance

- Provides a channel for analysis and communication across organizational layers

Lesson 18: Follow Your Project Management System

No reputable producer in Hollywood would seek to initiate a new production using a new or innovative production approach. No matter how intriguing the new system, that person would be laughed out of town. Hollywood follows a well-honed, well-established system for producing motion pictures; it is a system that has proved reliable and predictable time and time again. It serves as the standard methodology for bringing in a project on time, on budget, and to spec. From this we come to the final lesson, **Lesson 18: Follow your project management system.**

An organization's project management program will reflect the organization's values. When an IT shop commits to the use of its program, it sets in place methods to track current performance and monitor progress across all of its projects. The benefits:

- Encourages consistency, predictability, and repeatability of performance

- Promotes continuous improvement across the organization

Summary

We've now looked at 18 practices that Hollywood uses as part of its motion picture production process. We've seen how each has proved to be effective in reaching a production's goals for schedule, budget, and scope compliance. We've also seen how IT professionals can take these practices and with a little modification apply them in their specific project domains to achieve similar results. A look at standards and methods like the PMI's PMBOK, the SEI's CMMI, ISO 9001:2000, and Agile clearly shows these practices in place and highly recommended. Perhaps as more and more shops become familiar with these standards and methods, project performance will be enhanced throughout the industry.

Support for the prospect of improvement comes indirectly from The Standish Group, a research organization perhaps best known for its ground-breaking 1994 Chaos Study of IT project performance. We looked at the results of that study earlier in the Introduction, as well as results from the follow-up 2004 study. Both sets of findings underscore the need for more effective IT project management. As a complement to that view, the 2004 study also looked at successful projects and identified traits that they all seemed to share in common, either in part or in whole. Based on the 2004 study, the Standish Group identified the top ten traits of IT project success. These 10 traits should look immediately familiar: They are all represented in the 18 lessons taken from Hollywood motion picture production. If we examine the studio production process, we can easily trace each of those 10 traits directly to well-defined and established practices. This correlation is shown in Table 19-1.

TABLE 19-1. Traits Shared by Successful Projects

Standish Success Trait	Hollywood Lesson(s) in This Book
1. User involvement	Lessons 3, 4, 9, 13, and 16
2. Executive management support	Lessons 1, 9, and 18
3. Clear business objectives	Lessons 4 and 15
4. Optimized scope	Lessons 2, 3, and 6
5. Agile-like process	Lesson 5
6. Project management expertise	Lessons 1 and 18
7. Financial management	Lessons 8 and 13
8. Skilled resources	Lesson 7
9. Formal methodology	Lessons 1 and 18
10. Standard tools and infrastructure	Lessons 1 and 18

What becomes clear, then, is a threefold understanding. First, the practices that Hollywood studios follow when they initiate and produce a movie are proved to be effective, reliable, and dependable. More relevant is the next: From the foregoing 10 traits, we can construe that the IT industry probably already knows, taken as a whole, the kinds of things it *should* be doing to manage projects successfully. Yet it still stumbles, perhaps more often than it would like to admit. That brings us to the third understanding: In view of the remarkable similarities between production in the IT industry and the motion picture industry, we can confidently leverage Hollywood's practices, tailoring them and then embedding them into our own methods with expectations for full, tangible, and direct improvement.

For any IT shop, implementing some or all of these practices, as appropriate, not only will benefit day-to-day operations but should lead to a better grasp of project management success for the entire organization.

Credits

The following motion picture executives and producers contributed to the material in this book.

Jim Behnke

Jim Behnke has spent more than 25 years in the motion picture industry. He has served as an assistant director, production manager, and producer. His projects include *The Omen*, *A Perfect Stranger*, and *The Bridges of Madison County*.

Michael Beugg

Michael Beugg has worked as a producer, production manager, and an actor. As a producer, he has guided over 30 projects. These include *Little Miss Sunshine*, *Thank You for Smoking*, and *Welcome to Mooseport*. He has just completed the romantic comedy *He's Just Not That into You* and is now in preproduction on *Patriots*. Before entering the film business, Mr. Beugg worked in the White House Budget Office (OMB) in energy and environmental policy and in the management consulting industry for BCG. He received an MBA/Public Policy degree from Stanford University and a BA degree from Yale University.

Alan Blomquist

Alan Blomquist is a producer at Parallel Entertainment, where his work has included the Lionsgate project *Witless Protection*, as well as *Delta Farce* and *Larry the Cable Guy: Health Inspector*. In addition, Mr. Blomquist was executive producer for the Johnny Cash biopic *Walk the Line*, *Cider House Rules*, *Chocolat*, *Taking Lives*, *Bounce*, *What Dreams May Come*, *Spawn*, *A Little Princess*, *Beautiful Girls*, *Of Mice and Men*, and *Everybody's All-American*. He received an Emmy Award for producing the ABC "After School Special" *The War Between the Classes*.

Pat Crowley

Patrick Crowley is a veteran motion picture producer who has produced box office hits *Eight Below*, *The Bourne Identity*, and *The Bourne Ultimatum* and is currently shooting *Eagle Eye* for DreamWorks Productions. He was the executive producer on *Sleepless in Seattle* and *Legends of the Fall*. From 1994 to 2000, he was Executive Vice President, Production, for New Regency Productions. Crowley is also a principal in E-studio Network, an Internet-based document manager and database used by Walt Disney Studios.

Carey Dietrich

Carey Dietrich has worked as an assistant director on over 30 productions, including *The Butcher's Wife*, *American Beauty*, and *Zero Effect*. Her producer credits include *Shades of Ray* and *Walk Hard: The Dewey Cox Story*.

Stephen Dunn

Stephen Dunn has over 30 years' industry experience as an assistant director. His work includes *He's Just Not That into You*, *Walk the Line*, *The Shipping News*, and *Falling Down*.

Marty Ewing

As an executive producer, Marty Ewing has helmed pictures like *Yes Man*, *Blades of Glory*, *Ladder 49*, and *She's the Man*. He has worked in the industry as an assistant director, production manager, associate producer, coproducer, unit production manager, and executive producer.

Bill Fay

Bill Fay is President of Production with Legendary Pictures, an independent production company founded to create, develop, coproduce, cofinance, and distribute major motion pictures through a partnership with Warner Bros. Mr. Fay's work with Legendary includes *Batman Begins*, *Superman Returns*, *300*, and *We Are Marshall*. Previously, he was President of Centropolis Entertainment, one of the most successful production companies in Hollywood. Mr. Fay has worked in the industry as a producer, production manager, and writer.

Eric Jones

Eric Jones has a long record working with both television and theatrical productions. His TV work includes *When the Whistle Blows*, *BJ and the Bear*, and *The Misadventures of Sheriff Lobo*. He also worked on the award-winning miniseries *The Thorn Birds*. In 1990 he worked on the Academy Award–nominated feature film *Boyz n the Hood* and, later, *Amistad*. Mr. Jones was awarded the prestigious Directors Guild of America Award for Outstanding Achievement for his work on *Amistad*.

Amy Kaufman

Amy Kaufman is a feature film and television producer based in New York City. Currently, she is producing *Gossip Girl*, based on the bestselling book series. Previously, she produced Todd Haynes's critically acclaimed film *I'm Not There*, about the life and music of Bob Dylan. Other producing credits include Norman René's *Reckless*, Peter Chelsom's *Serendipity*, and Francois Girard's award-winning *Thirty Two Short Films about Glenn Gould*. Ms. Kaufman lives in Brooklyn with her husband, Robert, and 11-year-old son, Gabriel.

Patty Long

Patty Long is a production executive at Intermedia Films. Intermedia develops, produces, and distributes genre movies, primarily action films with midrange budgets between $15 million and $30 million. Her television and motion picture work includes *King of California*, *Coyote Waits*, *Skinwalkers*, and *Thief of Time*. She is currently in preproduction on *The Public*.

Peter Macgregor-Scott

Peter Macgregor-Scott is a producer whose work includes *The Guardian*, *A Perfect Murder*, *Batman & Robin*, *Batman Forever*, and *The Fugitive*. He is currently producing the Disney project *Liberty*.

Scott Rosenfelt

Scott Rosenfelt has worked as a director, producer, and executive producer. Now an independent producer, he has guided such projects as *Smoke Signals*, *Home Alone*, *Mystic Pizza*, *Teen Wolf*, and *Extremities*. He is the president of 8th Street Films, a member of the Directors Guild of America, and a member of the Academy of Motion Picture Arts and Sciences. He is a graduate of NYU's Tisch School of the Arts. His latest project, the drama *Gospel Hill*, has just been released.

Index

A

Abaca Labor Council, 105
accommodation of work, 158, 163
accountability, 5
"ad hoc" shops, 230
adjustments, in Hollywood production management, 14
Advantage Computers Inc., 237–238
advertising, in Hollywood production management, 16
advocates, as stakeholders, 132
after-market, green lighting and, 47
agents, as stakeholders, 132
Agile method, 79
Agilys, 224
alignment, of resources, 99
AMR Research, 30
analysis
   by bond companies, 169
   commitment to, 58
Anderson, Wes, 243
answer print, 193
APM. *See* applications portfolio management (APM)
Apocalypse Now, 143
applicability, in project portfolio management, 49
applications portfolio, 30
applications portfolio management (APM)
   benefits of, 31
   black box model of, 31
   boundaries and, 34
   cost management and, 39
   defined, 30–31
   development costs and, 33
   directed growth and, 32
   documentation in, 38
   environmental complexity and, 32
   implementation and, 35
   importance of, 29, 260
   interfaces in, 38
   inventory in, 37
   Kohl's department store example, 40–41
   launching, 37–40
   metadata in, 37
   need for, 32–35
   planning and, 33
   platforms in, 38
   production cycle and, 33
   project, 32
   project portfolio management and, 32
   redesigns and, 34
   rework and, 35
   scope and, 34
   stakeholders and, 34
   as strategic positioning, 30–32
   test results and, 35
   universe modeling in, 38
   upper-level management and, 39
   value management and, 29
appreciation, technical, 58
approval guidelines, 261
assessment guidelines, 261
assessment team
   requirements and, 97
   work breakdown structures and, 96
asset, project management as, 248–250
associate involvement, 254
Athena Technologies, 68–69
Athenati Integration Services, 112
audience testing, in Hollywood production management, 15, 218
authorization form, in work authorization system, 160–161
Avatar, 46

B

backend component, in potential analysis, 47
backlog, managed product, 80
backwards budgeting, 115
balancing, of requirements, 66–67
Behnke, Jim, 192, 271
benchmarks, weak performance, 95
Beugg, Michael, 179, 271
black box model, 31, 33–35
Blomquist, Alan, 55, 271
Blue Collar Comedy Tour, 56
bottom line, budgeting and, 119–120
boundaries, portfolio management and, 34
Bucket List, The, 227–229
budget overruns
   as common, 119
   scheduling and, 77–78
   statistics on, 182
   traits of projects with, 71
   upper-level management and, 71
budgeting
   backwards, 115
   benefits of, 123–124, 188–189
   bottom line and, 119–120
   cost controls and, 124
   data stream and, 185
   data-based forecasting and, 188
   debugging and, 120
   decision analysis and, 188

James R. Persse

James R. Persse is the managing partner of Altair Solutions, Inc. He holds a doctoral degree in Information Technology Management and has over 20 years experience in the fields of technology systems design and process improvement. Dr. Persse is an SEI-authorized CMMI Instructor, a certified Six Sigma professional, and an ISO 9001:2000 auditor. His practice specializes in helping Fortune 500 IT shops select, design, and implement process improvement programs in the fields of project management, systems engineering, software engineering, integrated product and process development, and supplier management.

He is the author of the following books:

Project Management Success with CMMI, Prentice Hall, 2007

Process Improvement Essentials, O'Reilly, 2006

Implementing the Capability Maturity Model, John Wiley & Sons, 2001

Bit x Bit: Topics in Technology Management, Little Hill, 2000

Additional Resources for Developers: Advanced Topics and Best Practices

Published and Forthcoming Titles from Microsoft Press

Code Complete, Second Edition
Steve McConnell • ISBN 0-7356-1967-0

For more than a decade, Steve McConnell, one of the premier authors and voices in the software community, has helped change the way developers write code—and produce better software. Now his classic book, *Code Complete*, has been fully updated and revised with best practices in the art and science of constructing software. Topics include design, applying good techniques to construction, eliminating errors, planning, managing construction activities, and relating personal character to superior software. This new edition features fully updated information on programming techniques, including the emergence of Web-style programming, and integrated coverage of object-oriented design. You'll also find new code examples—both good and bad—in C++, Microsoft® Visual Basic®, C#, and Java, although the focus is squarely on techniques and practices.

More About Software Requirements: Thorny Issues and Practical Advice
Karl E. Wiegers • ISBN 0-7356-2267-1

Have you ever delivered software that satisfied all of the project specifications, but failed to meet any of the customers expectations? Without formal, verifiable requirements—and a system for managing them—the result is often a gap between what developers think they're supposed to build and what customers think they're going to get. Too often, lessons about software requirements engineering processes are formal or academic, and not of value to real-world, professional development teams. In this follow-up guide to *Software Requirements*, Second Edition, you will discover even more practical techniques for gathering and managing software requirements that help you deliver software that meets project and customer specifications. Succinct and immediately useful, this book is a must-have for developers and architects.

Software Estimation: Demystifying the Black Art
Steve McConnell • ISBN 0-7356-0535-1

Often referred to as the "black art" because of its complexity and uncertainty, software estimation is not as hard or mysterious as people think. However, the art of how to create effective cost and schedule estimates has not been very well publicized. *Software Estimation* provides a proven set of procedures and heuristics that software developers, technical leads, and project managers can apply to their projects. Instead of arcane treatises and rigid modeling techniques, award-winning author Steve McConnell gives practical guidance to help organizations achieve basic estimation proficiency and lay the groundwork to continue improving project cost estimates. This book does not avoid the more complex mathematical estimation approaches, but the non-mathematical reader will find plenty of useful guidelines without getting bogged down in complex formulas.

Debugging, Tuning, and Testing Microsoft .NET 2.0 Applications
John Robbins • ISBN 0-7356-2202-7

Making an application the best it can be has long been a time-consuming task best accomplished with specialized and costly tools. With Microsoft Visual Studio® 2005, developers have available a new range of built-in functionality that enables them to debug their code quickly and efficiently, tune it to optimum performance, and test applications to ensure compatibility and trouble-free operation. In this accessible and hands-on book, debugging expert John Robbins shows developers how to use the tools and functions in Visual Studio to their full advantage to ensure high-quality applications.

The Security Development Lifecycle
Michael Howard and Steve Lipner • ISBN 0-7356-2214-0

Adapted from Microsoft's standard development process, the Security Development Lifecycle (SDL) is a methodology that helps reduce the number of security defects in code at every stage of the development process, from design to release. This book details each stage of the SDL methodology and discusses its implementation across a range of Microsoft software, including Microsoft Windows Server™ 2003, Microsoft SQL Server™ 2000 Service Pack 3, and Microsoft Exchange Server 2003 Service Pack 1, to help measurably improve security features. You get direct access to insights from Microsoft's security team and lessons that are applicable to software development processes worldwide, whether on a small-scale or a large-scale. This book includes a CD featuring videos of developer training classes.

Software Requirements, Second Edition
Karl E. Wiegers • ISBN 0-7356-1879-8

Writing Secure Code, Second Edition
Michael Howard and David LeBlanc • ISBN 0-7356-1722-8

CLR via C#, Second Edition
Jeffrey Richter • ISBN 0-7356-2163-2

For more information about Microsoft Press® books and other learning products,
visit: **www.microsoft.com/mspress** *and* **www.microsoft.com/learning**

Additional Resources for Web Developers

Published and Forthcoming Titles from Microsoft Press

Microsoft® Visual Web Developer™ 2005 Express Edition: Build a Web Site Now!
Jim Buyens ● ISBN 0-7356-2212-4

With this lively, eye-opening, and hands-on book, all you need is a computer and the desire to learn how to create Web pages now using Visual Web Developer Express Edition! Featuring a full working edition of the software, this fun and highly visual guide walks you through a complete Web page project from set-up to launch. You'll get an introduction to the Microsoft Visual Studio® environment and learn how to put the light-weight, easy-to-use tools in Visual Web Developer Express to work right away—building your first, dynamic Web pages with Microsoft ASP.NET 2.0. You'll get expert tips, coaching, and visual examples at each step of the way, along with pointers to additional learning resources.

Microsoft ASP.NET 2.0 Programming
Step by Step
George Shepherd ● ISBN 0-7356-2201-9

With dramatic improvements in performance, productivity, and security features, Visual Studio 2005 and ASP.NET 2.0 deliver a simplified, high-performance, and powerful Web development experience. ASP.NET 2.0 features a new set of controls and infrastructure that simplify Web-based data access and include functionality that facilitates code reuse, visual consistency, and aesthetic appeal. Now you can teach yourself the essentials of working with ASP.NET 2.0 in the Visual Studio environment— one step at a time. With *Step by Step*, you work at your own pace through hands-on, learn-by-doing exercises. Whether you're a beginning programmer or new to this version of the technology, you'll understand the core capabilities and fundamental techniques for ASP.NET 2.0. Each chapter puts you to work, showing you how, when, and why to use specific features of the ASP.NET 2.0 rapid application development environment and guiding you as you create actual components and working applications for the Web, including advanced features such as personalization.

Programming Microsoft ASP.NET 2.0
Core Reference
Dino Esposito ● ISBN 0-7356-2176-4

Delve into the core topics for ASP.NET 2.0 programming, mastering the essential skills and capabilities needed to build high-performance Web applications successfully. Well-known ASP.NET author Dino Esposito deftly builds your expertise with Web forms, Visual Studio, core controls, master pages, data access, data binding, state management, security services, and other must-know topics—combining definitive reference with practical, hands-on programming instruction. Packed with expert guidance and pragmatic examples, this *Core Reference* delivers the key resources that you need to develop professional-level Web programming skills.

Programming Microsoft ASP.NET 2.0
Applications: *Advanced Topics*
Dino Esposito ● ISBN 0-7356-2177-2

Master advanced topics in ASP.NET 2.0 programming—gaining the essential insights and in-depth understanding that you need to build sophisticated, highly functional Web applications successfully. Topics include Web forms, Visual Studio 2005, core controls, master pages, data access, data binding, state management, and security considerations. Developers often discover that the more they use ASP.NET, the more they need to know. With expert guidance from ASP.NET authority Dino Esposito, you get the in-depth, comprehensive information that leads to full mastery of the technology.

Programming Microsoft Windows® Forms
Charles Petzold ● ISBN 0-7356-2153-5

Programming Microsoft Web Forms
Douglas J. Reilly ● ISBN 0-7356-2179-9

CLR via C++
Jeffrey Richter with Stanley B. Lippman
ISBN 0-7356-2248-5

Debugging, Tuning, and Testing Microsoft .NET 2.0 Applications
John Robbins ● ISBN 0-7356-2202-7

CLR via C#, Second Edition
Jeffrey Richter ● ISBN 0-7356-2163-2

For more information about Microsoft Press® books and other learning products, visit: **www.microsoft.com/books** *and* **www.microsoft.com/learning**

Developer Books for Windows Vista™
Published and Forthcoming Titles

Applications = Code + Markup: A Guide to the Microsoft® Windows® Presentation Foundation
Charles Petzold
ISBN 9780735619579

Delve into Windows Presentation Foundation (WPF), the Microsoft .NET Framework 3.0 programming interface for client applications. Using hundreds of practical examples, esteemed author Charles Petzold shows you how to combine C# code and XAML to create next-gen interfaces for Windows Vista-based applications.

Microsoft Windows Communication Foundation Step by Step
John Sharp
ISBN 9780735623361

Teach yourself the essentials of Windows Communication Foundation (WCF)—a set of .NET technologies for building and running connected systems—with this practical, hands-on tutorial. You'll gain context for understanding how services interoperate, how to relate service-orientation to object-orientation, and how to create WCF-enabled services for Windows.

Microsoft Windows 3D
Charles Petzold
ISBN 9780735623941

Windows Vista is the first Microsoft operating system with built-in support for three-dimensional graphics. As part of the Windows Presentation Foundation (WPF), these 3D capabilities are also available in Windows XP with the Microsoft .NET Framework 3.0 installed. This book shows proficient developers how to understand the math and put the 3D API to work.

Inside Microsoft Windows Communication Foundation
Justin Smith
ISBN 9780735623064

Dive deep into the operation of WCF and the intricacies of service-oriented concepts—and discover a new paradigm for architecting solutions. Concise, practical, and incisive, this book provides essential information for building applications with a service-oriented architecture and shows how WCF implements the international standards for Web services.

Microsoft Windows Workflow Foundation Step by Step
Kenn Scribner
ISBN 9780735623354

Get hands-on guidance for using Windows Workflow Foundation (WWF) to create process-managed applications—one step at a time. New-to-topic developers can use this self-paced guide to understand workflows and learn how to create WWF–enabled applications and services.

Developing Drivers with the Microsoft Windows Driver Foundation
Microsoft Windows Hardware Platform Evangelism Team
ISBN 9780735623743

Embedded Programming with the Microsoft .NET Micro Framework
Donald Thompson and Rob S. Miles
ISBN 9780735623651

Microsoft® Windows® Presentation Foundation Developer Workbook
Billy Hollis
ISBN 9780735624184

See more resources at **microsoft.com/mspress** *and* **microsoft.com/learning**

Additional Resources for C# Developers
Published and Forthcoming Titles from Microsoft Press

Microsoft® Visual C#® 2005 Express Edition: Build a Program Now!
Patrice Pelland ● ISBN 0-7356-2229-9

In this lively, eye-opening, and hands-on book, all you need is a computer and the desire to learn how to program with Visual C# 2005 Express Edition. Featuring a full working edition of the software, this fun and highly visual guide walks you through a complete programming project—a desktop weather-reporting application—from start to finish. You'll get an unintimidating introduction to the Microsoft Visual Studio® development environment and learn how to put the lightweight, easy-to-use tools in Visual C# Express to work right away—creating, compiling, testing, and delivering your first, ready-to-use program. You'll get expert tips, coaching, and visual examples at each step of the way, along with pointers to additional learning resources.

Microsoft Visual C# 2005 *Step by Step*
John Sharp ● ISBN 0-7356-2129-2

Visual C#, a feature of Visual Studio 2005, is a modern programming language designed to deliver a productive environment for creating business frameworks and reusable object-oriented components. Now you can teach yourself essential techniques with Visual C#—and start building components and Microsoft Windows®–based applications—one step at a time. With *Step by Step*, you work at your own pace through hands-on, learn-by-doing exercises. Whether you're a beginning programmer or new to this particular language, you'll learn how, when, and why to use specific features of Visual C# 2005. Each chapter puts you to work, building your knowledge of core capabilities and guiding you as you create your first C#-based applications for Windows, data management, and the Web.

Programming Microsoft Visual C# 2005 Framework Reference
Francesco Balena ● ISBN 0-7356-2182-9

Complementing *Programming Microsoft Visual C# 2005 Core Reference*, this book covers a wide range of additional topics and information critical to Visual C# developers, including Windows Forms, working with Microsoft ADO.NET 2.0 and Microsoft ASP.NET 2.0, Web services, security, remoting, and much more. Packed with sample code and real-world examples, this book will help developers move from understanding to mastery.

Programming Microsoft Visual C# 2005 *Core Reference*
Donis Marshall ● ISBN 0-7356-2181-0

Get the in-depth reference and pragmatic, real-world insights you need to exploit the enhanced language features and core capabilities in Visual C# 2005. Programming expert Donis Marshall deftly builds your proficiency with classes, structs, and other fundamentals, and advances your expertise with more advanced topics such as debugging, threading, and memory management. Combining incisive reference with hands-on coding examples and best practices, this *Core Reference* focuses on mastering the C# skills you need to build innovative solutions for smart clients and the Web.

CLR via C#, Second Edition
Jeffrey Richter ● ISBN 0-7356-2163-2

In this new edition of Jeffrey Richter's popular book, you get focused, pragmatic guidance on how to exploit the common language runtime (CLR) functionality in Microsoft .NET Framework 2.0 for applications of all types—from Web Forms, Windows Forms, and Web services to solutions for Microsoft SQL Server™, Microsoft code names "Avalon" and "Indigo," consoles, Microsoft Windows NT® Service, and more. Targeted to advanced developers and software designers, this book takes you under the covers of .NET for an in-depth understanding of its structure, functions, and operational components, demonstrating the most practical ways to apply this knowledge to your own development efforts. You'll master fundamental design tenets for .NET and get hands-on insights for creating high-performance applications more easily and efficiently. The book features extensive code examples in Visual C# 2005.

Programming Microsoft Windows Forms
Charles Petzold ● ISBN 0-7356-2153-5

CLR via C++
Jeffrey Richter with Stanley B. Lippman
ISBN 0-7356-2248-5

Programming Microsoft Web Forms
Douglas J. Reilly ● ISBN 0-7356-2179-9

Debugging, Tuning, and Testing Microsoft .NET 2.0 Applications
John Robbins ● ISBN 0-7356-2202-7

For more information about Microsoft Press® books and other learning products,
visit: **www.microsoft.com/books** *and* **www.microsoft.com/learning**

2007 Microsoft® Office System Resources for Developers and Administrators

Microsoft Office SharePoint® Server 2007 Administrator's Companion

Bill English with the Microsoft SharePoint Community Experts
ISBN 9780735622821

Get your mission-critical collaboration and information management systems up and running. This comprehensive, single-volume reference details features and capabilities of SharePoint Server 2007. It delivers easy-to-follow procedures, practical workarounds, and key troubleshooting tactics—for on-the-job results.

Microsoft Windows SharePoint Services Version 3.0 Inside Out

Jim Buyens
ISBN 9780735623231

Conquer Microsoft Windows SharePoint Services— from the inside out! This ultimate, in-depth reference packs hundreds of time-saving solutions, troubleshooting tips, and workarounds. You're beyond the basics, so now learn how the experts tackle information sharing and team collaboration— and challenge yourself to new levels of mastery!

Microsoft SharePoint Products and Technologies Administrator's Pocket Consultant

Ben Curry
ISBN 9780735623828

Portable and precise, this pocket-sized guide delivers immediate answers for the day-to-day administration of Sharepoint Products and Technologies. Featuring easy-to-scan tables, step-by-step instructions, and handy lists, this book offers the straightforward information you need to get the job done—whether you're at your desk or in the field!

Inside Microsoft Windows® SharePoint Services Version 3

Ted Pattison and Daniel Larson
ISBN 9780735623200

Get in-depth insights on Microsoft Windows SharePoint Services with this hands-on guide. You get a bottom-up view of the platform architecture, code samples, and task-oriented guidance for developing custom applications with Microsoft Visual Studio® 2005 and Collaborative Application Markup Language (CAML).

Inside Microsoft Office SharePoint Server 2007

Patrick Tisseghem
ISBN 9780735623682

Dig deep—and master the intricacies of Office SharePoint Server 2007. A bottom-up view of the platform architecture shows you how to manage and customize key components and how to integrate with Office programs—helping you create custom enterprise content management solutions.

Microsoft Office Communications Server 2007 Resource Kit

Microsoft Office Communications Server Team
ISBN 9780735624061

Your definitive reference to Office Communications Server 2007—direct from the experts who know the technology best. This comprehensive guide offers in-depth technical information and best practices for planning, designing, deploying, managing, and optimizing your systems. Includes a toolkit of valuable resources on CD.

Programming Applications for Microsoft Office Outlook® 2007

Randy Byrne and Ryan Gregg
ISBN 9780735622494

Microsoft Office Visio® 2007 Programming Step by Step

David A. Edson
ISBN 9780735623798

See more resources at **microsoft.com/mspress**
and **microsoft.com/learning**

What do you think of this book?

We want to hear from you!

Do you have a few minutes to participate in a brief online survey?

Microsoft is interested in hearing your feedback so we can continually improve our books and learning resources for you.

To participate in our survey, please visit:

www.microsoft.com/learning/booksurvey/

...and enter this book's ISBN-10 or ISBN-13 number (located above barcode on back cover*). As a thank-you to survey participants in the United States and Canada, each month we'll randomly select five respondents to win one of five $100 gift certificates from a leading online merchant. At the conclusion of the survey, you can enter the drawing by providing your e-mail address, which will be used for prize notification only.

Thanks in advance for your input. Your opinion counts!

* Where to find the ISBN on back cover

ISBN-13: 000-0-0000-0000-0
ISBN-10: 0-0000-0000-0

Example only. Each book has unique ISBN.

www.microsoft.com/learning/booksurvey/